ACCESS
Building Literacy Through Learning™

W9-BBY-125

Newcomers

Witajcie

Ukaribithio

Enna vishayam

Tuloy po kayo

Rahmat

नमस्ते

Bienvenidos

WELCOME

Great Source Education Group

a division of Houghton Mifflin Company

Wilmington, Massachusetts

www.greatsource.com

AUTHORS

Dr. Elva Duran holds a Ph.D. from the University of Oregon in special education and reading disabilities. Duran has been an elementary reading and middle school teacher in Texas and overseas. Currently, she is a professor in the Department of Special Education, Rehabilitation, and School Psychology at California State University, Sacramento, where she teaches beginning reading and language and literacy courses. Duran is co-author of the Leamos Español reading program and has published two textbooks, *Teaching Students with Moderate/Severe Disabilities* and *Systematic Instruction in Reading for Spanish-Speaking Students.*

Jo Gusman grew up in a family of migrants and knows firsthand the complexities surrounding a second language learner. Gusman's career in bilingual education began in 1974. In 1981, she joined the staff of the Newcomer School in Sacramento, California. There she developed her brain-based ESL strategies. Her work has garnered national television appearances and awards, including the Presidential Recognition for Excellence in Teaching. Gusman is the author of *Practical Strategies for Accelerating the Literacy Skills and Content Learning of Your ESL Students.* She is a featured video presenter including, "Multiple Intelligences and the Second Language Learner." Currently, she teaches at California State University, Sacramento, and at the Multiple Intelligences Institute at the University of California, Riverside.

Dr. John Shefelbine is a professor in the Department of Teacher Education, California State University, Sacramento. His degrees include a Master of Arts in Teaching in reading and language arts, K–12, from Harvard University and a Ph.D. in educational psychology from Stanford. During 11 years as an elementary and middle school teacher, Shefelbine has worked with students from linguistically and culturally diverse populations in Alaska, Arizona, Idaho, and New Mexico. Shefelbine was a contributor to the California Reading Language Arts Framework, the California Reading Initiative, and the California Reading and Literature Project and has authored a variety of reading materials and programs for developing fluent, confident readers.

EDITORIAL: Developed by Nieman Inc. with Phil LaLeike

DESIGN: Ronan Design

CONSULTANTS

Shane Bassett
Mill Park Elementary School
David Douglas School District
Portland, OR

Jeanette Gordon
Senior Educational Consultant
Illinois Resource Center
Des Plaines, IL

Dr. Aixa Perez-Prado
College of Education
Florida International University
Miami, FL

Dennis Terdy
Director of Grants
and Special Programs
Newcomer Center
Township High School
Arlington Heights, IL

RESEARCH SITE LEADERS

Carmen Concepción
Lawton Chiles Middle School
Miami, FL

Andrea Dabbs
Edendale Middle School
San Lorenzo, CA

Daniel Garcia
Public School 130
Bronx, NY

Bobbi Ciriza Houtchens
Arroyo Valley High School
San Bernardino, CA

Portia McFarland
Wendell Phillips High School
Chicago, IL

RESEARCH SITE NEWCOMER REVIEWERS

Marlene Bicondova
Martin Luther King, Jr.
Middle School
San Bernardino, CA

Mayra Mateos
Lawton Chiles Middle School
Miami, FL

NEWCOMER TEACHER REVIEWERS

Elma Ayala
Magee Middle School
Round Lake, IL

Carole Doran
Richfield Middle School
Richfield, MN

Diane Lucas
First Avenue Middle School
Arcadia, CA

Patricia Previdi
Howard County Public Schools
Ellicott City, MD

Dr. Lisa R. Troute
School District of
Palm Beach County
West Palm Beach, FL

Katrin Venema
Daniel Morgan Middle School
Winchester, VA

Dianne Zalesky
Dundee-Crown High School
Carpentersville, IL

TABLE OF

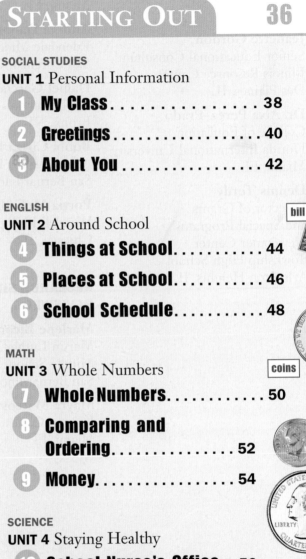

bill

coins

tell

CONTENTS

fire extinguisher

GETTING READY 110

▲ People have special ways of cooking.

▲ Dr. King fought for equal rights.

◀ Soccer is a popular sport.

CONTENTS

That canyon is deep. ▼

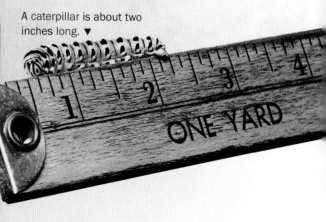

A caterpillar is about two inches long. ▼

TABLE OF

You can skip-count
your toes by 2s. ▶

SCHOOL READINESS 184

▲ The noun *lady* becomes *ladies* as a plural.

You can really enjoy yourself
at an amusement park. ▶

CONTENTS

▲ You need a microscope to see cells.

◄ The planet Earth is made of different layers.

Readiness

Saying the Alphabet

Big Idea Say the letters of the alphabet.

1. Look and Explore

Aa apple

Bb bug

Cc cat

Dd door

Ee eggs

Ff fish

Gg goat

Hh horse

Ii igloo

Jj jam

Kk kite

Ll lamp

Mm mop

Nn nap

Oo owl

Pp pots

Qq quiz

Rr rainbow

Ss seal

Tt train

Uu umbrella

Vv vase

Ww wagon

Xx x-ray

Yy yarn

Zz zebra

2. Say and Write

▶ Listen to your teacher say the word. Repeat each word. Then write the first letter of each word.

1. apple
2. bug
3. cat
4. door
5. eggs
6. fish
7. goat
8. horse
9. igloo
10. jam
11. kite
12. lamp
13. mop

14. nap
15. owl
16. pots
17. quiz
18. rainbow
19. seal
20. train
21. umbrella
22. vase
23. wagon
24. x-ray
25. yarn
26. zebra

B Writing the Alphabet

 **Big Idea** Write the letters of the alphabet.

1. Look and Explore

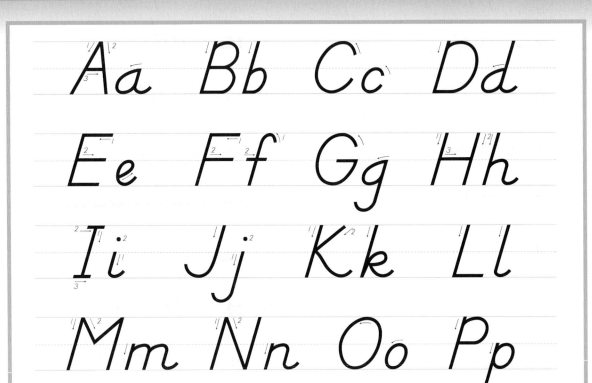

▶ Say each letter. Then write each uppercase and lowercase letter three times.

1. Aa _Aa_ _Aa_ _Aa_

2. Bb _Bb_ _Bb_ _Bb_

3. Cc _Cc_ _Cc_ _Cc_

4. Dd _Dd_ _Dd_ _Dd_

5. Ee _Ee_ _Ee_ _Ee_

6. Ff _Ff_ _Ff_ _Ff_

7. Gg _Gg_ _Gg_ _Gg_

8. Hh _Hh_ _Hh_ _Hh_

9. Ii _Ii_ _Ii_ _Ii_

10. Jj _Jj_ _Jj_ _Jj_

11. Kk _Kk_ _Kk_ _Kk_

12. Ll _Ll_ _Ll_ _Ll_

13. Mm _Mm_ _Mm_ _Mm_

14. Nn _Nn_ _Nn_ _Nn_

15. Oo _Oo_ _Oo_ _Oo_

16. Pp _Pp_ _Pp_ _Pp_

17. Qq _Qq_ _Qq_ _Qq_

18. Rr _Rr_ _Rr_ _Rr_

19. Ss _Ss_ _Ss_ _Ss_

20. Tt _Tt_ _Tt_ _Tt_

21. Uu _Uu_ _Uu_ _Uu_

22. Vv _Vv_ _Vv_ _Vv_

23. Ww _Ww_ _Ww_ _Ww_

24. Xx _Xx_ _Xx_ _Xx_

25. Yy _Yy_ _Yy_ _Yy_

26. Zz _Zz_ _Zz_ _Zz_

C Days and Months

Big Idea Say and write the days and the months.

1. Look and Explore

Days of the Week

Sunday	Monday	Tuesday	Wednesday	Thursday	Friday	Saturday

Months of the Year

January	February	March	April

May	June	July	August

September	October	November	December

2. Say and Write

▶ Say the days of the week. Then write them.

1. *Sunday*

2. *Monday*

3. *Tuesday*

4. *Wednesday*

5. *Thursday*

6. *Friday*

7. *Saturday*

▶ Use the Word Bank to write the months that fit the clues.

Write the months that start with *J*.

8. J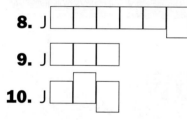

9. J

10. J

Write the months that start with *M*.

14. M

15. M

Write the months that start with vowels.

17. A

18. O

19. A

Write the month your birthday is in.

20. _____

Write the months that end with *ember*.

11. S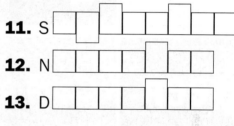

12. N

13. D

Write the month that starts with *F*.

16. F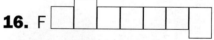

D Colors

Big Idea Learn the words for colors.

1. Look and Explore

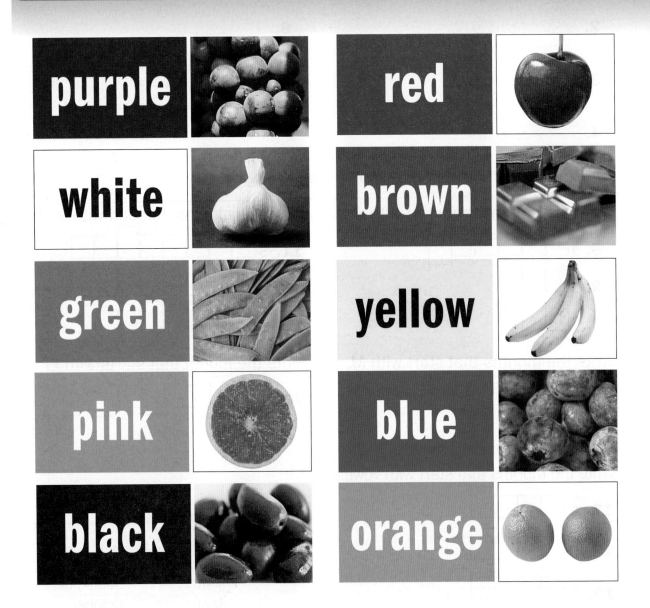

purple

red

white

brown

green

yellow

pink

blue

black

orange

2. Say and Write

▶ Say the color words. Then write them.

1. *red*

2. *black*

3. *white*

4. *green*

5. *pink*

6. *orange*

7. *blue*

8. *brown*

9. *purple*

10. *yellow*

▶ Use the Word Bank to complete the sentences.

11. The grapes are ⬜⬜⬜⬜⬜⬜ .

12. The cherry is ⬜⬜⬜ .

13. The garlic is ⬜⬜⬜⬜⬜ .

14. The chocolate is ⬜⬜⬜⬜⬜ .

15. The peas are ⬜⬜⬜⬜⬜ .

16. The bananas are ⬜⬜⬜⬜⬜⬜ .

17. The grapefruit is ⬜⬜⬜⬜ .

18. The blueberries are ⬜⬜⬜⬜ .

19. The olives are ⬜⬜⬜⬜ .

20. The oranges are ⬜⬜⬜⬜⬜⬜ .

Word Bank

brown
white
purple
orange
black
red
green
pink
yellow
blue

Common Verbs

Find out the meanings of common verbs.

1. Look and Explore

▶ Say the common verbs. Then write them.

1. pull
2. carry
3. walk
4. play
5. run
6. jump
7. fall
8. see
9. ask
10. sing
11. hold
12. take
13. read
14. buy
15. eat
16. drink
17. call
18. draw
19. clean
20. say

F Useful Words

Big Idea Learn useful English words.

1. Look and Explore

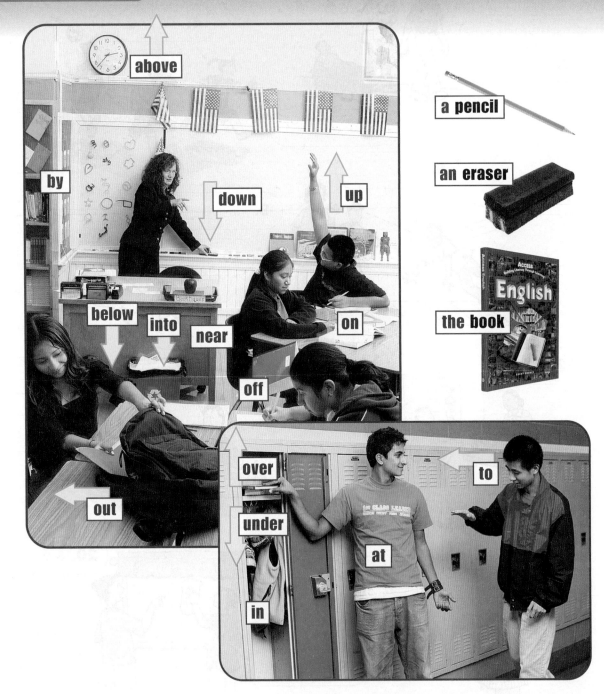

< hidden>
</>

▶ Say the useful words. Then write them.

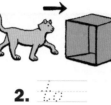
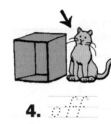

1. *at*   **2.** *to*   **3.** *on*   **4.** *off*   **5.** *in*

6. *out*   **7.** *near*   **8.** *under*   **9.** *over*

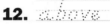

10. *down*   **11.** *up*   **12.** *above*   **13.** *below*

14. *into*   **15.** *by*

▶ Say the useful words. Then write them.

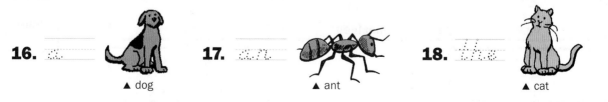

16. *a*   ▲ dog   **17.** *an*   ▲ ant   **18.** *the*   ▲ cat

G Numbers 0–100

Say and write numbers zero to one hundred.

1. Look and Explore

0 zero			
1 one	**11** eleven		-one
2 two	**12** twelve	**20** twenty	-two
3 three	**13** thirteen	**30** thirty	-three
4 four	**14** fourteen	**40** forty	-four
5 five	**15** fifteen	**50** fifty	-five
6 six	**16** sixteen	**60** sixty	-six
7 seven	**17** seventeen	**70** seventy	-seven
8 eight	**18** eighteen	**80** eighty	-eight
9 nine	**19** nineteen	**90** ninety	-nine
10 ten		**100** one hundred	

▶ Say and write the numbers three times. Then write the word for each number.

1. 1   1   1   1   ONE

2. 3   3   3   3   three

3. (12)   12   12   12   twelve

4. 17   17   17   17   seventeen

5. 25   25   25   25   twenty-five

6. 29   29   29   29   twenty-nine

7. 31   31   31   31   thirty-one

8. 34   34   34   34   thirty-four

9. 48   48   48   48   _____ - _____

10. 49   49   49   49   _____ - ____

11. 54   54   54   54   _____ - _____

12. 100   100   100   100   ___ _____

13. 63   63   63   63   _____ - _____

14. 67   67   67   67   _____ - _____

15. 70   70   70   70   _____

16. 71   71   71   71   _____ - ___

17. 82   82   82   82   _____ - ___

18. 0   0   0   0   ____

19. 90   90   90   90   _____

20. 95   95   95   95   _____ - ____

H Add and Subtract

Big Idea Add and subtract numbers one through ten.

1. Look and Explore

+ plus	− minus	= equals **or** is

Addition Facts

1+0=1	2+0=2	3+0=3	4+0=4	5+0=5	6+0=6	7+0=7	8+0=8	9+0=9	10+0=10
1+1=2	2+1=3	3+1=4	4+1=5	5+1=6	6+1=7	7+1=8	8+1=9	9+1=10	10+1=11
1+2=3	2+2=4	3+2=5	4+2=6	5+2=7	6+2=8	7+2=9	8+2=10	9+2=11	10+2=12
1+3=4	2+3=5	3+3=6	4+3=7	5+3=8	6+3=9	7+3=10	8+3=11	9+3=12	10+3=13
1+4=5	2+4=6	3+4=7	4+4=8	5+4=9	6+4=10	7+4=11	8+4=12	9+4=13	10+4=14
1+5=6	2+5=7	3+5=8	4+5=9	5+5=10	6+5=11	7+5=12	8+5=13	9+5=14	10+5=15
1+6=7	2+6=8	3+6=9	4+6=10	5+6=11	6+6=12	7+6=13	8+6=14	9+6=15	10+6=16
1+7=8	2+7=9	3+7=10	4+7=11	5+7=12	6+7=13	7+7=14	8+7=15	9+7=16	10+7=17
1+8=9	2+8=10	3+8=11	4+8=12	5+8=13	6+8=14	7+8=15	8+8=16	9+8=17	10+8=18
1+9=10	2+9=11	3+9=12	4+9=13	5+9=14	6+9=15	7+9=16	8+9=17	9+9=18	10+9=19

Subtraction Facts

0−0=0	1−1=0	2−2=0	3−3=0	4−4=0	5−5=0	6−6=0	7−7=0	8−8=0	9−9=0
1−0=1	2−1=1	3−2=1	4−3=1	5−4=1	6−5=1	7−6=1	8−7=1	9−8=1	10−9=1
2−0=2	3−1=2	4−2=2	5−3=2	6−4=2	7−5=2	8−6=2	9−7=2	10−8=2	11−9=2
3−0=3	4−1=3	5−2=3	6−3=3	7−4=3	8−5=3	9−6=3	10−7=3	11−8=3	12−9=3
4−0=4	5−1=4	6−2=4	7−3=4	8−4=4	9−5=4	10−6=4	11−7=4	12−8=4	13−9=4
5−0=5	6−1=5	7−2=5	8−3=5	9−4=5	10−5=5	11−6=5	12−7=5	13−8=5	14−9=5
6−0=6	7−1=6	8−2=6	9−3=6	10−4=6	11−5=6	12−6=6	13−7=6	14−8=6	15−9=6
7−0=7	8−1=7	9−2=7	10−3=7	11−4=7	12−5=7	13−6=7	14−7=7	15−8=7	16−9=7
8−0=8	9−1=8	10−2=8	11−3=8	12−4=8	13−5=8	14−6=8	15−7=8	16−8=8	17−9=8
9−0=9	10−1=9	11−2=9	12−3=9	13−4=9	14−5=9	15−6=9	16−7=9	17−8=9	18−9=9
10−0=10	11−1=10	12−2=10	13−3=10	14−4=10	15−5=10	16−6=10	17−7=10	18−8=10	19−9=10

▶ Write the number that completes the math problem. Then write the word for that number.

1. $1 +$ _____ $= 3$ One plus ☐☐☐ equals three.

2. $2 + 7 =$ _____   Two plus seven equals ☐☐☐☐.

3. _____ $+ 3 = 6$ ☐☐☐☐☐ plus three is six.

4. $4 + 7 =$ _____   Four plus seven equals ☐☐☐☐☐☐.

5. _____ $+ 2 = 7$ ☐☐☐☐ plus two is seven.

6. $6 +$ _____ $= 13$ Six plus ☐☐☐☐☐ equals thirteen.

7. $7 + 8 =$ _____   Seven plus eight equals ☐☐☐☐☐☐☐.

8. $8 +$ _____ $= 8$ Eight plus ☐☐☐☐ is eight.

9. $9 + 8 =$ _____   Nine plus eight equals ☐☐☐☐☐☐☐☐☐.

10. $10 + 4 =$ _____   Ten plus four equals ☐☐☐☐☐☐☐☐.

11. $11 -$ _____ $= 10$ Eleven minus ☐☐☐ equals ten.

12. $12 -$ _____ $= 8$ Twelve minus ☐☐☐☐ equals eight.

13. _____ $- 9 = 4$ ☐☐☐☐☐☐☐☐ minus nine is four.

14. $14 -$ _____ $= 6$ Fourteen minus ☐☐☐☐☐ equals six.

15. $15 - 5 =$ _____   Fifteen minus five equals ☐☐☐.

16. _____ $- 2 = 14$ ☐☐☐☐☐☐☐ minus two equals fourteen.

17. $17 - 5 =$ _____   Seventeen minus five is ☐☐☐☐☐☐.

18. _____ $- 7 = 11$ ☐☐☐☐☐☐☐☐ minus seven equals eleven.

19. $19 - 13 =$ _____   Nineteen minus thirteen equals ☐☐☐.

20. $19 -$ _____ $= 0$ Nineteen minus ☐☐☐☐☐☐☐☐ is zero.

Ⅰ Multiply and Divide

Big Idea   Multiply and divide by numbers one through ten.

1. Look and Explore

| × times | ÷ divided by | = equals or is |

Multiplication Facts

1×1=1	2×1=2	3×1=3	4×1=4	5×1=5	6×1=6	7×1=7	8×1=8	9×1=9
1×2=2	2×2=4	3×2=6	4×2=8	5×2=10	6×2=12	7×2=14	8×2=16	9×2=18
1×3=3	2×3=6	3×3=9	4×3=12	5×3=15	6×3=18	7×3=21	8×3=24	9×3=27
1×4=4	2×4=8	3×4=12	4×4=16	5×4=20	6×4=24	7×4=28	8×4=32	9×4=36
1×5=5	2×5=10	3×5=15	4×5=20	5×5=25	6×5=30	7×5=35	8×5=40	9×5=45
1×6=6	2×6=12	3×6=18	4×6=24	5×6=30	6×6=36	7×6=42	8×6=48	9×6=54
1×7=7	2×7=14	3×7=21	4×7=28	5×7=35	6×7=42	7×7=49	8×7=56	9×7=63
1×8=8	2×8=16	3×8=24	4×8=32	5×8=40	6×8=48	7×8=56	8×8=64	9×8=72
1×9=9	2×9=18	3×9=27	4×9=36	5×9=45	6×9=54	7×9=63	8×9=72	9×9=81
1×10=10	2×10=20	3×10=30	4×10=40	5×10=50	6×10=60	7×10=70	8×10=80	9×10=90

Division Facts

0÷1=0	0÷2=0	0÷3=0	0÷4=0	0÷5=0	0÷6=0	0÷7=0	0÷8=0	0÷9=0	0÷10=0
1÷1=1	2÷2=1	3÷3=1	4÷4=1	5÷5=1	6÷6=1	7÷7=1	8÷8=1	9÷9=1	10÷10=1
2÷1=2	4÷2=2	6÷3=2	8÷4=2	10÷5=2	12÷6=2	14÷7=2	16÷8=2	18÷9=2	20÷10=2
3÷1=3	6÷2=3	9÷3=3	12÷4=3	15÷5=3	18÷6=3	21÷7=3	24÷8=3	27÷9=3	30÷10=3
4÷1=4	8÷2=4	12÷3=4	16÷4=4	20÷5=4	24÷6=4	28÷7=4	32÷8=4	36÷9=4	40÷10=4
5÷1=5	10÷2=5	15÷3=5	20÷4=5	25÷5=5	30÷6=5	35÷7=5	40÷8=5	45÷9=5	50÷10=5
6÷1=6	12÷2=6	18÷3=6	24÷4=6	30÷5=6	36÷6=6	42÷7=6	48÷8=6	54÷9=6	60÷10=6
7÷1=7	14÷2=7	21÷3=7	28÷4=7	35÷5=7	42÷6=7	49÷7=7	56÷8=7	63÷9=7	70÷10=7
8÷1=8	16÷2=8	24÷3=8	32÷4=8	40÷5=8	48÷6=8	56÷7=8	64÷8=8	72÷9=8	80÷10=8
9÷1=9	18÷2=9	27÷3=9	36÷4=9	45÷5=9	54÷6=9	63÷7=9	72÷8=9	81÷9=9	90÷10=9

▶ Write the number that completes the math problem. Then write the word for that number.

1. $1 \times 0 =$ _____   One times zero equals _ _ _ _ .

2. $2 \times$ _____ $= 10$ Two times _ _ _ _ is ten.

3. $3 \times 4 =$ _____   Three times four equals _ _ _ _ _ _ _ .

4. $4 \times 7 =$ _____   Four times seven is _ _ _ _ _ _ - _ _ _ _ _ _ .

5. $5 \times 6 =$ _____   Five times six equals _ _ _ _ _ _ _ .

6. $6 \times 9 =$ _____   Six times nine is _ _ _ _ _ _ - _ _ _ _ .

7. $7 \times 3 =$ _____   Seven times three is _ _ _ _ _ _ _ - _ _ _ .

8. $8 \times 8 =$ _____   Eight times eight equals _ _ _ _ _ _ - _ _ _ _ .

9. $9 \times 2 =$ _____   Nine times two is _ _ _ _ _ _ _ _ _ .

10. $10 \times 8 =$ _____   Ten times eight is _ _ _ _ _ _ _ .

11. $7 \div 1 =$ _____   Seven divided by one is _ _ _ _ _ _ .

12. _____ $\div 2 = 8$ _ _ _ _ _ _ _ _ divided by two is eight.

13. _____ $\div 3 = 5$ _ _ _ _ _ _ _ _ divided by three equals five.

14. _____ $\div 4 = 3$ _ _ _ _ _ _ _ divided by four is three.

15. _____ $\div 5 = 4$ _ _ _ _ _ _ _ divided by five equals four.

16. _____ $\div 6 = 6$ _ _ _ _ _ _ _ - _ _ _ divided by six is six.

17. _____ $\div 7 = 3$ _ _ _ _ _ _ _ - _ _ _ divided by seven equals three.

18. _____ $\div 8 = 9$ _ _ _ _ _ _ _ _ - _ _ _ divided by eight equals nine.

19. _____ $\div 9 = 5$ _ _ _ _ _ _ - _ _ _ _ divided by nine is five.

20. _____ $\div 10 = 10$ _ _ _ _ _ _ _ _ _ _ _ divided by ten is ten.

J World Map

1. Look and Explore

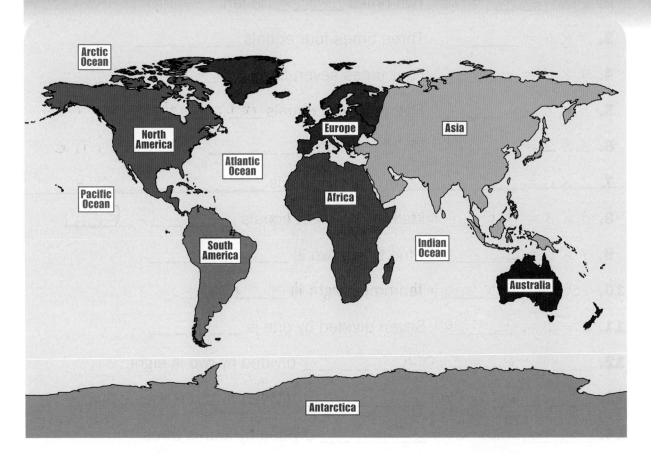

CONTINENTS
Africa
Antarctica
Asia
Australia
Europe
North America
South America

OCEANS
Arctic Ocean
Atlantic Ocean
Indian Ocean
Pacific Ocean

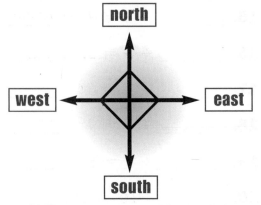

2. Say and Write

▶ Use the Word Bank to write the four continents that start with *A*.

1. A _ _ _ _ _ _

2. A _ _ _ _ _ _ _ _ _ _

3. A _ _ _

4. A _ _ _ _ _ _ _ _

▶ Use the Word Bank to write the two continents with *America* in their names.

5. _ _ _ _ _ _ America

6. _ _ _ _ _ _ America

▶ Use the Word Bank to write the continent that is left.

7. E _ _ _ _ _ _

▶ Use the Word Bank to write the four oceans in alphabetical order.

8. _ r _ _ _ _ _ Ocean

9. _ t _ _ _ _ _ _ _ Ocean

10. _ n _ _ _ _ Ocean

11. _ a _ _ _ _ _ _ Ocean

▶ Use the Word Bank to label the directions of this compass.

Word Bank
Asia
North America
Europe
Australia
Antarctica
Arctic Ocean
Pacific Ocean
north
South America
east
Indian Ocean
west
Africa
Atlantic Ocean
south

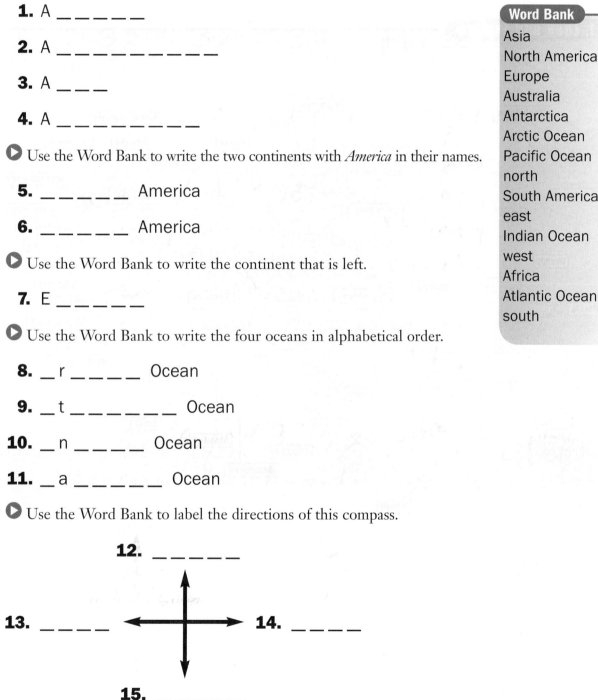

12. _ _ _ _ _

13. _ _ _ _

14. _ _ _ _

15. _ _ _ _ _

K U.S. Map

 **Big Idea** Learn the names of the fifty U.S. states.

1. Look and Explore

2. Say and Write

▶ Use the Word Bank to write the names of six states that end with *na*.

1. A _ _ _ _ na

2. I _ _ _ _ na

3. L _ _ _ _ _ _ _ na

4. M _ _ _ _ na

5. N _ _ _ _ _ _ _ _ _ _ na

6. S _ _ _ _ _ _ _ _ _ na

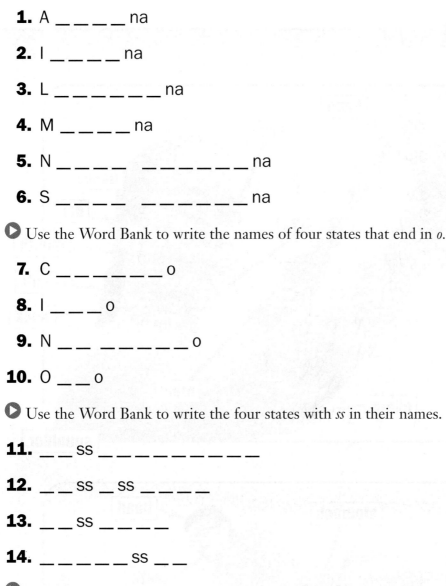

Word Bank

South Carolina
Indiana
Louisiana
Missouri
Colorado
Arizona
Montana
North Carolina
Idaho
New Mexico
Ohio
Massachusetts
Tennessee
Mississippi

▶ Use the Word Bank to write the names of four states that end in *o*.

7. C _ _ _ _ _ _ o

8. I _ _ _ o

9. N _ _ _ _ _ _ _ o

10. O _ _ o

▶ Use the Word Bank to write the four states with *ss* in their names.

11. _ _ ss _ _ _ _ _ _ _ _

12. _ _ ss _ ss _ _ _ _

13. _ _ ss _ _ _ _

14. _ _ _ _ _ ss _ _

▶ Write the name of the state you live in.

15. _____

L Parts of the Body

Big Idea Say and write the parts of the body.

1. Look and Explore

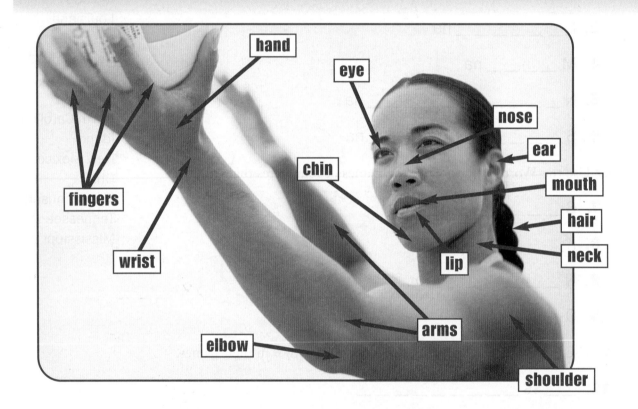

hand

eye

nose

ear

mouth

hair

neck

chin

fingers

wrist

lip

arms

elbow

shoulder

foot

stomach

head

toes

teeth

legs

knee

chest

ankle

▶ Use the Word Bank to write the words for the body parts.

1. _ _ _ _ _
2. eye
3. EAR
4. LIP
5. mouth
6. NECK
7. HAIR
8. NOSE
9. mouth
10. CHIN

11. STOMACH
12. WRIST
13. hAND
14. FINGERS
15. shoulDER
16. chEST
17. ELbow
18. ARMS

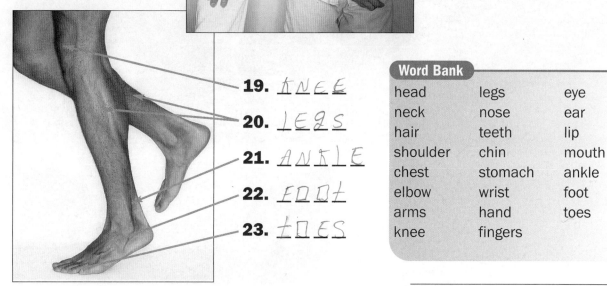

19. KNEE
20. LEGS
21. ANKLE
22. FOOt
23. tOES

Word Bank

head	legs	eye
neck	nose	ear
hair	teeth	lip
shoulder	chin	mouth
chest	stomach	ankle
elbow	wrist	foot
arms	hand	toes
knee	fingers	

Starting Out

1 My Class

1. Look and Explore

class

My name is Roberto.
Mr. Carter is my teacher.

teacher

I am a student.

Sara is my partner.
She is my friend.

student

friend

boy

girl

partner

2. Listen and Talk

WORDS 1–10

1. **Meet** the people in my class.
2. This is my **class.**
3. I am a **student.**
4. Mr. Carter is my **teacher.**
5. Sara is my **partner.**
6. She is my **friend.**
7. Roberto is a **boy.**
8. Sara is a **girl.**
9. **Who** are you?
10. **What** is your name?

WORDS 11–20

11. What is your **name?**
12. **I** am Roberto.
13. Who is **your** partner?
14. **My** partner is Sara.
15. Are **you** a student?
16. Yes, I **am.**
17. Sara **is** a student.
18. We **are** friends.
19. She is **a** student.
20. Mr. Carter is **the** teacher.

WORDS 1–10

▶ Choose the correct word from the Word Bank to fill in the letter boxes.

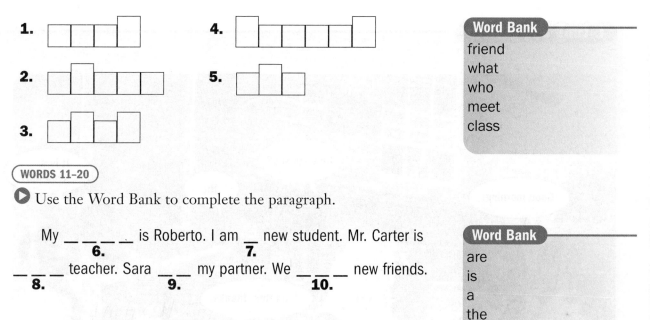

1.

2.

3.

4.

5.

Word Bank

friend
what
who
meet
class

WORDS 11–20

▶ Use the Word Bank to complete the paragraph.

My _ _ _ _ is Roberto. I am _ new student. Mr. Carter is
      6.   **7.**
_ _ _ teacher. Sara _ _ my partner. We _ _ _ new friends.
   8.   **9.**   **10.**

Word Bank

are
is
a
the
name

4. Develop Language

BE			
Singular		**Plural**	
I	**am**	we	**are**
you	**are**	you	**are**
he she it	**is**	they	**are**

▶ Complete the sentences with *am*, *is*, or *are*.

11. You _____ my friend.

12. He _____ my teacher.

13. They _____ students.

14. I _____ a girl.

15. We _____ partners.

2 Greetings

Greet your friends.

1. Look and Explore

Good morning!

How are you?

Hi!

It is a good day!

I am fine, thanks.

2. Listen and Talk

WORDS 1–10

1. **Welcome** to school.
2. Good **morning!**
3. Good **afternoon!**
4. Good **evening!**
5. **Hello,** Pam.
6. **How** are you?
7. I am **fine,** and you?
8. I am **great!**
9. It is a **good** day.
10. **Goodbye!**

WORDS 11–20

11. **He** is my friend Dan.
12. **She** is my friend Pam.
13. **His** name is Dan.
14. **Her** name is Pam.
15. Her name is **not** Linda.
16. Is **it** Pam?
17. **Yes,** it is.
18. **No,** it is not.
19. It is **nice** to meet you.
20. **Have** a good day!

3. Read and Write

▶ Say each word. Then copy it to complete each sentence.

1. welcome   Dan, [   ] to class.

2. Good   [   ] morning, teacher!

3. how   Hi, [   ] are you?

4. great   I am [   ], and you?

5. fine   I am [   ], thanks.

Word Bank

how
welcome
fine
great
good

▶ Use the Word Bank to write the missing word to complete each sentence.

6. This is my friend. [   ] name is Pam.

7. Her name is [   ] Linda.

8. Is [   ] your friend?

9. [   ], he is my friend.

10. [   ] name is Dan.

Word Bank

not
her
he
his
yes

4. Develop Language

YES/NO QUESTIONS WITH *AM, ARE, IS*		
	Yes	**No**
I	am	am not
you	are	are not
he, she, it	is	is not

▶ Complete the sentences with the correct form of *am, is,* or *are.*

11. Is she from Mexico? Yes, she _____.

12. Is your name Linda? No, it _____ not.

13. Are you my partner? No, I _____ not.

14. Are they your parents? Yes, they _____.

15. Is this my classroom? Yes, it _____.

About You

Big Idea Know your telephone number and home address.

1. Look and Explore

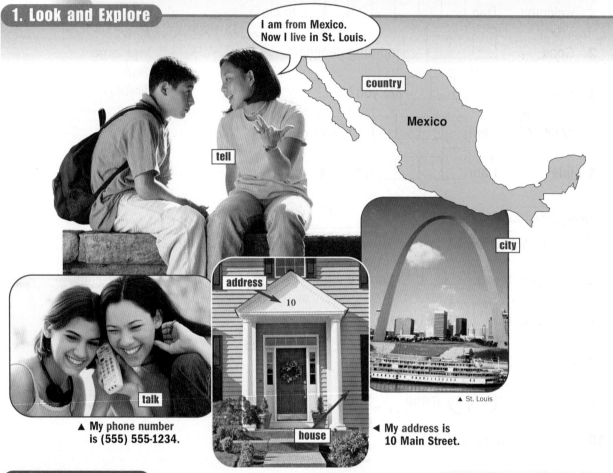

I am **from Mexico.**
Now I **live in St. Louis.**

country

Mexico

tell

city

address

10

house

▲ St. Louis

▲ My phone number
is (555) 555-1234.

talk

◄ My address is
10 Main Street.

2. Listen and Talk

WORDS 1–10

1. **Where** are you from?
2. I am **from** Mexico.
3. Mexico is my home **country.**
4. I live in the **city** of St. Louis.
5. I live in a **house.**
6. **Write** your address.
7. My **address** is 10 Main Street.
8. Do you **know** your address?
9. My **phone number** is (555) 555-1234.
10. **Read** the questions.

WORDS 11–20

11. **Talk** to me.
12. Erica **and** Roberto are friends.
13. **We** are from Mexico.
14. **They** are from Chilé.
15. Roberto is a student, **too.**
16. I **live** in the United States.
17. We go to school **together.**
18. **Tell** me your phone number.
19. Say it again, **please.**
20. **Thank** you very much.

3. Read and Write

▶ Use the Word Bank to complete the conversation.

1. *Roberto*: Tell me ☐☐☐☐ you are from.

2. *Erica*: I am ☐☐☐ Mexico. Now I live in St. Louis.
Roberto: What is your address?

3. *Erica*: My ☐☐☐☐☐ is 10 Main Street.
Roberto: What is your phone number?

4. *Erica*: My ☐☐☐ ☐☐☐☐ is (555) 555-1234.

5. *Roberto*: Please ☐☐☐☐ down your phone number.

Word Bank

write
address
phone number
where
from

▶ Use the Word Bank to complete each sentence.

6. I _ _ _ _ in the United States.

7. I _ _ _ _ to my partner.

8. Erica _ _ _ Roberto are friends.

9. _ _ _ _ me your phone number.

10. Say your name, _ _ _ _ _ _.

Word Bank

tell
and
live
talk
please

4. Develop Language

CONTRACTIONS WITH PRONOUNS		
Singular		**Plural**
I am	= **I'm**	we are = **we're**
you are	= **you're**	you are = **you're**
he is	= **he's**	
she is	= **she's**	they are = **they're**
it is	= **it's**	

▶ Complete the sentences with contractions.

11. _____ from India. (I am)

12. _____ my address. (It is)

13. _____ students. (We are)

14. _____ in my class. (You are)

15. _____ a student, too. (He is)

Things at School

Big Idea Things at school help us learn.

1. Look and Explore

2. Listen and Talk

WORDS 1–10

1. Do you have a **pencil?**
2. I need an **eraser.**
3. Take out a **pen.**
4. Write on the **paper.**
5. Is it your **notebook?**
6. Open your **book.**
7. Put it on the **desk.**
8. Push in the **chair.**
9. Where is the **board?**
10. Write your name with **chalk.**

WORDS 11–20

11. **Go** to the board.
12. Go to the board **again.**
13. Go **to** your desk.
14. **Bring** your notebook to class.
15. **Get** your book.
16. Put it **upon** your desk.
17. **Put** your pen on the desk.
18. **Use** a pencil to write.
19. Put your paper **here.**
20. **Give** me your paper, please.

3. Read and Write

WORDS 1–10

▶ Use the Word Bank to complete the paragraph.

You can use a _ _ _ to write in color. I have blue and red
1.
pens. You can use a _ _ _ _ _ _ to write, too. I always use a
2.
pencil to write in my _ _ _ _ _ _ _ _. My pencil has an
3.
_ _ _ _ _ _ so I can erase any mistakes. You can write on the
4.
board with _ _ _ _ _. There is an eraser for the board, too.
5.

Word Bank

notebook
chalk
eraser
pen
pencil

WORDS 11–20

▶ Underline the word from the Word Bank in each sentence.
Then write each word.

6. Give the pencil to me.   _ _ _ _

7. Bring your book to class.   _ _ _ _ _ _

8. Come here, please.   _ _ _ _

9. May I use your pen?   _ _ _

10. Put the book on the desk.   _ _ _

Word Bank

here
use
bring
give
put

4. Develop Language

NEGATIVE CONTRACTIONS

Singular
is not = **isn't**
It isn't *my pencil.*

Plural
are not = **aren't**
They aren't *my papers.*

▶ Complete each sentence with *isn't* or *aren't*.

11. It _____ my notebook.

12. The chalkboard _____ clean.

13. The chairs _____ in the classroom.

14. My notebook _____ in my bag.

15. The lights _____ on.

5 Places at School

Big Idea ➤ You can name the places at your school.

1. Look and Explore

2. Listen and Talk

WORDS 1–10

1. I'm in my **classroom**.
2. Where is the **bathroom**?
3. Walk to the **office**.
4. We run and play in the **gym**.
5. We eat in the **cafeteria**.
6. Take me to the **field**.
7. Let's get a book from the **library**.
8. Put your backpack in the **locker**.
9. Go up the **stairs**.
10. Walk down the **hall**.

WORDS 11–20

11. **May** I go to the bathroom?
12. **Find** room 201.
13. **Ask** the teacher for help.
14. **Come** over here.
15. We **need** to go up the stairs.
16. Follow **me** to the field.
17. Ask **him** for a book.
18. Show **her** the way to the library.
19. Please take **us** to the gym.
20. Show **them** where it is.

WORDS 1–10

▶ Use the Word Bank to answer the questions.

1. Where do you find many books? _ _ _ _ _ _ _

2. Where do you wash your hands? _ _ _ _ _ _ _ _

3. Where do you eat lunch? _ _ _ _ _ _ _ _ _

4. Where do you play basketball? _ _ _

5. Where do you learn math? _ _ _ _ _ _ _ _ _

Word Bank

bathroom
cafeteria
classroom
gym
library

WORDS 11–20

▶ Use the Word Bank to complete each sentence.

6. I eat lunch in the cafeteria. Please take _ _ there.

7. I sit next to Luis. I sit next to _ _ _.

8. Lupé sits next to Jennifer. She sits next to _ _ _.

9. Jennifer talks to Lupé and me. She talks to _ _.

10. Lupé and I talk to Luis and Jennifer. We talk to _ _ _ _.

Word Bank

her
him
them
me
us

4. Develop Language

OBJECT PRONOUNS

Singular		Plural	
I	**me**	we	**us**
he	**him**		
she	**her**	they	**them**
it	**it**		

Take <u>Ana</u> to the office.
Take her to the office.

▶ Complete each sentence with the correct object pronoun.

11. They ask _____ a question. (Mrs. Xiu)

12. She talks to _____ after class. (the students)

13. Follow _____ to the gym. (Tim)

14. Take _____ to the office, please. (Jess and me)

15. Put _____ in your locker. (the book)

6 School Schedule

Big Idea   We follow a schedule at school.

1. Look and Explore

math

science

Art class starts at 2:00 P.M.

art

history

schedule

8:00 Math
9:00 English
10:00 Science
11:00 Gym
12:00 Lunch
1:00 History
2:00 Art

2. Listen and Talk

WORDS 1–10

1. We have a daily **schedule.**
2. We **attend** many classes.
3. **Math** is at 8:00 A.M.
4. **English** ends at 10:00 A.M.
5. In **science** class we learn about animals.
6. **Gym** class is fun.
7. **History** starts at 1:00 P.M.
8. History is my favorite **subject.**
9. What time is **art** class?
10. We **study** these subjects.

WORDS 11–20

11. We **hurry** to class!
12. I get to class **early.**
13. We're not **late** for class.
14. **When** is lunch?
15. Lunch is starting **now.**
16. We have lunch **once** a day.
17. Is art at 1:00 P.M. **or** 2:00 P.M. ?
18. Our schedule is **full.**
19. I'm **done** with my art project.
20. After art, the school day is **over.**

WORDS 1–10

▶ Say each word. Then copy it to complete each sentence.

1. schedule   We follow a _ _ _ _ _ _ _ _ at school.

2. study   Trang and Alejandra _ _ _ _ _ English.

3. subject   Art is Deepak's favorite _ _ _ _ _ _ _.

4. history   _ _ _ _ _ _ _ starts after lunch.

5. attend   We _ _ _ _ _ _ math class.

Word Bank
attend
study
subject
schedule
history

WORDS 11–20

▶ Use the Word Bank to write the word that matches each definition.

6. only one time

7. not on time

8. at the present time

9. finished

10. go fast

Word Bank
done
hurry
late
now
once

4. Develop Language

PREPOSITIONS OF TIME	
Use	**To tell about**
in	months, seasons, and years *in October; in summer; in 1999*
at	clock times *at 10:00 A.M.; at night; at noon*
on	days *on Monday; on Friday*

▶ Complete the sentences with *in*, *at*, or *on*.

11. I have art class _____ the summer.

12. Luke practices _____ Mondays.

13. History class starts _____ 1:00 P.M.

14. School is over _____ June.

15. They have gym _____ Wednesdays and Fridays.

7 Whole Numbers

 We use whole numbers to count things.

1. Look and Explore

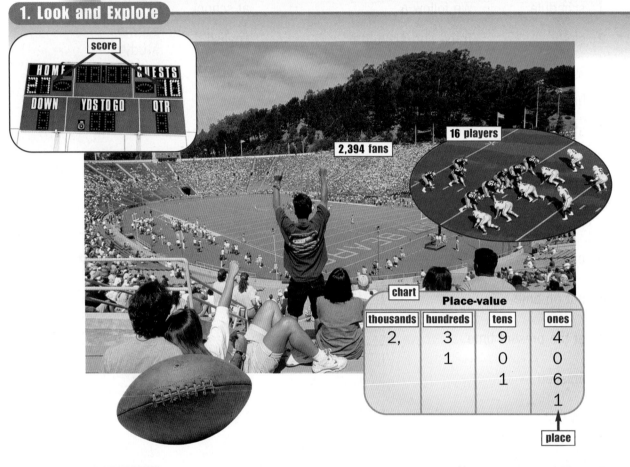

score

HOME · GUESTS
DOWN · YDS TO GO · QTR

2,394 fans

16 players

chart

Place-value

thousands	hundreds	tens	ones
2,	3	9	4
1	0	0	
	1	0	6
			1

place

2. Listen and Talk

WORDS 1–10

1. 2,394 is a **whole number**.
2. We use whole numbers to **count** things.
3. A number has one or more **digits**.
4. Each digit has a **place**.
5. Each place has a **value**.
6. A place-value **chart** shows the values.
7. In 2,394, the 2 is in the **thousands** place.
8. The **hundreds** place has a 3.
9. The **tens** place has a 9.
10. The **ones** place has a 4.

WORDS 11–20

11. **Numbers** from 0 to 9 are digits.
12. We count things **every** day.
13. Tell the place for **each** digit.
14. A chart **shows** how to say the number.
15. We **say** numbers from left to right.
16. How many fans **came** to the game?
17. There are 2,394 **fans** here.
18. The **score** is 27 to 10.
19. How many **players** are there?
20. **There** are 16 players on the field.

3. Read and Write

WORDS 1–10

▶ Use the place-value chart and the Word Bank to complete each sentence.

THOUSANDS	HUNDREDS	TENS	ONES
5,	7	6	3

Word Bank

count
digits
place
value
chart

1. This number has four ⬚⬚⬚⬚ .

2. The numbers are in a place-value ⬚⬚⬚⬚ .

3. The number 7 is in the hundreds ⬚⬚⬚ .

4. The digit in the tens place has a ⬚⬚⬚ of 60.

5. We use numbers to ⬚⬚⬚⬚ things.

WORDS 11–20

▶ Use the Word Bank to fill in the missing blanks.

6. e __ __ r __

7. s __ __ r __

8. p __ __ __ __ __ r __

9. t __ __ r __

10. __ __ __ __ __ __ r __

Word Bank

there
every
numbers
score
players

4. Develop Language

USING *THERE IS* AND *THERE ARE*

Singular	Plural
there is	**there are**
There is 1 ball.	*There are 2,394 fans.*

▶ Complete the sentences with *is* or *are*.

11. There _____ 16 players on the field.

12. There _____ 1 player from Japan.

13. There _____ 3 players from Mexico.

14. There _____ 1 football.

15. There _____ many people cheering.

 Comparing and Ordering

Big Idea We use numbers to compare and order things.

1. Look and Explore

Pie-Eating Contest

pies

prize

◀ Mark won the contest.

Compare the number of pies. ▼

Results of the Contest

Person	Number of pies	
Mark	8	first
Jan	7	second
Sam	6	third
Bill	3	fourth
Mira	2	fifth

2. Listen and Talk

WORDS 1–10

1. **Compare** the number of pies.
2. Put the number of pies in **order**.
3. **Ordinal** numbers show the order.
4. Mark won **first** prize.
5. Jan came in **second** place.
6. Sam came in **third** place.
7. Bill came in **fourth** place.
8. Mira came in **fifth** place.
9. 8 is the **greatest** number of pies.
10. 2 is the **least** number of pies.

WORDS 11–20

11. Mark ate **more** pies than Sam did.
12. Sam ate more pies **than** Mira did.
13. Bill ate **fewer** pies than Mark did.
14. Mira ate the least number of **pies**.
15. Mark ate the **most** pies.
16. **Which** student ate the most pies?
17. Who won first **prize?**
18. How many did Sam **eat?**
19. Mark won the **contest**.
20. Bill **ate** only 3 pies.

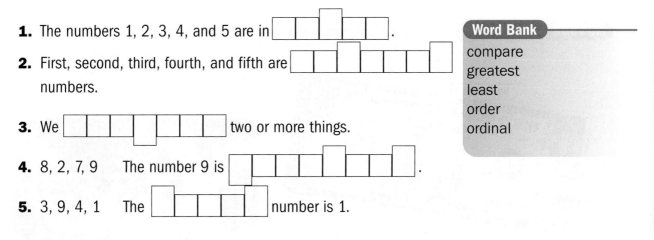

WORDS 1–10

▶ Use the Word Bank to complete each sentence.

1. The numbers 1, 2, 3, 4, and 5 are in ☐☐☐☐ .

2. First, second, third, fourth, and fifth are ☐☐☐☐☐☐ numbers.

3. We ☐☐☐☐☐☐☐ two or more things.

4. 8, 2, 7, 9   The number 9 is ☐☐☐☐☐☐☐ .

5. 3, 9, 4, 1   The ☐☐☐☐☐ number is 1.

Word Bank

compare
greatest
least
order
ordinal

WORDS 11–20

▶ Underline the word from the Word Bank in each sentence. Then write each word.

6. Our school had a contest.   _ _ _ _ _ _ _

7. Mark won first prize.   _ _ _ _ _

8. He ate the most pies.   _ _ _

9. How many pies did you eat?   _ _ _

10. Which student won?   _ _ _ _ _

Word Bank

prize
which
contest
eat
ate

4. Develop Language

COMPARING USING *MORE THAN/LESS THAN*	
Use	**When**
more + than	the first number is greater 8 is more than 6.
less + than	the first number is less 4 is less than 7.

▶ Complete the sentences with *more* or *less*.

11. 9 is _____ than 2.

12. 2 is _____ than 3.

13. 4 is _____ than 1.

14. 5 is _____ than 4.

15. 9 is _____ than 99.

9 Money

Big Idea We use bills and coins to buy things.

1. Look and Explore

This sweater costs $18.50.

one dollar bill

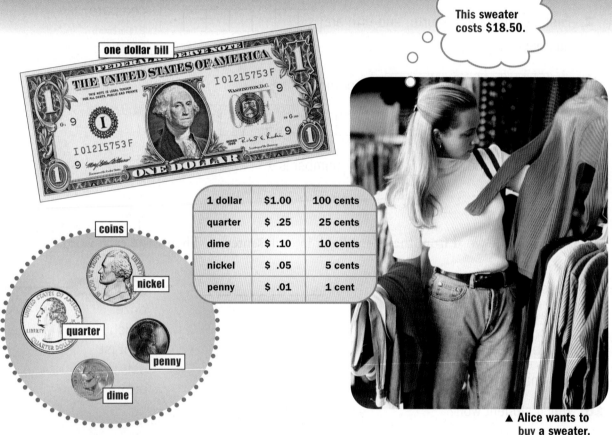

1 dollar	$1.00	100 cents
quarter	$ .25	25 cents
dime	$ .10	10 cents
nickel	$ .05	5 cents
penny	$ .01	1 cent

coins

nickel

quarter

penny

dime

▲ Alice wants to buy a sweater.

2. Listen and Talk

WORDS 1–10

1. Alice wants to **buy** a sweater.
2. She will **pay** with cash.
3. How **much** does it cost?
4. This sweater **costs** $18.50.
5. Alice has almost twenty-two **dollars**.
6. How much **change** does she get back?
7. A **quarter** is worth twenty-five cents.
8. A **dime** is worth ten cents.
9. A **nickel** is worth five cents.
10. A **penny** is worth one cent.

WORDS 11–20

11. **This** red sweater costs $34.95.
12. **That** sweater is $32.00.
13. How much are **those** sweaters?
14. **These** sweaters are on sale.
15. They are on **sale** for $18.50.
16. The **total** cost is $20.98.
17. The **price** of the sweater is $20.98.
18. Alice has a twenty and a one dollar **bill**.
19. She has some **coins** in her pocket, too.
20. She gives money to the **cashier**.

3. Read and Write

WORDS 1-10

▶ Use the Word Bank to complete the conversation.

1. *Mateo:* I want to _ _ _ this sweater.

2. *Cashier:* It _ _ _ _ _ $29.99 plus tax.

3. *Mateo:* How _ _ _ _ is the tax?

4. *Cashier:* You need to _ _ _ $32.39.

   Mateo: Here's $33.00.

5. *Cashier:* Your _ _ _ _ _ _ is 61 cents.

Word Bank

buy
much
change
costs
pay

WORDS 11-20

▶ Use the Word Bank to label the pictures.

6. _ _ _ _ _ _ _ _

7. _ _ _ _

Word Bank

bill
sale
coins
price
cashier

8. _ _ _ _ _

9. _ _ _ _

10. _ _ _ _ _

4. Develop Language

USING *THIS/THAT/THESE/THOSE*	Near	Far
Singular	**this** *This* sweater is red.	**that** *That* sweater costs $19.99.
Plural	**these** *These* sweaters cost $30.	**those** *Those* sweaters are blue.

▶ Complete the sentences with *this, that, these,* or *those.*

11. _____ sweater here is red.

12. _____ sweater over there is blue.

13. _____ sweaters over there are red.

14. I like _____ sweater I have on.

15. She likes _____ sweaters over there.

School Nurse's Office

Big Idea The nurse helps you when you get sick or hurt.

1. Look and Explore

headache

How do you feel?

I feel sick.

nurse

stomachache

sneezing

bandage

2. Listen and Talk

WORDS 1-10

1. Frank has a **headache**.
2. Angie has a **stomachache**.
3. Tamara has a **cold**.
4. She is **coughing**.
5. Tamara is **sneezing**.
6. Tom is **bleeding**.
7. He **hurt** his finger.
8. Tom is in **pain**.
9. I hurt **myself**.
10. Did you cut **yourself**?

WORDS 11-20

11. How do you **feel**?
12. I feel **sick**.
13. I don't feel **well**.
14. I am **ill**.
15. What's the **matter**?
16. She has a **fever**.
17. Tom **has** a cut on his finger.
18. Tom **cut** himself.
19. You need a **bandage**.
20. Go see the **nurse**.

3. Read and Write

WORDS 1–10

▶ Use the Word Bank to complete the conversation.

1. *Nurse:* What's the matter? Did you hurt __ __ __ __ __ __ __ __ __?

2. *Tom:* I cut __ __ __ __ __ __ __.

3. *Tom:* My finger is __ __ __ __ __ __ __ __ __.

4. *Nurse:* Does it __ __ __ __?

5. *Tom:* Yes, it hurts. I am in __ __ __ __.

Word Bank

bleeding
hurt
myself
pain
yourself

WORDS 11–20

▶ Use the Word Bank to write the word that fits each clue.

Word Bank

bandage
cut
fever
nurse
sick

6. __ u __ __ __

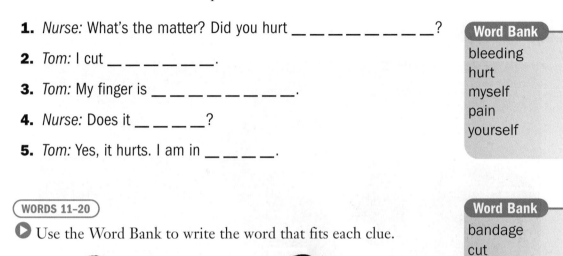

7. __ e __ e __

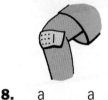

8. __ a __ __ a __ __

9. __ u __

10. __ i __ __

4. Develop Language

USING HAS/HAVE

Singular		Plural	
I	**have**	we	**have**
you	**have**	you	**have**
he she it	**has**	they	**have**

▶ Complete the sentences with *has* or *have*.

11. She _____ a fever.

12. I _____ a cold.

13. Angie _____ a stomachache.

14. Do you _____ a cold?

15. Frank and Laurie _____ headaches.

11 Doctor's Office

Big Idea Talk about your health with a doctor.

1. Look and Explore

- patient
- doctor
- I feel weak. I have the chills.
- You might have the flu.
- medicine
- aspirin
- thermometer

2. Listen and Talk

WORDS 1–10

1. Anju has a **sore** throat.
2. She needs to **visit** the doctor's office.
3. She has a doctor's **appointment**.
4. Anju feels **weak**.
5. She has the **chills**.
6. The doctor takes Anju's **temperature**.
7. He uses a **thermometer**.
8. She might have the **flu**.
9. She should take some **medicine**.
10. The doctor gave her some **aspirin**.

WORDS 11–20

11. The **doctor** is very busy.
12. Anju is the doctor's **patient**.
13. Anju talks about her **health**.
14. The doctor gives **advice**.
15. Anju **got** sick.
16. What **should** Anju do?
17. She should **rest**.
18. Go home **as** soon as you can.
19. You'll feel **better** in a few days.
20. Get well **soon**.

3. Read and Write

WORDS 1–10

▶ Use the Word Bank to complete each sentence.

1. I have a headache. I will take some _ _ _ _ _ _ _ .

2. I am sick. I need to _ _ _ _ _ the doctor.

3. I have a temperature and my stomach hurts. I think I have the _ _ _ .

4. I am tired and I can't move. I am _ _ _ _ .

5. I need to see a doctor. I will make an _ _ _ _ _ _ _ _ _ _ _ .

Word Bank
appointment
aspirin
flu
weak
visit

WORDS 11–20

▶ Underline the word from the Word Bank in each sentence. Then write each word.

6. Anju had trouble with her health.　　_ _ _ _ _ _

7. She went to see the doctor.　　_ _ _ _ _ _

8. Anju was a good patient.　　_ _ _ _ _ _ _

9. Dr. Kumar gave her advice.　　_ _ _ _ _ _

10. She felt better the next week.　　_ _ _ _ _ _

Word Bank
advice
health
patient
doctor
better

4. Develop Language

USING *SHOULD/SHOULDN'T*	
Use	**To give**
should	advice *You should study hard.*
should not = **shouldn't**	a warning *You shouldn't study hard.*

▶ Complete the sentences with *should* or *shouldn't*.

11. Monica has a headache. She _____ take some aspirin.

12. You are always tired. You _____ stay up so late.

13. They have the flu. They _____ stay in bed.

14. Brice is late. He _____ hurry to class.

15. Lin has a stomachache. She _____ eat candy.

12 Emergency!

Big Idea

You need to know what to do in an emergency.

1. Look and Explore

2. Listen and Talk

WORDS 1–10

1. There was an **accident**.
2. It's an **emergency**!
3. Peter has an **injury**.
4. His leg might be **broken**.
5. Here comes the **ambulance**.
6. Did he **break** his leg?
7. The **paramedic** will help.
8. You need to go to the **hospital**.
9. Your ankle might be **sprained**.
10. The **police** are here.

WORDS 11–20

11. **Call** 911!
12. 911 is the number **for** an emergency.
13. Can you **help** my son?
14. What **happened?**
15. He **fell** off his bike.
16. **Let** the paramedic help him.
17. Don't **pull** him up.
18. Where **does** it hurt?
19. **Did** you hurt your leg?
20. You **must** be careful!

60 STARTING OUT

3. Read and Write

WORDS 1–10

▶ Use the Word Bank to complete the conversation.

1. *Mother:* Help! It's an ⬚⬚⬚⬚⬚⬚⬚⬚⬚!

Paramedic: What happened?

2. *Mother:* There was an ⬚⬚⬚⬚⬚⬚⬚⬚.

3. *Paramedic:* Your son is hurt. He has an ⬚⬚⬚⬚⬚⬚.

4. *Mother:* Is his leg ⬚⬚⬚⬚⬚⬚?

5. *Paramedic:* No, I think it might be ⬚⬚⬚⬚⬚.

Word Bank

accident
broken
emergency
injury
sprained

WORDS 11–20

▶ Use the Word Bank to write the missing word to complete each sentence.

6. Help, _ _ _ _ 911!

7. What _ _ _ _ _ _ _ _ to his leg?

8. He _ _ _ _ be more careful.

9. Peter _ _ _ _ off his bike.

10. The paramedic will _ _ _ _ you.

Word Bank

call
fell
happened
help
must

4. Develop Language

QUESTIONS WITH *DO/DOES*	
Use	**With**
Do	**I, you, we, they** Do *you speak Spanish?*
Does	**he, she, it** Does *he need help?*

▶ Complete each question with *Do* or *Does*.

11. _____ Janice and Mila ride bicycles?

12. _____ Rico know his phone number?

13. _____ paramedics help people?

14. _____ they know what to do in an emergency?

15. _____ he wear a helmet?

13 Getting Around

Big Idea There are many ways to get around town.

1. Look and Explore

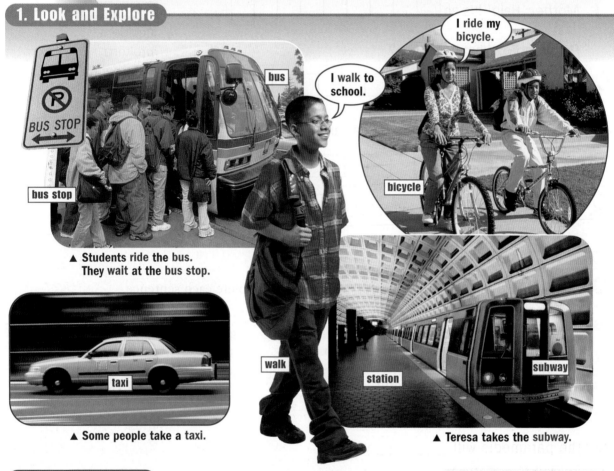

bus

I walk to school.

I ride my bicycle.

bicycle

bus stop

▲ Students ride the bus.
They wait at the bus stop.

taxi

walk

station

subway

▲ Some people take a taxi.

▲ Teresa takes the subway.

2. Listen and Talk

WORDS 1–10

1. People wait for the bus at the **bus stop**.
2. Students take the **bus** to school.
3. My friend takes the **train**.
4. She takes the **subway** to school.
5. Teresa walks to the subway **station**.
6. Some people take a **taxi**.
7. I ride my **bicycle**.
8. My mother drives a **car** to work.
9. I walk on the **sidewalk**.
10. People drive on the **street**.

WORDS 11–20

11. How do you get **around** town?
12. My father **drives** me to school.
13. They **ride** the bus.
14. I **walk** to school on nice days.
15. I get to school **by** bus.
16. The students **wait** for the bus.
17. The bus stop is **far** from Yoshi's house.
18. It's **near** my house.
19. The bus **stops** at the corner.
20. It **goes** around town.

3. Read and Write

▶ Use the Word Bank to complete the crossword puzzle.

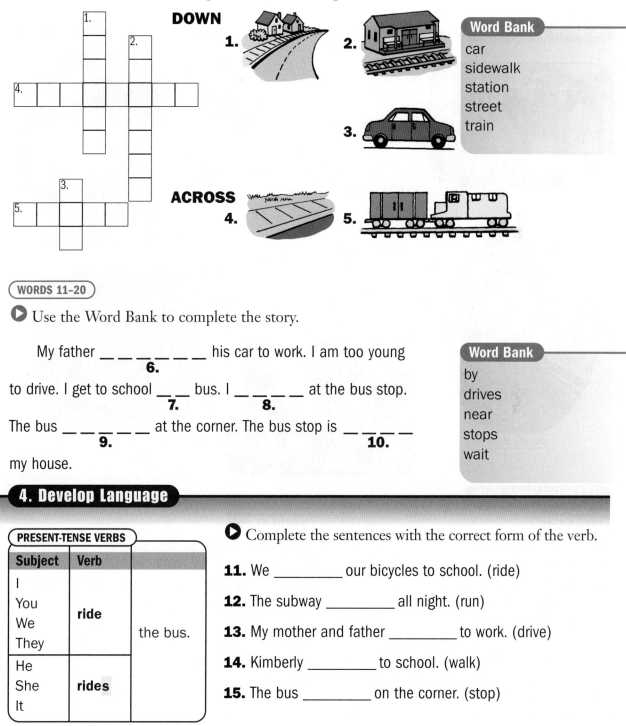

DOWN

1.

2.

3.

ACROSS

4.

5.

Word Bank

car
sidewalk
station
street
train

▶ Use the Word Bank to complete the story.

My father _ _ _ _ _ _ his car to work. I am too young

6.

to drive. I get to school _ _ bus. I _ _ _ _ _ at the bus stop.

7.   **8.**

The bus _ _ _ _ _ at the corner. The bus stop is _ _ _ _

9.   **10.**

my house.

Word Bank

by
drives
near
stops
wait

4. Develop Language

PRESENT-TENSE VERBS		
Subject	**Verb**	
I You We They	**ride**	the bus.
He She It	**rides**	

▶ Complete the sentences with the correct form of the verb.

11. We _____ our bicycles to school. (ride)

12. The subway _____ all night. (run)

13. My mother and father _____ to work. (drive)

14. Kimberly _____ to school. (walk)

15. The bus _____ on the corner. (stop)

14 Places in Town

Big Idea We have many places to go in our town.

1. Look and Explore

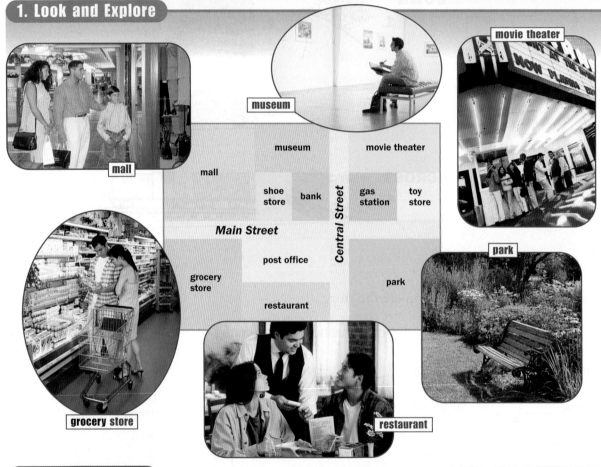

2. Listen and Talk

WORDS 1–10

1. Let's go **downtown**.
2. We can eat lunch at the **restaurant**.
3. It's across from the **park**.
4. What is next to the **movie theater?**
5. I need to buy something at the **store**.
6. Then we can visit the **museum**.
7. I need to send a letter at the **post office**.
8. The grocery store is across from the **mall**.
9. The **bank** is on the corner.
10. The park is across from the **gas station**.

WORDS 11–20

11. We are **at** the park now.
12. We can **see** the bank.
13. **Could** you give us directions to the bank?
14. It's on the **corner**.
15. We **found** it!
16. The bank is **across** from the post office.
17. The shoe store is to the **right** of the mall.
18. The mall is to the **left** of the shoe store.
19. The bank is **next to** the museum.
20. What store is **between** the bank and the mall?

3. Read and Write

WORDS 1–10

▶ Use the Word Bank to write the word or words for the place where you do the activities.

1. buy clothes   _ _ _ _

2. eat dinner   _ _ _ _ _ _ _ _ _ _

3. send a letter   _ _ _ _   _ _ _ _ _ _

4. get money   _ _ _ _

5. get gas for a car   _ _ _   _ _ _ _ _ _ _

Word Bank

bank
gas station
mall
post office
restaurant

WORDS 11–20

▶ Use the Word Bank to write the missing words to complete the conversation.

6. *Li:* Sir, _ _ _ _ _ _ you help me find Sam's Restaurant?

   Policeman: Sure, what's the address?

7. *Li:* It is located _ _ 1528 Central Street.

8. *Policeman:* It's _ _ _ _ _   _ _ the post office.

9. *Policeman:* Do you see it on the _ _ _ _ _ _ over there?

10. *Li:* I _ _ _ it now. Thanks!

Word Bank

at
corner
could
next to
see

4. Develop Language

PREPOSITIONS OF PLACE	
Use	**To tell about**
at	an address *It's at 123 Main Street.*
on	a street *It's on Main Street.*
in	a city, state, country *It's in Chicago.*

▶ Complete the sentences with *at*, *on*, or *in*.

11. The mall is _____ Main Street.

12. It's _____ 14 Main Street.

13. Ramona lives _____ New York City.

14. New York City is _____ the state of New York.

15. The state of New York is _____ the United States.

What People Do

People have different jobs.

1. Look and Explore

People have different jobs.

pilot

police officer

mail carrier

crossing guard

gardener

artist

2. Listen and Talk

WORDS 1–10

1. People have different **jobs.**
2. He's a **mail carrier.**
3. My father is a **trash collector.**
4. Whitney is a **police officer.**
5. Johannes knows an **artist.**
6. Courtney is a **pilot.**
7. Maria is a **crossing guard.**
8. My brother is a **factory worker.**
9. He **works** in a factory.
10. My uncle is a **gardener.**

WORDS 11–20

11. A pilot flies an **airplane.**
12. My uncle grows **plants.**
13. A mail carrier **delivers** mail.
14. He carries **mail** in a bag.
15. A trash collector **collects** trash.
16. Police officers **keep** people safe.
17. Some artists **paint** pictures.
18. A pilot knows how to **fly** an airplane.
19. What job would you **want** to have?
20. Gardeners **grow** plants in a garden.

3. Read and Write

WORDS 1–10

▶ Use the Word Bank to complete the story.

There are so many __ __ __ __. My father is a
1.

__ __ __ __ __ __ __, __ __ __ __ __ __ __. He __ __ __ __ __ hard.
2. **3.**

I want to be a __ __ __ __ __ when I grow up because I like
4.

airplanes. I also love to paint. Maybe I will become an

__ __ __ __ __ __.
5.

Word Bank

artist
factory worker
jobs
pilot
works

WORDS 11–20

▶ Use the Word Bank to complete each sentence.

6. Pilots __ __ __ airplanes.

7. Gardeners __ __ __ __ plants.

8. A mail carrier __ __ __ __ __ __ __ __ mail.

9. The trash collector __ __ __ __ __ __ __ __ trash.

10. Police officers __ __ __ __ people safe.

Word Bank

fly
grow
keep
delivers
collects

4. Develop Language

WH QUESTIONS WITH *DO* AND *DOES*	
Use	**With**
do	**I, you, we, they** *Where do you work?*
does	**he, she, it** *When does it arrive?*

▶ Complete the questions with *do* or *does*.

11. Where _____ you live?

12. What _____ a teacher do?

13. What _____ your mother do?

14. Where _____ you go to school?

15. What time _____ you get up?

At the Grocery Store

Big Idea You shop for food at the grocery store.

1. Look and Explore

soup

fruit

list

juice
cheese
fruit
vegetables
soup
butter
milk
sugar
bread

grocery store

milk

bread

cheese

butter

sugar

vegetables

juice

cart

2. Listen and Talk

WORDS 1–10

1. Let's shop for the things on our **list**.
2. Orange **juice** is on our list.
3. **Cheese** is on our list, too.
4. Let's buy apples for the **fruit** salad.
5. Peas are one of my favorite **vegetables**.
6. We need to buy some **soup** for dinner.
7. Where's the **butter** to put on the bread?
8. How much is the **milk?**
9. Get a bag of **sugar**.
10. I'll go get some **bread**.

WORDS 11–20

11. We buy food at the **grocery** store.
12. Put the groceries in the **cart**.
13. We need another bag **of** sugar.
14. How **many** eggs do we need?
15. We need a **few** more apples.
16. How **much** milk should we get?
17. We need **a lot** of milk.
18. Do we need **any** cheese?
19. We need to get **some** sugar.
20. **Our** cart is full of food.

▶ Use the Word Bank to label the different types of food.

1. _ _ _ _ _ _
Swiss
cream
Cheddar

2. _ _ _ _ _ _
apples
oranges
bananas

3. _ _ _ _ _
chicken
tomato
pea

Word Bank
bread
cheese
fruit
soup
vegetables

4. _ _ _ _ _
white
French
wheat

5. _ _ _ _ _ _ _ _ _ _
carrots
lettuce
potatoes

▶ Use the Word Bank to complete the conversation.

6. *Mica:* How ☐☐☐☐ eggs do we need?

7. *Mother:* We only need a ☐☐☐ eggs.

8. *Mica:* How ☐☐☐☐ sugar do we need?

Mother: Two cups.

9. *Mica:* Do we need ☐☐☐ cheese?

10. *Mother:* No, we don't. I think we already have ☐☐☐☐.

Word Bank
any
few
many
much
some

4. Develop Language

USING *SOME/ANY*	
Use	**With**
some	*yes* statements *I have some bread.*
any	*no* statements *I don't have any bread.*
	questions *Do you want any bread?*

▶ Complete the statements and questions with *some* or *any*.

11. We don't have _____ juice.

12. Is there _____ cheese?

13. They need _____ milk.

14. Let's buy _____ oranges.

15. There aren't _____ bagels left.

17 Meals

1. Look and Explore

meals

breakfast

lunch

dinner

fork plate knife napkin spoon glass

2. Listen and Talk

WORDS 1–10

1. I eat **breakfast** every morning.
2. We eat **lunch** at noon.
3. My family eats **dinner** together.
4. I always eat everything on my **plate.**
5. Pour hot chocolate into the **cup.**
6. I drink a **glass** of milk with dinner.
7. Dad eats his rice with a **fork.**
8. My mother cuts meat with a **knife.**
9. A **spoon** works well for eating soup.
10. Use a **napkin** to wipe your mouth.

WORDS 11–20

11. We love to eat **meals** together.
12. Everybody in my family **drinks** milk.
13. My mother **makes** my lunch.
14. Today she **made** a sandwich for me.
15. I **usually** bring my lunch to school.
16. I **often** eat ham and cheese sandwiches.
17. I **sometimes** eat cereal for breakfast.
18. We **never** drink soda at dinner.
19. Dad **always** washes the dishes.
20. I **rarely** eat dessert.

3. Read and Write

WORDS 1–10

▶ Use the Word Bank to complete each sentence.

1. Most people eat _ _ _ _ _ _ _ _ _ in the morning.

2. At school we eat _ _ _ _ _ _ around noon.

3. Many families eat _ _ _ _ _ _ together in the evenings.

4. I always drink a _ _ _ _ _ of milk at dinner.

5. I put a _ _ _ _ _ _ on my lap.

Word Bank

dinner
breakfast
glass
napkin
lunch

WORDS 11–20

▶ Use the Word Bank to complete the table.

Action	Times per week	Adverbs
6. drinks soda at dinner	0	_ _ _ _ _ _
7. puts plates on the table	5	_ _ _ _ _ _
8. eats dessert	2	_ _ _ _ _ _
9. helps Mom cook	6	_ _ _ _ _ _ _
10. eats breakfast	7	_ _ _ _ _ _

Word Bank

always
often
never
rarely
usually

4. Develop Language

ADVERBS OF FREQUENCY

Go after the verb *to be*

I am always hungry in the morning.

Go before other verbs

I usually eat cereal.

▶ Write the adverbs on the blanks. Then circle the verbs.

11. Sean _____ eats sandwiches. (always)

12. My dog is _____ thirsty. (often)

13. The students are _____ late. (rarely)

14. Bill _____ makes lunch. (sometimes)

15. I _____ eat sushi for dinner! (never)

18 Clothes Shopping

Big Idea   We shop for clothes to wear.

1. Look and Explore

I need to buy new jeans.

shirt

belt

skirt

pants

sweater

jeans

shoes

2. Listen and Talk

WORDS 1–10

1. I like to **wear** pretty clothes.
2. Do you like this blue **shirt?**
3. I am looking for a black **skirt**.
4. She is wearing **pants**.
5. I always wear blue **jeans**.
6. What color are your **socks?**
7. He is wearing a black **belt**.
8. I am going to buy a new **dress**.
9. Let's look for some cool **shoes**.
10. I think your **sweater** is nice.

WORDS 11–20

11. What do you **like** to wear?
12. I **hate** to wear baseball caps.
13. She needs to **try on** that shirt.
14. My shirt is too **large** for me.
15. **Yours** is too small.
16. I need a size **small** shirt.
17. My jeans are **old**.
18. I need to buy **new** jeans.
19. What a **pretty** shirt!
20. I think it is **ugly**.

3. Read and Write

WORDS 1–10

▶ Write the word from the Word Bank that fits each clue.

1. You wear these on your feet.   _ _ _ _ _

2. This helps hold your pants up.   _ _ _ _

3. You wear this when it is cold.   _ _ _ _ _ _ _

4. Girls wear this.   _ _ _ _ _

5. These are usually blue.   _ _ _ _ _

Word Bank
jeans
dress
sweater
socks
belt

WORDS 11–20

▶ Use the Word Bank to complete the chart.

Antonyms	Synonyms
big ≠ _ _ _ _ _ **6.**	big = _ _ _ _ _ **9.**
_ _ _ _ ≠ old **7.**	_ _ _ _ _ _ = beautiful **10.**
pretty ≠ _ _ _ _ **8.**	

Word Bank
large
new
ugly
pretty
small

4. Develop Language

PRESENT CONTINUOUS VERBS

Subject	Be	Verb + *ing*
I	am	
He She It	is	talk*ing*.
You We They	are	

▶ Complete the sentences to show that the action is happening right now.

11. Steve _____ a baseball cap. (wear)

12. My parents _____ tea. (drink)

13. Monica _____ shoes. (buy)

14. We _____ at the mall. (shop)

15. Luz _____ that sweater. (try on)

19 Add and Subtract

Big Idea Add to find the sum. Subtract to find the difference.

1. Look and Explore

fish

little

big

addends

6 **add**

plus + 2

sum 8

2 big fish + 6 little fish
= 8 fish in all

▲ How many fish are there?

8 **subtract**

minus − 3

5

8 − 3 = 5 fish left

difference

2. Listen and Talk

WORDS 1–10

1. **Add** to find how many in all.
2. In 2 + 6, 2 and 6 are the **addends**.
3. 2 big fish **plus** 6 little fish equals 8 fish.
4. **Subtract** to find how many are left.
5. 8 fish **minus** 3 fish equals 5 fish.
6. In 2 + 6 = 8, 8 is the **sum**.
7. In 8 − 3 = 5, 5 is the **difference**.
8. Plus and minus **signs** tell us what to do.
9. We add and subtract to get the **answer**.
10. 8 minus 3 **equals** 5.

WORDS 11–20

11. There are 2 **big** fish in the tank.
12. There are 6 **little** fish in the tank.
13. How many **fish** are there in the tank?
14. **Combine** 2 and 6 to get the answer.
15. There are 8 fish in the **tank.**
16. Jonathan **had** 8 fish.
17. He **gave** 3 fish to Trisha.
18. How many does that **leave?**
19. We take **away** 3 from 8.
20. There are 5 fish **left.**

3. Read and Write

▶ Use the Word Bank to complete the sentences.

1. What is the sum of 9 __ __ __ __ 1?

2. Find the difference of 9 __ __ __ __ __ 5.

3. Do you know the __ __ __ __ __ __ ?

4. We __ __ __ to find the sum.

5. We __ __ __ __ __ __ __ __ to find the difference.

Word Bank

subtract
answer
minus
plus
add

▶ Use the Word Bank to complete the story problem.

Jonathan __ __ __ eight pet fish. He __ __ __ __ three fish to
        6.   **7.**

Trisha. How many __ __ __ __ does that __ __ __ __ __ ?
         8.   **9.**

Five fish are __ __ __ __ in the tank.
      10.

Word Bank

left
gave
had
fish
leave

4. Develop Language

COMMANDS

Add 1 and 5.

Subtract 3 from 4.

Take away 2 from 9.

Combine 10 and 4.

Find the sum of 2 plus 9.

▶ Circle the command words in the sentences. Then write the answer to each problem.

11. Add 5 + 5. _____

12. Take away 4 from 9. _____

13. Combine 4 and 3. _____

14. Find the sum. 7 + 5 = _____

15. Subtract 4 from 5. _____

Multiply and Divide

Big Idea   Multiply to find the product. Divide to find the quotient.

1. Look and Explore

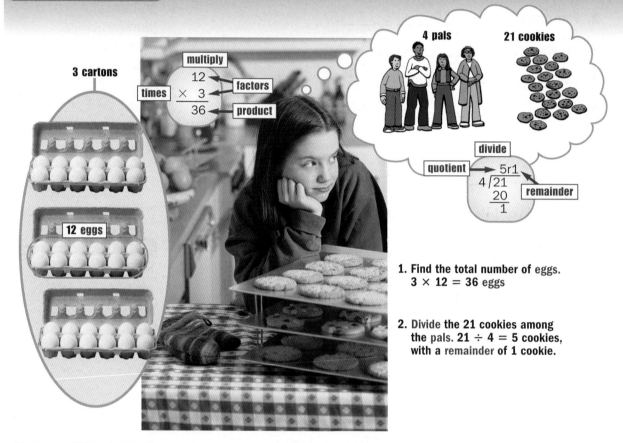

4 pals   **21 cookies**

3 cartons

multiply

times   12   factors
   ×   3
   36   product

12 eggs

divide

quotient   5r1
   4⟌21
    20   remainder
     1

1. Find the total number of eggs.
$3 \times 12 = 36$ eggs

2. Divide the 21 cookies among the pals. $21 \div 4 = 5$ **cookies, with a remainder of 1 cookie.**

2. Listen and Talk

WORDS 1–10

1. **Multiply** to find the total number of things.
2. In 3 times $12 = 36$, *3* and *12* are **factors**.
3. 3 **times** 12 equals 36.
4. The **product** is 36.
5. **Divide** to separate a group into equal parts.
6. 36 **divided by** 3 is 12.
7. 36 has 3 **equal** parts.
8. In 36 divided by 3, *12* is the **quotient**.
9. 21 does not divide into 4 equal **parts**.
10. There is a **remainder** of 1.

WORDS 11–20

11. Denise has three cartons of **eggs**.
12. A carton can **hold** twelve eggs.
13. Twelve eggs fit **into** one carton.
14. A **dozen** equals twelve.
15. She wants to share with four **pals**.
16. Some numbers don't divide **equally**.
17. **All** the cookies are divided.
18. There is one cookie **left over**.
19. The remainder is the one **extra** cookie.
20. **Only** one cookie is left.

3. Read and Write

WORDS 1–10

▶ Use the Word Bank to complete the sentences.

1. _ _ _ _ _ _ _ _ the factors.

2. The _ _ _ _ _ _ _ are 12 and 3.

3. What is the _ _ _ _ _ _ _ ?

4. _ _ _ _ _ _ 21 by 4.

5. What is the _ _ _ _ _ _ _ _ ?

Word Bank

product
factors
multiply
divide
quotient

WORDS 11–20

▶ Use the Word Bank to write the words to complete the story problem.

There are twenty-five _ _ _ _ on the table. A carton can
6.

_ _ _ _ twelve eggs. A dozen eggs fit _ _ _ _ one carton. A
7. **8.**

_ _ _ _ _ is equal to twelve. Twenty-four eggs fit into two
9.

cartons. Only one egg is _ _ _ _ _ _ _ _ .
10.

Word Bank

left over
eggs
into
dozen
hold

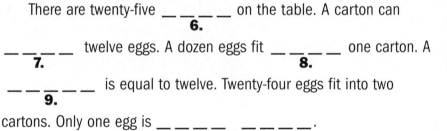

4. Develop Language

DEFINITE/INDEFINITE ARTICLES

Use	To tell about
a **an**	any noun *I need an egg. I want a cookie.*
the	a certain noun or certain nouns *He ate the cookies.*

▶ Complete the sentences with *a*, *an*, or *the*.

11. There is _____ exact recipe I need.

12. _____ carton has only eleven eggs in it.

13. I have _____ cookie for every student.

14. I am making _____ cake tomorrow.

15. _____ cake will be chocolate.

21 Rounding Numbers

Big Idea You can round numbers.

1. Look and Explore

We **round** numbers to make an **estimate**.

▲ There are 235 cars.

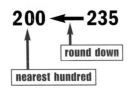

200 ◄— 235

round down

nearest hundred

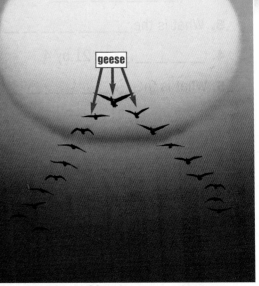

geese

▲ There are almost 20 geese.

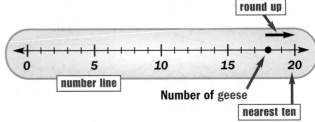

round up

number line

Number of geese

nearest ten

2. Listen and Talk

WORDS 1–10

1. We **round** numbers to make an estimate.
2. Bill's **estimate** is 20 geese.
3. Round 18 geese to the **nearest ten**.
4. Ruth's estimate is **close to** the exact amount.
5. Ruth's estimate is **less** than 235.
6. The exact number is **greater** than her guess.
7. You can use a **number line** to estimate.
8. Round 235 to the **nearest hundred**.
9. **Round up** if the digit to the right is 5 or more.
10. **Round down** if the digit is lower than 5.

WORDS 11–20

11. We can round numbers up or **down**.
12. Sally thinks there are **almost** 300 cars.
13. Sami thinks there are **just** 100 cars.
14. **Their** estimates are very different.
15. The cars have not been **counted**.
16. What is the exact number of **geese**?
17. Is this true or **false**?
18. It's **true** there are almost 250 cars.
19. Something that is true is **correct**.
20. Something that is false is **incorrect**.

▶ Use the Word Bank to complete each sentence.

1. We _ _ _ _ _ numbers to make an estimate.

2. An estimate is _ _ _ _ _ _ _ the exact amount.

3. 250 is _ _ _ _ _ _ _ than 235.

4. 235 is _ _ _ _ than 250.

5. Ruth made an _ _ _ _ _ _ _ _.

Word Bank
close to
greater
round
estimate
less

▶ Use the Word Bank to find the word that fits each clue.

6. only _____ _ _ _ _

7. not true _____ _ _ _ _ _

8. belonging to them _____ _ _ _ _ _

9. close to, but not exactly _____ _ _ _ _ _ _

10. correct _____ _ _ _ _

Word Bank
false
just
true
almost
their

4. Develop Language

IRREGULAR PLURALS	
Singular	**Plural**
goose	**geese**
foot	**feet**
child	**children**
tooth	**teeth**
mouse	**mice**

▶ Complete the sentences with the plural form of the word.

11. The _____ are late for school. (child)

12. I have about 30 _____. (tooth)

13. I see almost 100 _____ in the sky. (goose)

14. Please keep your _____ off the desk. (foot)

15. Do _____ really like cheese? (mouse)

22 How's the Weather?

Big Idea We talk about the weather.

1. Look and Explore

It is hot and sunny today.

hot
warm
cool
cold

weather forecast

Yesterday | Today | Tomorrow

cloudy | sunny | rainy

umbrella

It is a rainy day. ▶

2. Listen and Talk

WORDS 1–10

1. How's the **weather** today?
2. It is **sunny** today.
3. The weather is **hot** outside.
4. I like **warm** weather.
5. It was **cool** yesterday.
6. I hate **cold** weather.
7. It will be **rainy** tomorrow.
8. Then it will be **cloudy** too.
9. It is **clear** today.
10. Last winter was **freezing**!

WORDS 11–20

11. Look **up** at the sky.
12. The **forecast** says it will be rainy tomorrow.
13. It will **also** be cold.
14. **If** it's rainy tomorrow, I'll wear a coat.
15. If it rains, I **will** carry an umbrella.
16. I **won't** wear shorts.
17. I am **going** to stay inside.
18. The temperature is warm **inside**.
19. It will be cold and rainy **outside**.
20. Open your **umbrella**.

WORDS 1–10

▶ Use the Word Bank to complete each sentence.

1. How's the __ __ __ __ __ __ __ in your city?

2. It's 89° F in Phoenix. It's __ __ __ in Phoenix.

3. It's 72° F in Sacramento. It's __ __ __ __ in Sacramento.

4. It's 5° F in Milwaukee. It's __ __ __ __ in Milwaukee.

5. It's 58° F in New York City. It's __ __ __ __ in New York City.

Word Bank

warm
cool
hot
weather
cold

WORDS 11–20

▶ Use the Word Bank to complete the poem.

I __ __ __□ __ play soccer
     6.

__ __ the weather is bad.
 7.

If I don't play soccer,

then I __ __ __ __ be sad.
         8.

I will stay __ __ __ __ __ all day.
            9.

What does the __ __ __ __ __ __ __ __ say?
              10.

Word Bank

won't
will
forecast
inside
if

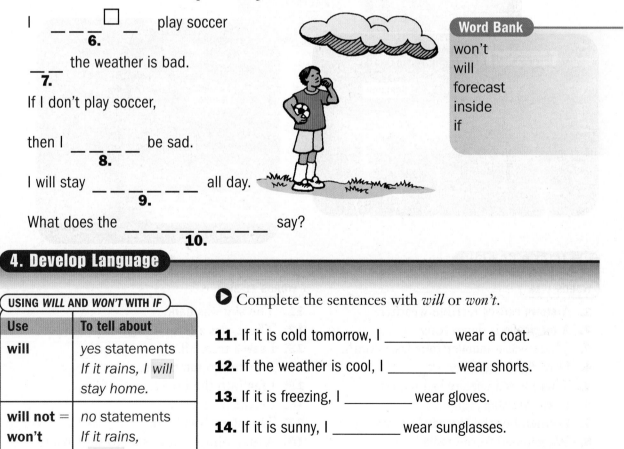

USING *WILL* AND *WON'T* WITH *IF*	
Use	**To tell about**
will	*yes* statements *If it rains, I will stay home.*
will not = **won't**	*no* statements *If it rains,* *I won't play.*

▶ Complete the sentences with *will* or *won't*.

11. If it is cold tomorrow, I _____ wear a coat.

12. If the weather is cool, I _____ wear shorts.

13. If it is freezing, I _____ wear gloves.

14. If it is sunny, I _____ wear sunglasses.

15. If it rains, I will use an umbrella so I _____ get wet.

23 Storms

Storms cause terrible weather.

1. Look and Explore

A storm **causes terrible weather.**

windy

hurricane

snowing

blizzard

thunderstorm

lightning

tornado

2. Listen and Talk

WORDS 1–10

1. A **storm** causes terrible weather.
2. A **hurricane** is dangerous.
3. There was a **thunderstorm** last month.
4. I saw **lightning** in the sky.
5. There was a **blizzard** last winter.
6. It was **snowing** really hard.
7. I remember the **tornado** last year.
8. We listened to the **radio**.
9. There was a tornado **warning**.
10. It was so **windy**.

WORDS 11–20

11. The sky was **dark**.
12. There was a flash of **light** in the sky.
13. I **saw** a tree fall.
14. I started to **run** home.
15. I **ran** into the house.
16. I **heard** an alarm.
17. The **alarm** was loud.
18. A man on the radio **said** to stay inside.
19. We ran to find **shelter**.
20. My family **went** down into the basement.

3. Read and Write

▶ Use the Word Bank to find the word that fits each clue. Then fill in the blanks.

1. a flash of light in the sky   _ i _ _ _ _ i _ _

2. another name for a twister   _ o _ _ a _ o

3. a storm with loud noises   _ _ u _ _ e _ _ _ o _ _

4. a storm with a lot of snow   _ _ i _ _ a _ _

5. a storm with a lot of wind   _ u _ _ i _ a _ e

Word Bank

hurricane
blizzard
tornado
thunderstorm
lightning

▶ Use the Word Bank to complete the chart.

Present	Past
go	_ _ _ _ **6.**
see	_ _ _ **7.**
_ _ _ **8.**	ran
say	_ _ _ _ **9.**
hear	_ _ _ _ _ **10.**

Word Bank

run
saw
went
heard
said

4. Develop Language

SIGNAL WORDS

Use signal words to tell about the past.	
last	*I saw her last night.*
yesterday	*I ran home yesterday.*

▶ Circle the signal word in each sentence. Then complete each sentence with the past tense form of the verb.

11. There _____ a bad storm last week. (is)

12. I _____ lightning last night. (see)

13. I _____ the thunderstorm yesterday. (hear)

14. I _____ from the tornado last month. (run)

15. I don't remember what you _____ yesterday. (say)

 Seasons

Big Idea You can do different activities during each season.

1. Look and Explore

winter

sledding

spring

garden

fall / autumn

leaves

play

summer

2. Listen and Talk

WORDS 1–10

1. **Winter** begins in December.
2. Summer **starts** in June.
3. July is a **summer** month.
4. **Fall** ends in December.
5. Fall is also called **autumn.**
6. When does **spring** begin?
7. The **seasons** change four times a year.
8. Winter **ends** and spring begins.
9. My **favorite** season is the spring.
10. What is your favorite fall **activity?**

WORDS 11–20

11. **Can** you play tennis?
12. No, **I can't.**
13. I can't **play** tennis very well.
14. **Shall** we practice together?
15. I wish winter **would** end soon.
16. I **wish** it could always be summer.
17. The **leaves** fall in the fall.
18. I plant a **garden** in the spring.
19. We're **going** to the beach this summer.
20. We go **sledding** in the winter.

3. Read and Write

▶ Use the Word Bank to complete each sentence.

1. There are four __ __ __ __ __ __ __ per year.

2. Fall __ __ __ __ __ __ in September.

3. Autumn __ __ __ __ in December.

4. Summer is Sunjay's __ __ __ __ __ __ __ __ season.

5. Sledding is a winter __ __ __ __ __ __ __ __.

Word Bank

ends
seasons
favorite
starts
activity

▶ Use the Word Bank to write the word that fits each clue.

6. They fall off trees in the fall. __ __ __ __ __ __

7. You need snow to go do this. __ __ __ __ __ __ __ __ __

8. This means *to be able to*. __ __ __

9. You plant flowers here. __ __ __ __ __ __

10. This means *to hope for something*. __ __ __ __

Word Bank

leaves
wish
can
garden
sledding

4. Develop Language

USING *CAN* AND *CAN'T*

Use	With
can	*yes statements* *I can play the guitar.*
cannot = **can't**	*no statements* *I can't drive a car.*

▶ Answer the questions with *Yes, I can* or *No, I can't*.

11. Can you dance? _____.

12. Can you touch your tongue to your nose?
_____.

13. Can you speak Japanese? _____.

14. Can you make spaghetti? _____.

15. Can you drive a car? _____.

25 Family

Big Idea Talk about the members of your family.

1. Look and Explore

Marisa's Family Tree

grandparents

mother | father | aunt | uncle

sister | **Marisa** | brother | cousin

2. Listen and Talk

WORDS 1–10

1. Marisa has a large **family.**
2. Her **parents** are smiling.
3. Marisa's **father** is serving tamales.
4. Her **mother** is eating.
5. Marisa's **sister** is helping serve.
6. Her **brother** is young.
7. Her **uncle** is drinking water.
8. Marisa's **aunt** is sitting.
9. Her **cousin** is standing.
10. Marisa's **grandparents** are happy.

WORDS 11–20

11. **Both** of her siblings are young.
12. Her grandparents are **sitting.**
13. Her father is **standing.**
14. Marisa has two **siblings.**
15. Marisa's sister is **beautiful.**
16. Her uncle is **handsome.**
17. Her sister is **thin.**
18. Marisa's cousin is not **heavy.**
19. Marisa's brother is **young.**
20. One of her siblings has **long** hair.

▶ Use the Word Bank to complete each sentence.

1. Your mother and father are your __ __ __ __ __ __ __ __.

2. Your parents' parents are your __ __ __ __ __ __ __ __ __ __ __ __.

3. Your father's brother is your __ __ __ __ __ __.

4. Your mother's sister is your __ __ __ __.

5. Your uncle's daughter is your __ __ __ __ __ __.

Word Bank

grandparents
uncle
parents
cousin
aunt

▶ Say the word for each picture. Then use the Word Bank to write the word.

Word Bank

long
young
thin
sitting
standing

6. __ __ __ __ __ __ __

7. __ __ __ __ __ __ __ __

8. __ __ __ __ __ __

9. __ __ __ __ __

10. __ __ __ __

4. Develop Language

POSITIVE SHORT ANSWERS		
	I am.	
Yes,	he she **is.** it	
	you we **are.** they	

▶ Complete the questions about the picture on page 86.

11. Is Marisa's sister standing? _____.

12. Is Marisa's father serving? _____.

13. Are Marisa's grandparents smiling?

_____.

14. Is Marisa's brother sitting? _____.

15. Is Marisa's mother laughing? _____.

26

Things to Do at Home

Big Idea We do many things at home.

1. Look and Explore

fixing

washing

practicing

singing

listening

sleeping

2. Listen and Talk

WORDS 1–10

1. The brothers are **washing** the car.
2. Sandra is **sleeping** on the sofa.
3. Latoya is **listening** to music.
4. How do you **relax?**
5. Eva is **jumping** rope.
6. Phil and his father are **fixing** his bike.
7. Maria and Latoya are **singing** songs.
8. I **enjoy** watching movies.
9. Vera is **practicing** the violin.
10. My father is **watching** TV.

WORDS 11–20

11. Lacy likes to **do** many things at home.
12. Do you have a **hobby?**
13. What do you do in your **free** time?
14. Everybody in my house is **busy.**
15. How do you have **fun?**
16. I like doing **nothing.**
17. Is there **anything** you don't like to do?
18. Cleaning is **something** I don't like to do.
19. Is **anyone** making dinner at your house?
20. **Someone** is doing exercises.

3. Read and Write

WORDS 1–10

▶ Underline the word from the Word Bank in each sentence. Then write each word.

1. What do you enjoy doing? _ _ _ _ _ _

2. How do you relax? _ _ _ _ _ _

3. Yun Ju is washing her hands. _ _ _ _ _ _ _ _

4. My brother is watching TV. _ _ _ _ _ _ _ _ _

5. Adrian is listening to music. _ _ _ _ _ _ _ _ _

Word Bank

relax
washing
enjoy
listening
watching

WORDS 11–20

▶ Use the Word Bank to complete the conversation.

6. *Eric:* What do you _ _ for fun?

7. *Brinda:* My favorite _ _ _ _ _ is bowling.

8. *Brinda:* But, I am very _ _ _ _ with school.

9. *Eric:* Are you _ _ _ _ on Saturday?

10. *Brinda:* Sure, let's go then. It will be _ _ _.

Word Bank

fun
busy
free
do
hobby

4. Develop Language

PRESENT TENSE VERBS

Subject	Verb	
I You We They	**eat**	dinner early.
He She It	**eats**	

▶ Complete the sentences using the correct form of the verb.

11. They _____ bikes. (fix)

12. Martha _____ English at night. (practice)

13. Jan _____ a movie. (watch)

14. Mike _____ cooking. (enjoy)

15. Alycia _____ rope. (jump)

27

Places at Home

Big Idea   Learn the names of places in your home.

1. Look and Explore

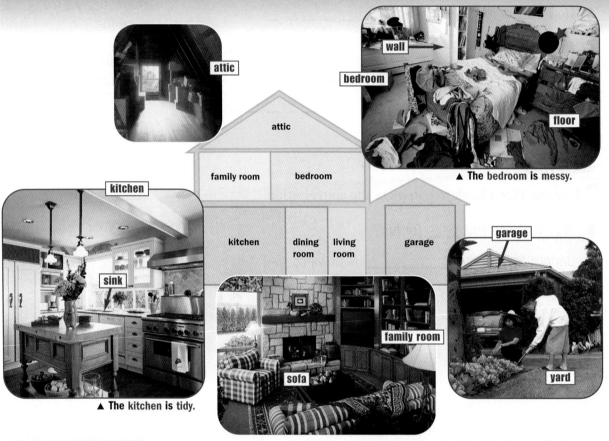

▲ The bedroom is messy.

▲ The kitchen is tidy.

2. Listen and Talk

WORDS 1–10

1. There's a lamp in the **living room**.
2. There's a TV in the **family room**.
3. The bed is in the **bedroom**.
4. The sink is in the **kitchen**.
5. There's a table in the **dining room**.
6. They are working in the **yard**.
7. There is a truck in the **garage**.
8. There are boxes in the **attic**.
9. The picture is on the **wall**.
10. There are clothes on the **floor**.

WORDS 11–20

11. The bedroom is **messy**.
12. The kitchen is **tidy**.
13. There are lights **above** the table.
14. The fireplace is **below** the picture.
15. The window is **behind** the chair.
16. There's a table in **front** of the fireplace.
17. Clothes are **under** the bed.
18. A **sofa** is in the family room.
19. There is a **lamp** on the table.
20. There is a **sink** in the kitchen.

3. Read and Write

WORDS 1–10

▶ Look at the pictures on page 90. Use the Word Bank to complete the sentences.

1. There's a sofa in the __ __ __ __ __ __ __ __ __ __.

2. The bed is in the __ __ __ __ __ __ __.

3. There's a garden in the __ __ __ __.

4. There are boxes in the __ __ __ __ __.

5. The clothes are on the __ __ __ __ __.

Word Bank

floor
family room
bedroom
attic
yard

WORDS 11–20

▶ Use the Word Bank to complete the word that fits each clue.

6. where you wash dishes   __ i __ __

7. an object that gives light   __ a __ __

8. couch   __ o __ a

9. not clean   __ e __ __ __

10. neat   __ i __ __

Word Bank

messy
tidy
sink
sofa
lamp

4. Develop Language

QUESTIONS WITH *IS THERE/ARE THERE*	
Singular	**Plural**
Is there	**Are there**
Is there <u>a cat</u>?	Are there <u>chairs</u>?

▶ Complete the sentences with *Is* or *Are*. Then answer the questions aloud about the pictures on page 90.

11. _____ there a TV in the family room?

12. _____ there people in the yard?

13. _____ there a sink in the kitchen?

14. _____ there boxes in the attic?

15. _____ there clothes on the floor?

28 How We Act

Big Idea Friends have different character traits.

1. Look and Explore

kind

strict

smiling

laughing

frowning

funny

generous

2. Listen and Talk

WORDS 1–10

1. Sergio is **kind**.
2. That boy's brother is **generous**.
3. He's not **selfish** at all.
4. Mr. Martinez is very **strict**.
5. He looks **mean**.
6. He seems **serious**.
7. Stella is so **funny**.
8. He looks very **friendly**.
9. Cecilia is always so **quiet**.
10. I think she's very **shy**.

WORDS 11–20

11. How do your friends **act?**
12. She **looks** serious.
13. She is always **frowning**.
14. They **seem** happy.
15. They are always **smiling**.
16. Why are they **laughing?**
17. Why is Cecilia **so** shy?
18. His brother **shares** his umbrella.
19. I **think** Stella is funny, too.
20. He's always telling a **joke**.

3. Read and Write

WORDS 1–10

▶ Use the Word Bank to complete each sentence.

1. My brother is so __ __ __ __ __ __ __. He never shares.

2. My father is __ __ __ __. He helps me with my homework.

3. My friend, Leita, is always __ __ __ __ __ __ __. She never laughs.

4. Bob is so __ __ __ __ __ __ __ __. He always greets me with a smile.

5. Marta is so __ __ __ __ __. She never talks in class.

Word Bank

friendly
kind
serious
quiet
selfish

WORDS 11–20

▶ Use the Word Bank to complete each sentence.

6. She is __ __ __ __ __ __ __ because she is happy.

7. I am __ __ __ __ __ __ __ __ because the movie is funny.

8. They are __ __ __ __ __ __ __ __ because they are mad.

9. He is generous because he __ __ __ __ __ __ everything.

10. She is funny because she always has a good __ __ __ __.

Word Bank

joke
frowning
laughing
shares
smiling

4. Develop Language

NEGATIVE SHORT ANSWERS

Singular

Is <u>Sergio</u> mean?
No, he isn't.

Plural

Are <u>the brothers</u> selfish?
No, they aren't.

▶ Complete the questions with *isn't* or *aren't*.

11. Is Tomani mean? No, she _____.

12. Are the students quiet? No, they _____.

13. Is Mrs. Jansen strict? No, he _____.

14. Are Arturo and Alonso frowning? No, they _____.

15. Is Colin serious? No, he _____.

How We Feel

Big Idea People have different emotions.

1. Look and Explore

confused

upset

excited

embarrassed

angry

nervous

2. Listen and Talk

WORDS 1-10

1. What gets you **upset?**
2. She's **nervous** about driving a car.
3. They're **happy** because it's a great day.
4. I'm **sad** because my grandmother is sick.
5. Why do you get **embarrassed?**
6. She's **excited** because it's her birthday.
7. He's **bored** because he is done reading.
8. She's **lonely** without her friends.
9. She is **angry** at her little sister.
10. The children are **confused.**

WORDS 11-20

11. Have you ever **been** embarrassed?
12. **Why** are you so happy?
13. I'm happy **because** I passed the test.
14. I didn't mean to hurt your **feelings.**
15. Don't **be** so sad.
16. I was sad, **but** now I'm happy.
17. What's on your **mind?**
18. I **don't** know why I'm sad.
19. What's **wrong?**
20. Why are you in such a good **mood?**

3. Read and Write

▶ Use the Word Bank to say how the events make you feel.

Event	How you feel
1. You win a game.	_ _ _ _ _
2. Your best friend moves away.	_ _ _
3. You drop your books.	_ _ _ _ _ _ _ _ _ _ _
4. You don't understand the directions.	_ _ _ _ _ _ _ _
5. You are home alone.	_ _ _ _ _ _

Word Bank

sad
embarrassed
happy
lonely
confused

WORDS 11–20

▶ Use the Word Bank to complete the conversation.

6. *Joon:* _ _ _ _ are you upset?

7. *Kyle:* I'm upset _ _ _ _ _ _ _ _ my friend is sick.

8. *Kyle:* I've been in a bad _ _ _ _ _ all day.

9. *Joon:* Don't be sad. _ _ happy.

10. *Kyle:* Thanks for thinking about my _ _ _ _ _ _ _ _.

Word Bank

mood
feelings
be
because
why

4. Develop Language

ADJECTIVES	
Use	**With**
***ed* form**	people *The players are excited.*
***ing* form**	things *The game is exciting.*

▶ Complete the sentences with the correct word.

11. English can be _____ sometimes. (confused/confusing)

12. Ben is _____ in class. (bored/boring)

13. The movie is _____. (excited/exciting)

14. Waiting in line is _____. (bored/boring)

15. Soccer is _____. (excited/exciting)

Talk About It

You can express your emotions.

1. Look and Explore

counselor

argue

agree

letter

2. Listen and Talk

WORDS 1–10

1. Is there something **bothering** you?
2. A **counselor** helps you talk about it.
3. **Express** your feelings when you feel bad.
4. You can write a **letter** to a friend.
5. This will show that you **care**.
6. Sometimes people **argue**.
7. People don't always **agree**.
8. Have you ever had a **fight**?
9. How did you **make up**?
10. I would like to **apologize**.

WORDS 11–20

11. Carla sends funny email **messages**.
12. Bill said he was **sorry**.
13. People care **about** you.
14. You are never **alone**.
15. It is helpful to talk **with** someone.
16. How do you express **yourselves**?
17. Brad expresses **himself** by singing.
18. Belinda expresses **herself** by drawing.
19. The students talk things out **themselves**.
20. Counselors help us talk about **ourselves**.

3. Read and Write

WORDS 1–10

▶ Use the Word Bank to complete each sentence.

1. Jana, is something _ _ _ _ _ _ _ _ _ _ you?

2. How do you _ _ _ _ _ _ _ _ yourself?

3. Leticia had a _ _ _ _ _ with her sister.

4. I want to _ _ _ _ _ _ _ _ _ _ for being late.

5. My friends and family _ _ _ _ about me.

Word Bank

express
bothering
care
apologize
fight

WORDS 11–20

▶ Use the Word Bank to complete the chart.

Singular		Plural	
I	myself	we	_ _ _ _ _ _ _ _ _ **6.**
you	yourself	you	_ _ _ _ _ _ _ _ _ **7.**
he	_ _ _ _ _ _ _ **8.**	they	_ _ _ _ _ _ _ _ _ **10.**
she	_ _ _ _ _ _ _ **9.**		

Word Bank

himself
herself
themselves
yourselves
ourselves

4. Develop Language

ARTICLES A AND AN

Use	Before
a	a noun that starts with a consonant
I wrote a letter to apologize.	
an	a noun that starts with a vowel sound
I had an argument.	

▶ Complete the sentences with *a* or *an*.

11. I owe you _____ apology.

12. Sheila wrote _____ letter to her grandparents.

13. My teacher and I made _____ agreement.

14. Our school has _____ counselor.

15. I have _____ happy family life.

31 The Calendar

Big Idea   We have special ways to say dates in English.

1. Look and Explore

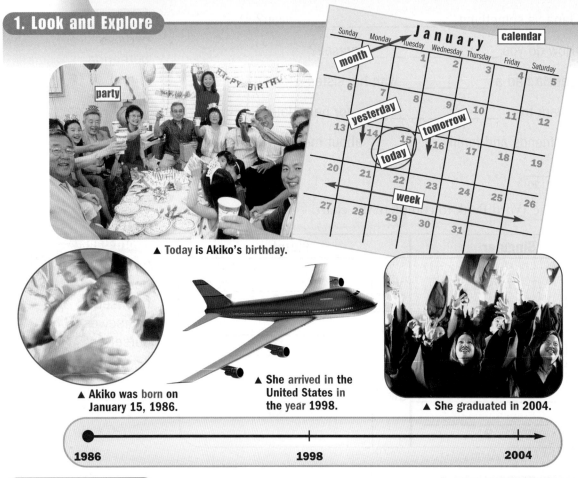

▲ Today is Akiko's birthday.

▲ Akiko was born on January 15, 1986.

▲ She arrived in the United States in the year 1998.

▲ She graduated in 2004.

1986   1998   2004

2. Listen and Talk

WORDS 1–10

1. A **calendar** shows dates.
2. The circled **date** today is January 15.
3. Today is Akiko's **birthday!**
4. She was **born** in 1986.
5. She **arrived** in the United States in 1998.
6. She **graduated** high school in 2004.
7. What **year** were you born?
8. What **month** were you born?
9. How many **days** are in a week?
10. I was born in the third **week** of January.

WORDS 11–20

11. The **party** is for Akiko's birthday.
12. Akiko **was** born in Japan.
13. When **were** you born?
14. She was born **in** January.
15. She moved here six years **ago.**
16. What is the date **today?**
17. **Yesterday** was the 14th.
18. **Tomorrow** is Wednesday.
19. My birthday was **last** month.
20. Her birthday is not **until** July.

3. Read and Write

WORDS 1–10

▶ Use the Word Bank to complete each sentence about the calendar.

1. We use a _ _ _ _ _ _ _ _ _ to write down dates.

2. August is a _ _ _ _ _ in the summer.

3. Monday, Wednesday, and Friday are _ _ _ _ of the week.

4. A _ _ _ _ has 7 days.

5. August 7, 1974, is a _ _ _ _.

Word Bank

date
days
month
week
calendar

WORDS 11–20

▶ Look at the calendar. Then use the Word Bank to complete each sentence.

Monday	Tuesday	Wednesday	Thursday	Friday	Saturday
December 31 New Year's Eve	January 1 New Year's Day	January 2	January 3 *Today*	January 4	January 5

6. _ _ _ _ _ is January 3.

7. _ _ _ _ _ _ _ _ _ _ was January 2.

8. _ _ _ _ _ _ _ _ is Friday.

9. New Year's Day was _ _ _ _ Tuesday.

10. New Year's Eve was _ _ December.

Word Bank

in
last
today
tomorrow
yesterday

4. Develop Language

SIMPLE PAST WITH *WAS/WERE*			
I	**was**	we	**were**
you	**were**	you	**were**
he she **was** it		they	**were**

▶ Complete the sentences with *was* or *were*.

11. I _____ 10 years old when I moved to the United States.

12. The Khans _____ in Costa Rica last month.

13. My little brother, Timothy, _____ born in 2001.

14. Linda and Judith _____ late for class yesterday.

15. We _____ invited to the birthday party.

32 Time

Big Idea   We use special words to tell time.

1. Look and Explore

What **time** is it?

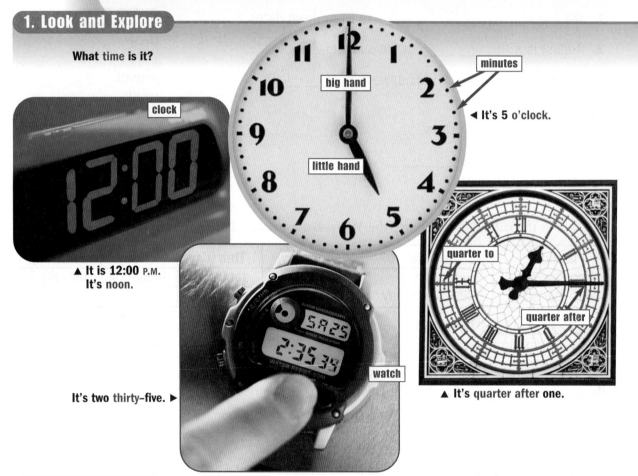

clock

big hand

minutes

◀ It's 5 o'clock.

little hand

▲ It is 12:00 P.M.
It's noon.

quarter to

quarter after

watch

It's two thirty-five. ▶

▲ It's quarter after one.

2. Listen and Talk

WORDS 1-10

1. We use a **clock** to tell time.
2. The **little hand** shows the hours.
3. The **big hand** shows the minutes.
4. There are 60 **seconds** in a minute.
5. There are 60 **minutes** in an hour.
6. There are 24 **hours** in a day.
7. What **time** is it now?
8. I think your **watch** is slow.
9. What time was the **sunrise** today?
10. When was the **sunset** yesterday?

WORDS 11-20

11. **A.M.** is before noon.
12. **P.M.** is after noon.
13. 12:00 P.M. is **noon**.
14. 12:00 A.M. is **midnight**.
15. 1:30 is read one **thirty**.
16. 12:45 is read **quarter to** one.
17. 1:15 is read **quarter after** one.
18. It is one **o'clock**.
19. The clock at school is two minutes **fast**.
20. Our clock at home is five minutes **slow**.

WORDS 1–10

▶ Use the Word Bank to complete each sentence.

1. What __ __ __ __ is it?

2. The __ __ __ __ __ __ on the wall is five minutes slow.

3. I wear a __ __ __ __ __ __ on my left wrist.

4. The __ __ __ __ __ __ __ __ was around 6:00 A.M.

5. The __ __ __ __ __ __ __ was around 6:00 P.M.

Word Bank

clock
sunset
sunrise
time
watch

WORDS 11–20

▶ Use the Word Bank to label each clock.

What time is it?

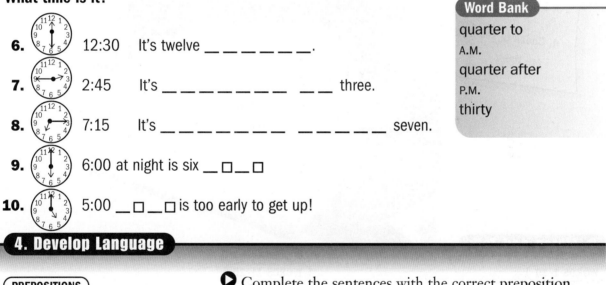

6. 12:30   It's twelve __ __ __ __ __ __ .

7. 2:45   It's __ __ __ __ __ __ __ __ __ __ __ three.

8. 7:15   It's __ __ __ __ __ __ __ __ __ __ __ __ seven.

9. 6:00 at night is six __ ☐ __ ☐

10. 5:00 __ ☐ __ ☐ is too early to get up!

Word Bank

quarter to
A.M.
quarter after
P.M.
thirty

4. Develop Language

PREPOSITIONS	
at	at 2:30 P.M. (exact times)
	at night
in	in the morning
	in the afternoon
	in a few minutes, hours

▶ Complete the sentences with the correct preposition.

11. School starts _____ a few minutes.

12. Lisa gets up _____ 7:00 A.M.

13. Mohammed has soccer practice _____ the afternoon.

14. School is over _____ two hours.

15. Cecile watches television _____ night.

Big Idea Math problems can be easy if you have a strategy.

1. Look and Explore

I'll guess the answer. Then I'll check to see if I'm right.

plan

1. Understand **the** problem.

2. Make a **plan.**

3. Solve **the** problem.

4. Check to see if you are right.

problem

2. Listen and Talk

WORDS 1–10

1. Yuri wants to solve the math **problem.**
2. He needs to find **its** answer.
3. Math problems give **clues** for what to do.
4. First, try to **understand** the problem.
5. Then, make a **plan.**
6. Next, **solve** the problem.
7. Finally, check to see if you are **right.**
8. He **thinks** about the question.
9. He thinks about what he will **try** to do.
10. Does his answer **make sense?**

WORDS 11–20

11. Yuri reads **over** the problem.
12. He tries to solve it on his **own.**
13. Yuri **looks for** clues.
14. He finds the **best** way to solve the problem.
15. There is more than one **way** to solve it.
16. Math problems can seem **difficult** at first.
17. They can be **easy** if you follow this strategy.
18. **Pick** a way to solve the problem.
19. You can also **guess** the answer.
20. Then, **check** to see if the answer is correct.

3. Read and Write

WORDS 1–10

▶ Use the Word Bank to complete each sentence.

1. Think about the _ _ _ _ _ _ _ .

2. Try to _ _ _ _ _ _ _ _ _ _ _ the problem.

3. Make a _ _ _ _ .

4. _ _ _ _ _ the problem.

5. Check to see if it is _ _ _ _ _ .

Word Bank

plan
right
solve
problem
understand

WORDS 11–20

▶ Underline the word or words from the Word Bank in each sentence. Then write each word.

6. Yuri read over the problem.   _ _ _ _

7. Pick a way to solve it.   _ _ _ _

8. You can guess the answer.   _ _ _ _ _

9. Yuri looks for word clues.   _ _ _ _ _ _ _ _

10. That problem was easy!   _ _ _ _

Word Bank

guess
looks for
pick
over
easy

4. Develop Language

ADVERBS

Adjective	Adverb
careful	**carefully**
careless	**carelessly**
easy	**easily**
slow	**slowly**
quick	**quickly**

▶ Complete each sentence by changing the adjective to an adverb.

11. Kristy reads the problem _____. (careful)

12. Peter rides his bike _____. (careless)

13. Our teacher speaks _____. (slow)

14. My father drives _____. (quick)

15. We solve word problems _____. (easy)

34 Computers

Big Idea Learn to use computer words.

1. Look and Explore

File
Open
Close
Save
Print

document → **file**

monitor

type | → **cursor**

→ **window**

screen

printer

disk drive

keyboard

documents

mouse

2. Listen and Talk

WORDS 1–10

1. A **keyboard** is used for typing.
2. You look at the **monitor.**
3. The **screen** is part of the monitor.
4. You use the **printer** to print pages.
5. Select things with your **cursor.**
6. You use a **mouse** to move the cursor.
7. Put your disk into the **disk drive.**
8. Save your work to a **diskette.**
9. Close the **window** on the screen.
10. Find the on/off **switch.**

WORDS 11–20

11. Turn **on** the computer.
12. **Click** the file you want to open.
13. **Type** your first and last name.
14. You save a **file** to a diskette.
15. **Save** your document to a diskette.
16. Click here to **open** the document.
17. Click there to **close** the document.
18. You can print **documents.**
19. **Print** your document.
20. Turn the monitor **off.**

► Use the Word Bank to complete each sentence.

1. Open and close the _ _ _ _ _ _ with your mouse.

2. Type at the _ _ _ _ _ _ _.

3. Save your work to a _ _ _ _ _ _ _ _ _.

4. Shut down the computer with the on/off _ _ _ _ _ _.

5. Print your document with the _ _ _ _ _ _ _.

Word Bank

cursor
diskette
switch
printer
window

► Use the words in the Word Bank to complete the chart.

What do you do with it?	
On/off switch	**Mouse**
turn _ _ **6.**	 _ _ _ _ **9.**
turn _ _ _ **7.**	
Keyboard	**Printer**
_ _ _ _ **8.**	_ _ _ _ **10.**

Word Bank

on
click
type
print
off

4. Develop Language

USING DON'T/DOESN'T

Subject	Don't/Doesn't
I you we they	**don't**
he she it	**doesn't**

► Complete the sentences with *don't* or *doesn't*.

11. Do you know how to type? No, I _____.

12. Does he always save his work? No, he _____.

13. Does your computer play CDs? No, it _____.

14. Do they go online often? No, they _____.

15. Do your friends send email? No, they _____.

 # Lab Safety

Big Idea We need to follow safety rules in the science lab.

1. Look and Explore

goggles

gloves

LAB RULES

1. If you spill something, clean it up.
2. Always wash your hands.
3. Wear an apron, gloves, and goggles.
4. Know where the exit is in case of a fire.

EXIT

exit sign

fire extinguisher

hands

2. Listen and Talk

WORDS 1–10

1. You need to **behave** in the science lab.
2. You have to be **careful.**
3. There are **rules** to follow in the lab.
4. Pay **attention** to the rules.
5. Protect your eyes with **goggles.**
6. Wear an **apron** over your clothes.
7. Wearing **gloves** protects your hands.
8. Know where the **exit** is at all times.
9. Where's the **fire extinguisher?**
10. The science lab can be **dangerous.**

WORDS 11–20

11. Knowing the rules helps keep you **safe.**
12. You need to be **very** careful.
13. If you **spill** something, clean it up.
14. Eating is not **allowed** in the lab!
15. Drinking in the lab is **prohibited!**
16. **Protect** yourself against injury.
17. Always wash your **hands.**
18. Know where to go **in case** of a fire.
19. What do we do if there is a **fire?**
20. Don't you know the fire **drill?**

3. Read and Write

WORDS 1-10

▶ Use the Word Bank to complete the sentences. Then read each sentence aloud.

1. The students _ _ _ _ _ _ very well.

2. Be _ _ _ _ _ _ _ _ or you will spill something.

3. Rami pays _ _ _ _ _ _ _ _ _ to the teacher.

4. Chewing gum is against the _ _ _ _ _.

5. Don't do anything that is _ _ _ _ _ _ _ _ _.

Word Bank

attention
rules
behave
dangerous
careful

WORDS 11-20

▶ Use the Word Bank to complete the safety rules.

6. Always wash your _ _ _ _ _ after an experiment.

7. If you _ _ _ _ _ something, clean it up.

8. Eating is not _ _ _ _ _ _ _ in the lab!

9. Know where to go _ _ _ _ _ _ of a fire.

10. Always be _ _ _ _ in the lab.

Word Bank

in case
hands
allowed
safe
spill

4. Develop Language

COMMANDS

Positive = verb only
Wash *your hands.*
Pay *attention.*

Negative = Don't + verb
Don't _spill_.
Don't _bring_ *food to the lab.*

▶ Complete the positive or negative commands.

11. _____ attention to the teacher. (pay)

12. _____. (spill)

13. _____ the fire drill. (know)

14. Always _____ an apron. (wear)

15. _____ in the lab. (eat)

Do an Experiment

Big Idea We learn about science by doing experiments.

1. Look and Explore

Let's do an experiment. **Follow** the **directions.**

You Will Need:
- **1 cup** baking soda
- **1 cup** vinegar
- **1 plastic bag that can be sealed**

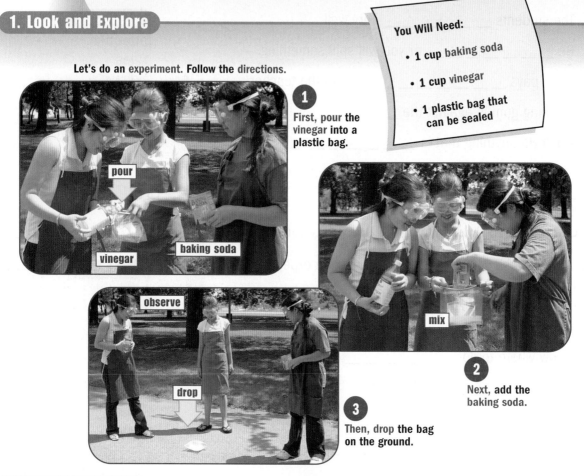

1 First, pour the vinegar **into** a plastic bag.

pour

vinegar

baking soda

observe

mix

drop

2 Next, **add** the baking soda.

3 Then, drop **the bag on the ground.**

2. Listen and Talk

WORDS 1–10

1. We do an **experiment** in science class.
2. The teacher gives us **directions.**
3. We **follow** the directions carefully.
4. What is the first **step?**
5. We need **vinegar** for the experiment.
6. We also need **baking soda.**
7. What are we going to **learn** about?
8. Vinegar and baking soda make a **gas.**
9. Read the directions **before** you start.
10. Clean up **after** you are done.

WORDS 11–20

11. **First,** open the plastic bag.
12. **Pour** some vinegar in the bag.
13. **Then,** add some baking soda.
14. **Next,** close the bag quickly.
15. **Drop** the bag to the ground.
16. Stand **back!**
17. **Observe** what happens.
18. What happens when you **mix** them?
19. **Finally,** clean up any mess.
20. What did you **find out?**

3. Read and Write

WORDS 1–10

▶ Use the Word Bank to complete each sentence.

1. We did an _ _ _ _ _ _ _ _ _ _ in science class.

2. The teacher gave us _ _ _ _ _ _ _ _ _ _.

3. _ _ _ _ _ _ the directions carefully.

4. The first _ _ _ _ is to open the bag.

5. What did you _ _ _ _ _ about?

Word Bank

directions
experiment
follow
learn
step

WORDS 11–20

▶ Use the Word Bank to complete the directions. Then number the steps from 1 to 5.

6. _ _ _ _ _, pour some vinegar in the bag. _____

7. _ _ _ _ _ _, open the plastic bag. _____

8. _ _ _ _ _ _ _ _, clean up. _____

9. Next, drop the bag and stand _ _ _ _ _! _____

10. _ _ _ _ _, add some baking soda. _____

Word Bank

back
finally
first
next
then

4. Develop Language

ORDER WORDS

Use	To tell about the
First	1st action
Then **Next**	2nd action 3rd action 4th action
Finally	last action

▶ Use the order words to complete the directions.

11. _____, open the cereal box.

12. _____, get a bowl.

13. _____, pour cereal in the bowl.

14. _____, pour milk over the cereal.

15. _____, eat it.

Getting Ready

Big Idea Earth has different landforms.

1. Look and Explore

mountains

hills

◄ Mountains **are** tall and steep.

A plain **is an area of flat land.** ►

plain

Sand covers a desert. ▼

◄ **That** canyon is deep.

canyon

desert

island

Water surrounds an island. ►

shore

2. Listen and Talk

WORDS 1–10

1. **Mountains** are tall and steep.
2. **Hills** are smaller than mountains.
3. That **area** of land is a plain.
4. A **plain** is an area of flat land.
5. She looks down at the **canyon.**
6. An area of dry land is a **desert.**
7. Sand **covers** a desert.
8. An **island** is surrounded by water.
9. Water **surrounds** an island.
10. The **shore** is the land next to the sea.

WORDS 11–20

11. **Soil** covers a plain.
12. **Grass** grows in soil.
13. The surface of a plain is **flat.**
14. That canyon is **deep.**
15. The sides of mountains are **steep.**
16. The **sand** on the beach is tan.
17. Sand covers the **beach.**
18. **Rocks** cover the ground.
19. Rocks are made of **hard** material.
20. The sand feels **soft.**

WORDS 1–10

► Use the Word Bank to complete the crossword puzzle.

ACROSS

1. an area of dry land

3. a part of a place

4. spreads over something

5. a flat area of land

DOWN

2. is all around something

Word Bank

covers
surrounds
plain
desert
area

WORDS 11–20

► Use the Word Bank to write the word that describes the things.

6. a swimming pool, a canyon, an ocean _____

7. a desk's surface, a plain, the floor _____

8. a mountain, a ski hill, stairs _____

9. a helmet, rocks, steel _____

10. a bed, sand, your skin _____

Word Bank

deep
soft
flat
hard
steep

4. Develop Language

USING IT OR THEY

Use	To tell about
it	1 thing *The mountain is steep.* *It is steep.*
they	more than 1 thing *Mountains are steep.* *They are steep.*

► Complete the sentences with *it* or *they*.

11. _____ is flat. (a plain)

12. _____ are deep. (canyons)

13. _____ surrounds an island. (water)

14. Farmers plant crops in _____. (soil)

15. _____ are not as big as mountains. (hills)

38

Bodies of Water

Big Idea Different bodies of water cover Earth.

1. Look and Explore

People surf on the waves in oceans. ▶

pond

A river flows over land. ▼

lake

▲ Land surrounds a lake.

▲ The children are fishing in a pond.

river

2. Listen and Talk

WORDS 1–10

1. Seven **oceans** cover Earth.
2. An ocean is a large **body** of water.
3. A **sea** is smaller than an ocean.
4. Land surrounds a **lake.**
5. A **pond** is smaller than a lake.
6. A **river** flows over land.
7. A **stream** is a small river.
8. All oceans have **salt water.**
9. Saltwater contains **salt.**
10. Some seas have **fresh water.**

WORDS 11–20

11. Look at the big **waves.**
12. The **tide** goes up and down every day.
13. People **surf** on the waves in oceans.
14. The ocean's waves can be **rough.**
15. A pond's surface is **smooth.**
16. The boat is **floating** in the pond.
17. The children go **fishing** in a pond.
18. People go **swimming** in the ocean.
19. That stream is **shallow.**
20. Some rivers **run into** the ocean.

3. Read and Write

WORDS 1–10

▶ Use the Word Bank to complete each sentence.

1. The largest bodies of water are _____.

2. A sea is a large _____ of water.

3. _____ tastes salty in your mouth.

4. _____ is the water we drink.

5. Salt water contains _____.

Word Bank

salt water
body
oceans
salt
fresh water

WORDS 11–20

▶ Use the Word Bank to label each picture.

Word Bank

fishing
swimming
surf
waves
floating

6. _____

7. _____

8. _____

9. _____

10. _____

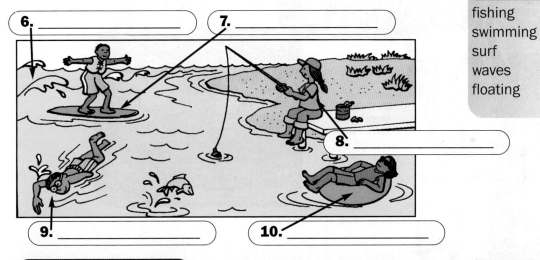

4. Develop Language

USING *GO* OR *GOES* WITH *ING* VERBS		
Subject	**Go/Goes**	**Verb**
I You We They	**go**	swimming.
He She It	**goes**	

▶ Complete each sentence with *go* or *goes*.

11. Karla _____ swimming in the pond.

12. Ana and Tomas _____ shopping at the mall.

13. Will you _____ fishing with me?

14. Apu's family _____ skiing every winter.

15. The children _____ sledding down the hill.

39

Cultures

> **Big Idea** ▶ People around the world have different cultures.

1. Look and Explore

People have special ways of cooking. ▶

Music is passed down through generations. ▶

Some people dress in special ways. ▼

Dance is important to some cultures. ▶

2. Listen and Talk

WORDS 1–10

1. People have different **cultures**.
2. Cultures have their own **traditions**.
3. **Art** is an important part of culture.
4. Parents help children learn their **beliefs**.
5. Families are made up of **generations**.
6. **Ethnic** groups share customs.
7. Wearing kilts is a **custom** in Scotland.
8. People eat different kinds of **food**.
9. **Dance** is an important part of culture.
10. Cultures have their own type of **music**.

WORDS 11–20

11. **Elders** teach children about customs.
12. **Grandchildren** continue the traditions.
13. People share **memories** with each other.
14. Traditions are **passed down**.
15. Parents tell **stories** to their children.
16. Close **relatives** take care of children, too.
17. People celebrate holidays in **special** ways.
18. Does your culture have a **style** of dress?
19. Some people **dress** in special ways.
20. People also have special ways of **cooking**.

3. Read and Write

WORDS 1–10

▶ Say each word. Then copy it to complete each sentence.

1. ethnic   Many _____ groups live in my community.

2. generations My father and I belong to different _____ .

3. custom   Wearing kilts is a _____ in Scotland.

4. traditions   Our family has its own special _____ .

5. beliefs   It's OK that your _____ are different from mine.

Word Bank
generations
ethnic
beliefs
traditions
custom

WORDS 11–20

▶ Use the Word Bank to complete the paragraphs.

I have many _____ who come from Japan. My
6.
culture's traditions were _____ from my father's father.
7.
   My grandfather shared our Japanese culture with us, his

_____ . My grandfather shares his
8.
_____ about growing up in Tokyo. Before I go to bed,
9.
he tells me Japanese _____ .
10.

Word Bank
grandchildren
stories
memories
relatives
passed down

4. Develop Language

ASKING *DO/DOES* QUESTIONS

Use	With
does	singular nouns *How does a Scottish man dress?*
do	plural nouns *How do Scottish men dress?*

▶ Complete the questions with *do* or *does*.

11. What _____ many Chinese people celebrate?

12. How _____ your family celebrate birthdays?

13. How _____ people pass down traditions?

14. What special foods _____ people in your culture eat?

15. How _____ your culture celebrate weddings?

40 Letters and Sounds

Big Idea Vowels and consonants make special sounds.

1. Look and Explore

The **alphabet has 26** letters.

◄ The **alphabet has** vowels and **consonants. The** letters *a, e, i, o,* and *u* **are** vowels.

◄ hat

The *a* **in** *hat* **is a short vowel.** ►

◄ The words *bat* and *hat* rhyme.

cake

bat ►

The *a* in *cake* is a long vowel. ►

2. Listen and Talk

WORDS 1–10

1. The **alphabet** has 26 letters.
2. There are 2 kinds of **letters.**
3. The letters *a, e, i, o,* and *u* are **vowels.**
4. The letters *c, n, t,* and *s* are **consonants.**
5. The *a* in *hat* is a **short vowel.**
6. The *a* in *cake* is a **long vowel.**
7. Long vowels sound **like** their names.
8. A **cluster** is a group of consonants.
9. In a cluster, consonants **blend** together.
10. The words *cat* and *hat* **rhyme.**

WORDS 11–20

11. Vowels make different **sounds.**
12. You can **hear** different vowel sounds.
13. Learning sounds helps you **speak** English.
14. Words with the same **final** sounds rhyme.
15. You can't hear the *e* in *cake.*
16. The *e* in *cake* is **silent.**
17. A vowel **pair** can make a long vowel sound.
18. The *o* and *a* in *boat* make a long *o* sound.
19. The *g* and *l* in *glad* blend together.
20. What words rhyme with *cat*?

WORDS 1–10

▶ Use the Word Bank to complete the crossword puzzle.

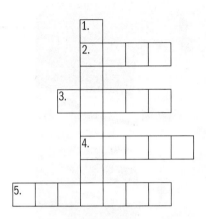

DOWN

1. the letters of any language

ACROSS

2. almost the same as

3. to have the same final sound, like *cat* and *hat*

4. to mix together

5. symbols you use to write words

Word Bank

alphabet
like
rhyme
blend
letters

WORDS 11–20

▶ Use the Word Bank to write the word that rhymes with each group of words.

6. *lake, rake, take* _____

7. *note, coat, wrote* _____

8. *hat, bat, sat* _____

9. *mad, sad, dad* _____

10. *hair, chair, care* _____

Word Bank

cake
pair
cat
glad
boat

4. Develop Language

ANSWERING *DOES* QUESTIONS	
Use	**To answer**
does	yes *Yes, it* does.
does not = **doesn't**	no *No, it* doesn't.

▶ Complete the questions with *does* or *doesn't*.

11. Does *cake* rhyme with *lake*? Yes, it _____.

12. Does the *e* in *cake* make a sound? No, it _____.

13. Does *hat* have a short vowel sound? Yes, it _____.

14. Does *cake* have a short vowel sound? No, it _____.

15. Does *cake* rhyme with *hat*? No, it _____.

# 41 Alphabetical Order

Big Idea We use alphabetical order to organize lists of things.

1. Look and Explore

glossary

▲ A glossary **puts words in** alphabetical order.

flights

Departures

▲ Flights at airports are in
alphabetical order by city.

attendance

Anderson, Monique
Kelly, Shannon
Krieger, Philip
Lopez, Eric
Martin, Teri
Sanchez, David

The last names
are arranged in
alphabetical
order. ▶

last names

2. Listen and Talk

WORDS 1–10

1. English letters are in **alphabetical** order.
2. The letters are in a **particular** order.
3. **Alphabetize** the names, please.
4. It is a **convenient** way to arrange names.
5. We **arranged** words in alphabetical order.
6. They **ordered** their names from A to Z.
7. **Flights** at airports are in ABC order by city.
8. Class **attendance** is in ABC order by names.
9. A **glossary** puts words in alphabetical order.
10. *Anderson* **appears** first on the list.

WORDS 11–20

11. Lillian knows how to say the **ABC's.**
12. **Sort** these words into alphabetical order.
13. Put the names in the correct **position.**
14. How are the **last names** arranged?
15. **Place** *Lopez* before *Martin.*
16. *Sanchez* goes **toward** the end.
17. *Lopez* **goes before** *Martin.*
18. *Martin* **goes after** *Lopez.*
19. *Krieger* **goes between** *Kelly* and *Lopez.*
20. What letter does the word **start with?**

3. Read and Write

WORDS 1–10

▶ Use the Word Bank to write the word that has the same meaning as the underlined word or words.

1. The city names are <u>arranged in order from A to Z</u>. _____

2. Lists in alphabetical order are <u>easy to use</u>. _____

3. The letters of the alphabet are in a <u>special</u> order. _____

4. The teacher takes <u>roll call</u> every morning. _____

5. The airport puts <u>airplane trips</u> in ABC order. _____

Word Bank

convenient
alphabetical
particular
attendance
flights

WORDS 11–20

▶ Use the Word Bank to write the word that fits each clue.

6. another name for the alphabet _____

7. to arrange _____

8. where something is located _____

9. to put _____

10. in the direction of _____

Word Bank

toward
sort
place
ABC's
position

4. Develop Language

GO OR GOES	
Use	**With**
goes	singular nouns Flynn goes before Newman.
go	plural nouns The letters s and t go before u.

▶ Complete each sentence with *go* or *goes*.

11. *Apple* _____ to the front of the list.

12. *Ship* and *shoe* _____ before *shop*.

13. *New* _____ before *shoe*.

14. *A* and *B* _____ before *C*.

15. *Zoo* _____ at the end of the list.

42 Spelling Basics

> **Big Idea** Learn the spelling of action words occurring right now.

1. Look and Explore

Use these rules to guide you.

Adding *ing*

Words that end in y

Add **ing**

fly   fly + ing   → | flying |

Words that end in e

Drop silent **e** and add **ing**

rake   rake + ing   → | raking |

Words that end in consonant–vowel–consonant, like c-l-a-p

Double the final consonant and add **ing**

clap   clap + p + ing   → | clapping |

▲ The helicopter is flying in the sky.

The students are clapping their hands. ▶

▲ The family is raking leaves.

2. Listen and Talk

WORDS 1–10

1. Kalial is studying the present **tenses**.
2. Some actions are **everyday**.
3. Some actions are **continuous**.
4. Use the **present simple** for everyday actions.
5. For **present continuous** action, use *ing*.
6. These rules are true **in general**.
7. Use these rules to **guide** you.
8. **Double** the *p* in *clap* to make *clapping*.
9. **Delete** the final *e* in *rake* and add *ing*.
10. For words **ending** in *y*, add *ing*.

WORDS 11–20

11. These actions are **occurring** now.
12. The helicopter is **flying** in the sky.
13. The family is **raking** leaves.
14. The students are **clapping** their hands.
15. What are you **doing** right now?
16. We are studying English **right now**.
17. At this **moment**, we are studying English.
18. It is happening at the **present** time.
19. We **spell** these words with *ing*.
20. It is easy to **misspell** words.

3. Read and Write

WORDS 1–10

▶ Use the Word Bank to write the word that matches the definition.

1. to help _____

2. usually _____

3. to add one more of the same letter _____

4. to take away _____

5. finishing _____

Word Bank

in general
double
guide
delete
ending

WORDS 11–20

▶ Use the Word Bank to complete the chart.

Present Simple	Present Continuous
Actions that occur every day	Actions that are _____ now **6.**
What do you do?	What are you _____? **7.**
The helicopters fly.	The helicopters are _____. **8.**
They clap their hands.	They are _____ their hands. **9.**
They rake the leaves.	They are _____ the leaves. **10.**

Word Bank

doing
flying
occurring
raking
clapping

4. Develop Language

PRESENT CONTINUOUS SENTENCES		
Subject	**Be**	**Verb + ing**
I	am	
He She It	is	studying.
We You They	are	

▶ Complete the sentences with *is*, *am*, or *are*.

11. My family _____ different things. (do)

12. I _____ English. (study)

13. My father _____ the lawn. (rake)

14. My sisters _____ lemonade. (drink)

15. My pets _____. (sleep)

43

Bar Graphs

Big Idea Bar graphs compare different information.

1. Look and Explore

Students took a poll about sports.

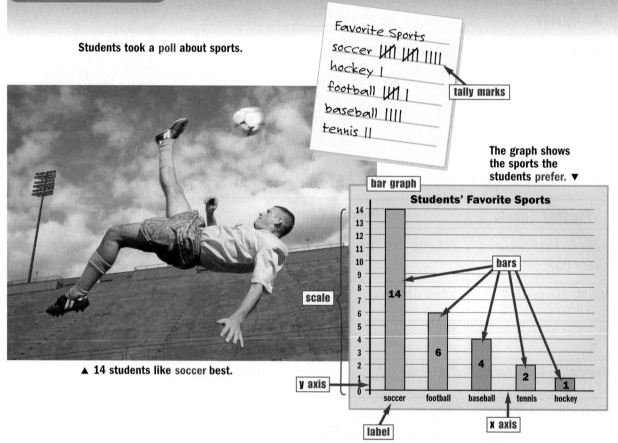

Favorite Sports
soccer ||||| ||||| ||||
hockey |
football ||||| |
baseball ||||
tennis ||

tally marks

The graph shows the sports the students prefer. ▼

bar graph

Students' Favorite Sports

scale

bars

soccer 14 · football 6 · baseball 4 · tennis 2 · hockey 1

y axis

label

x axis

▲ 14 students like soccer best.

2. Listen and Talk

WORDS 1–10

1. We use bar graphs to show **information**.
2. Students took a **poll** about sports.
3. **Tally marks** show students' favorite sports.
4. Ali uses the data to make a **bar graph**.
5. The bar graph shows the poll **results**.
6. **Title** the bar graph.
7. The number of answers is on the *y* **axis**.
8. A **label** for each sport is on the *x* axis.
9. The **scale** lists the exact numbers of students.
10. The **bars** stand for the numbers of students.

WORDS 11–20

11. The graph shows the sport students **prefer**.
12. The most **popular** sport is soccer.
13. There are 14 students who like **soccer** best.
14. The **majority** of students like to play soccer.
15. Six students prefer **football**.
16. **Baseball** is the favorite sport of four students.
17. **Several** students like baseball best.
18. Two students enjoy playing **tennis** best.
19. Only a **couple** of students enjoy tennis best.
20. One student likes to play **hockey** best.

3. Read and Write

WORDS 1–10

▶ Use the Word Bank to complete each sentence.

1. A _____ is an easy way to show information.

2. _____ the bar graph to tell what it shows.

3. You take a _____ to find something out.

4. The _____ are what you find out from the poll.

5. Bar graphs give _____ about poll results.

Word Bank

information
poll
title
results
bar graph

WORDS 11–20

▶ Use the Word Bank to write the word that fits each clue.

6. to like one thing better than another   _____

7. liked by many people   _____

8. most of the people or things in a group   _____

9. more than two, but not many   _____

10. two things   _____

Word Bank

majority
couple
several
prefer
popular

4. Develop Language

POSSESSIVE NOUNS	
Add	**With**
's	singular nouns *Yuko's team won.*
s'	plural nouns *Our students' favorite sport is soccer.*

▶ Complete each sentence with the correct possessive form of the noun.

11. What are _____ opinions about their teachers? (students)

12. That is Ms. _____ class. (Ms. Summer)

13. She answers every _____ question. (student)

14. _____ teacher is Mr. Newbie. (Bill)

15. Listen to _____ grammar. (teachers)

44

Showing Data

Big Idea You can display data in many different ways.

1. Look and Explore

The students took a **survey** to **pick** a **mascot**.

mascot

There are many ways to display the data.

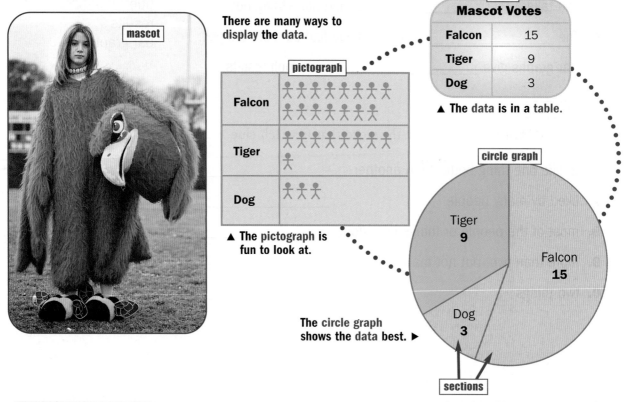

table

Mascot Votes

Falcon	15
Tiger	9
Dog	3

▲ The data is in a table.

pictograph

Falcon	👤👤👤👤👤👤👤👤👤👤👤👤👤👤👤
Tiger	👤👤👤👤👤👤👤👤👤
Dog	👤👤👤

▲ The pictograph is fun to look at.

circle graph

Tiger 9
Falcon 15
Dog 3

sections

The circle graph shows the data best. ▶

2. Listen and Talk

WORDS 1–10

1. The students took a **survey** to select a mascot.
2. A survey is a way to **gather** information.
3. The information you collect is called **data**.
4. The students **record** the data.
5. Use graphs to **show** the data clearly.
6. There are many ways to **display** the data.
7. You can **illustrate** the data in many ways.
8. The data is in a **table**.
9. The **pictograph** is fun to look at.
10. The **circle graph** shows the results best.

WORDS 11–20

11. We need to pick a **mascot**.
12. **Decide** which mascot you want.
13. The students counted the **ballots**.
14. In the pictograph, stick men **stand for** students.
15. A pictograph uses **pictures** to show data.
16. A circle graph divides a circle into **sections**.
17. Fifteen students voted for the **falcon**.
18. Nine students preferred the **tiger**.
19. Three students picked the **dog**.
20. There were 15 **votes** for the falcon.

3. Read and Write

WORDS 1–10

▶ Use the Word Bank to write the word that has the same meaning as the underlined word or words.

1. The students take a <u>poll</u> to select a new mascot. _____

2. They <u>collect</u> the information on a piece of paper. _____

3. They <u>display</u> the data in a bar graph. _____

4. There are many ways to <u>show</u> data. _____

5. You can even <u>explain</u> the results <u>with pictures</u>. _____

Word Bank

gather
display
show
illustrate
survey

WORDS 11–20

▶ Use the Word Bank to write the word that fits each clue.

6. represent _____

7. pieces of paper used to record votes _____

8. choose _____

9. parts _____

10. decisions in a survey _____

Word Bank

ballots
stand for
decide
sections
votes

4. Develop Language

PERSONAL PRONOUNS

Singular	
he	the boy, Max, Mr. Lu
she	the woman, Mira, Ms. Quivers
it	the dog, the desk, the chair
Plural	
they	Max and Mira, the dogs

▶ Complete each sentence with *he, she, it,* or *they.*

11. Did the students pick the falcon? Yes, _____ did.

12. How did you pick the mascot? I voted for _____ .

13. What did Lucy vote for? _____ voted for the dog.

14. Did Scott and Sue vote? No, _____ didn't.

15. Which animal did Terry vote for? _____ voted for the falcon.

45 Finding Averages

Big Idea We have many ways to describe data.

1. Look and Explore

We find the **average** of a set of numbers.

| mean |

| 71 | 71 | 72 | 73 | 74 | 75 | 76 | 76 | 79 |

Heights (in inches)

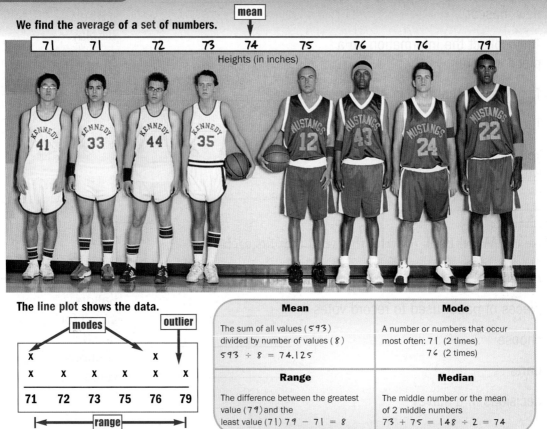

The line plot shows the data.

modes   outlier

	x			x	
x	x	x	x	x	x
71	72	73	75	76	79

range

Mean	**Mode**
The sum of all values (593) divided by number of values (8) 593 ÷ 8 = 74.125	A number or numbers that occur most often: 71 (2 times) 76 (2 times)
Range	**Median**
The difference between the greatest value (79) and the least value (71) 79 − 71 = 8	The middle number or the mean of 2 middle numbers 73 + 75 = 148 ÷ 2 = 74

2. Listen and Talk

WORDS 1–10

1. We find the average of a **set** of numbers.
2. We have special words to **summarize** data.
3. The mean is the same as the **average**.
4. The **mean** height of the boys is 74 inches.
5. The **range** is 8 inches, from 71 to 79.
6. The **modes** are 71 inches and 76 inches.
7. The **line plot** shows the data.
8. The **median** is 74, the middle value.
9. In math, **values** are shown with numbers.
10. The height of 79 inches is the **outlier**.

WORDS 11–20

11. There is a **gap** between 79 and 76.
12. The mode value **occurs** most often.
13. The **highest** height is 79 inches.
14. The **lowest** height is 71 inches.
15. What is the average **height** of the players?
16. The **middle** number is often the median.
17. Malcolm is not as **tall** as Isaac.
18. Yoshima is not as **short** as Rudy.
19. Malcolm is the **tallest** player.
20. Rudy is the **shortest** player.

3. Read and Write

WORDS 1–10

▶ Use the Word Bank to complete each sentence.

1. A _____ is a group of numbers.

2. You can _____ data by finding averages.

3. A _____ shows all the data.

4. Numbers give you the _____ of things.

5. The mean is the most commonly used _____.

Word Bank

line plot
values
average
summarize
set

WORDS 11–20

▶ Use the Word Bank to write the word that fits each clue.

6. an empty space between two things   _____

7. happens   _____

8. how tall you are   _____

9. in the center   _____

10. the most high   _____

Word Bank

occurs
height
gap
middle
highest

4. Develop Language

SUPERLATIVES

	Adjective + est
the	tallest building
	shortest path
	highest point
	lowest price

▶ Complete the sentences by writing the superlative form of the word.

11. Gloria is the _____ girl in the class. (tall)

12. Celine is the _____. (short)

13. The _____ height is 71 inches. (low)

14. What is the _____ place in the world? (high)

15. What is the _____ mountain? (tall)

46 Healthy Foods

Big Idea Eating nutritious food keeps you healthy.

1. Look and Explore

An apple makes a good snack. ▶

Kim drinks milk for calcium. ▼

Sonya has good eating habits. ▼

▲ **A well-balanced meal is nutritious.**

2. Listen and Talk

WORDS 1–10

1. Sonya has good eating **habits.**
2. She has a healthy **diet.**
3. Kim drinks milk for **calcium.**
4. Calcium makes teeth and **bones** strong.
5. Fruits and vegetables are **nutritious.**
6. She eats many **servings** of fruits a day.
7. Vegetables are high in **vitamins.**
8. Carla eats a **well-balanced** meal.
9. A food's **ingredients** tell you if it is healthy.
10. It's okay to eat **sweets** once in a while.

WORDS 11–20

11. Sonya stays **healthy** by eating good foods.
12. An apple makes a good **snack.**
13. She eats fruits and other **natural** foods.
14. **Fresh** foods are usually nutritious.
15. Fresh foods make you **strong.**
16. Ruth never **skips** breakfast.
17. She avoids food with **artificial** things in it.
18. Eating junk food all the time is **unhealthy.**
19. Junk food makes you feel **tired.**
20. Carla **avoids** unhealthy food, like candy.

3. Read and Write

WORDS 1–10

▶ Use the Word Bank to complete the crossword puzzle.

DOWN

1. portions of food

3. desserts and candy

ACROSS

2. the food that you eat

4. good for you

5. things you do without thinking

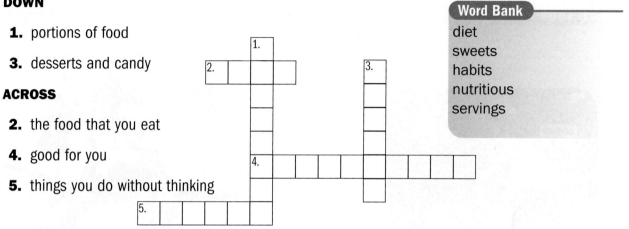

Word Bank

diet
sweets
habits
nutritious
servings

WORDS 11–20

▶ Use the Word Bank to write the word with the opposite meaning.

6. unhealthy ≠ _____

7. weak ≠ _____

8. artificial ≠ _____

9. alert ≠ _____

10. natural ≠ _____

Word Bank

tired
strong
artificial
healthy
natural

4. Develop Language

HAS/HAVE		
I You We They	**have**	healthy eating habits.
He She It	**has**	

▶ Complete the sentences with *has* or *have*.

11. Vegetables _____ a lot of vitamins.

12. Donna _____ a healthy diet.

13. Philip and Rhonda _____ good eating habits.

14. Junk food _____ artificial ingredients.

15. Sweets _____ a lot of sugar.

47 Fitness and Exercise

Big Idea You can stay in shape by exercising regularly.

1. Look and Explore

helmet

▲ Biking makes her muscles strong.

Leslie plays on the basketball team to stay fit. ▶

practice

pads

◀ Bill is wearing arm pads.

2. Listen and Talk

WORDS 1–10

1. Leslie has excellent **fitness.**
2. She is a good **athlete.**
3. She is on the school's basketball **team.**
4. **Physical** exercise helps her feel good.
5. Biking makes her **muscles** strong.
6. She is wearing a **helmet.**
7. Bill is wearing arm **pads.**
8. Sandra is **active** in sports.
9. Exercise makes Sandra more **flexible.**
10. Always **stretch** before you exercise.

WORDS 11–20

11. Leslie exercises **daily.**
12. She takes care of her **body.**
13. The players **practice** in the gym.
14. The players **work out** often.
15. They **warm up** before the game.
16. The basketball players lift **weights.**
17. Tanya gets a lot of **exercise.**
18. Nate and Tina **jog** around the track.
19. That's how they stay **in shape.**
20. Playing sports is a fun way to stay **fit.**

3. Read and Write

WORDS 1-10

▶ Use the Word Bank to write the word that fits each clue.

1. how you take care of your body _____

2. sports player _____

3. having to do with the body _____

4. doing things _____

5. easy to bend _____

Word Bank

athlete
physical
fitness
active
flexible

WORDS 11-20

▶ Use the Word Bank to write the word that has the same meaning as the underlined word or words.

6. Pamela plays soccer <u>every day</u>. _____

7. Nate and Tim <u>run</u> every morning. _____

8. That is how Mia stays <u>physically fit</u>. _____

9. The basketball players <u>exercise</u> in the gym. _____

10. Before playing a game, they <u>do short exercises</u>. _____

Word Bank

jog
daily
in shape
work out
warm up

4. Develop Language

MAKING PRESENT CONTINUOUS VERBS	
Use	**To tell about**
present tense verbs	habits and facts *Sonya always wears a helmet.*
present continuous verbs	actions happening now *Sonya is wearing a helmet now.*

▶ Complete each sentence by changing the present tense verb into the present continuous form.

11. The team _____ a game. (play)

12. Leslie _____ . (warm up)

13. The players _____ weights. (lift)

14. Bill and Sandra _____ helmets. (wear)

15. Lita _____ before the game. (exercise)

48 Germs and Hygiene

 **Big Idea** Practice good hygiene to prevent the spread of germs.

1. Look and Explore

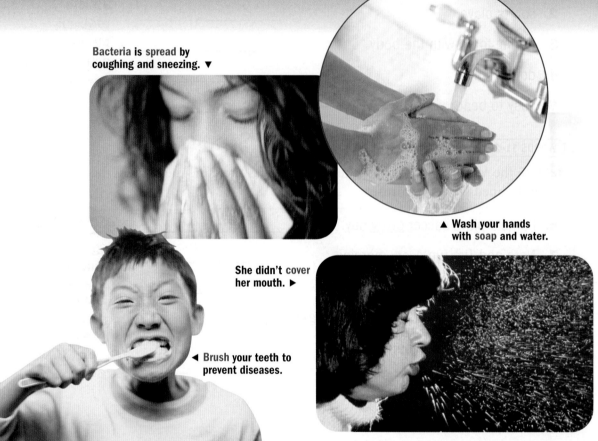

Bacteria **is spread by** coughing and sneezing. ▼

▲ **Wash your hands** with **soap** and water.

She didn't **cover** her mouth. ▶

◀ **Brush your teeth to** prevent diseases.

2. Listen and Talk

WORDS 1–10

1. Germs **cause** people to get sick.
2. You can't see **germs** in the air.
3. Julie practices good **hygiene**.
4. She **prevents** the spread of germs.
5. **Cover** your nose when you sneeze, please.
6. **Bacteria** are germs that make people sick.
7. Bacteria is **spread** by coughing and sneezing.
8. Wash your hands with **soap** and water.
9. **Brush** your teeth to prevent diseases.
10. Min Ho uses a **toothbrush**.

WORDS 11–20

11. Germs are **everywhere**.
12. They **enter** your body when you breathe.
13. **Everything** you touch has germs on it.
14. Wash your hands to **remove** germs.
15. Get the dirt out from under your **fingernails**.
16. You get germs when you **touch** things.
17. Some germs stay on your **skin**.
18. Wash your hands to **kill** germs.
19. It's easy to get germs from someone **else**.
20. Germs can be **harmful**.

WORDS 1–10

▶ Use the Word Bank to complete the crossword puzzle.

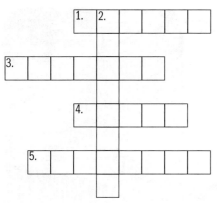

ACROSS

1. to pass something on

3. practices that keep you healthy

4. they carry diseases

5. germs that make people sick

DOWN

2. stops something from happening

Word Bank

prevents
bacteria
spread
hygiene
germs

WORDS 11–20

▶ Use the Word Bank to write the word that has the same meaning as the underlined word or words.

6. You can find germs <u>in all places.</u> _____

7. Wash your hands to <u>get rid of</u> germs. _____

8. <u>All things</u> have germs on them. _____

9. Germs <u>go into</u> your body when you breathe. _____

10. You get germs when you <u>handle</u> things. _____

Word Bank

enter
everything
remove
everywhere
touch

4. Develop Language

GERUNDS

Use	To say
by + verb (+ing)	how to do something
Kill germs by washing your hands.	

▶ Complete the sentences using the *ing* form of the verb.

You can stay healthy and stop the spread of germs by:

11. _____ good hygiene. (practice)

12. _____ your teeth. (brush)

13. _____ your mouth when you cough. (cover)

14. _____ germs from your hands. (remove)

15. _____ germs. (kill)

49 Washington, D.C.

Big Idea Our nation's capital is full of history.

1. Look and Explore

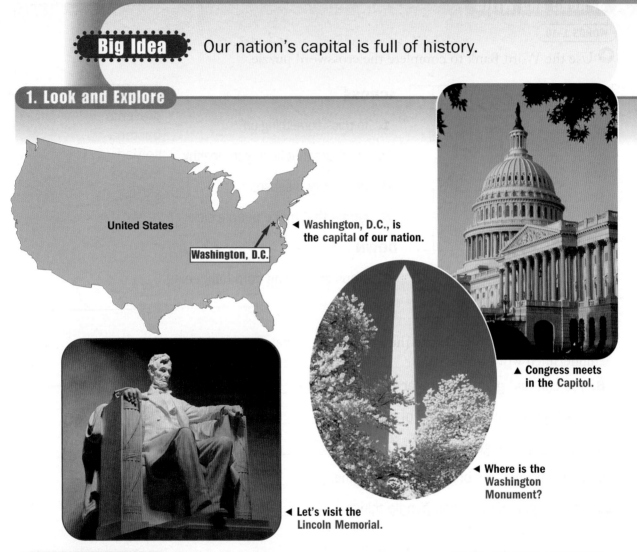

United States

Washington, D.C.

◄ Washington, D.C., is the capital of our nation.

▲ Congress meets in the Capitol.

◄ Where is the Washington Monument?

◄ Let's visit the Lincoln Memorial.

2. Listen and Talk

WORDS 1–10

1. **Washington, D.C.,** is the capital of our nation.
2. The main government is in the **capital.**
3. D.C. stands for **District of Columbia.**
4. Congress meets in the **Capitol.**
5. The **Library of Congress** is very big.
6. Where is the **Washington Monument?**
7. Let's visit the **Lincoln Memorial.**
8. Take a picture of the Lincoln **statue.**
9. This **memorial** honors President Lincoln.
10. **Tourists** visit Washington, D.C., every year.

WORDS 11–20

11. Washington, D.C., is a **district.**
12. Government buildings are **located** there.
13. The capital has many **historic** buildings.
14. The Lincoln Memorial is a historic **building.**
15. Memorials are made in **memory** of something.
16. Some were **built** to honor presidents.
17. One is **named after** George Washington.
18. Memorials **honor** historic people and events.
19. In the spring, the cherry blossoms **bloom.**
20. Visitors can **tour** the monuments.

3. Read and Write

WORDS 1–10

▶ Use the Word Bank to write the word that fits each clue.

1. the U.S. capital   _____

2. where the main government is located in a country   _____

3. what D.C. stands for   _____

4. holds the largest collection of books in the world   _____

5. something made to remember an important person or event   _____

Word Bank

memorial
capital
District of Columbia
Washington, D.C.
Library of Congress

WORDS 11–20

▶ Use the Word Bank to complete each sentence.

6. A _____ is a special area.

7. The Lincoln Memorial was built in _____ of President Lincoln.

8. The White House is a large _____ where the president lives.

9. Something that is _____ is an important part of history.

10. We make memorials to _____ important people or events.

Word Bank

honor
historic
building
district
memory

4. Develop Language

FOR/TO

Use	Before
for	a noun *We went to D.C. for vacation.*
to	a verb or a noun *We went to D.C. to see sights.*

▶ Complete each sentence with *to* or *for*.

11. Memorials are made _____ honor past presidents.

12. I surfed the Internet _____ information about the monuments.

13. Let's go to the capital _____ see the cherry blossoms.

14. We asked a travel agent _____ hotels.

15. We went _____ the White House.

50 Holidays

Big Idea Holidays honor people and special events in history.

1. Look and Explore

◄ We celebrate **Independence Day** on the 4th of July.

Look at these **Halloween costumes.** ▼

You give your **sweetheart** a gift on **Valentine's Day.** ►

Veterans Day honors U.S. soldiers. ►

◄ **Martin Luther King, Jr.,** **fought for** equal rights.

2. Listen and Talk

WORDS 1–10

1. People celebrate **holidays** with traditions.
2. **Independence Day** is on the 4th of July.
3. It is an important **celebration.**
4. When is **Martin Luther King, Jr., Day?**
5. It is **observed** on the 3rd Monday in January.
6. **Veterans Day** honors U.S. soldiers.
7. Soldiers wear **uniforms** on Veterans Day.
8. **Valentine's Day** is February 14.
9. Look at these Halloween **costumes.**
10. **Halloween** is on the 31st of October.

WORDS 11–20

11. There's a 4th of July **parade** every year.
12. People watch **fireworks** at night.
13. Martin Luther King, Jr., **fought** for civil rights.
14. He gave an important **speech.**
15. We honor **soldiers** who fought for our country.
16. Many soldiers died in **wars.**
17. Give your **sweetheart** a gift on Valentine's Day.
18. She gave **flowers** to her sweetheart.
19. Dr. King fought for **equal rights.**
20. On Halloween you get **candy.**

3. Read and Write

WORDS 1–10

▶ Use the Word Bank to complete each sentence.

1. Valentine's Day and Halloween are _____.

2. Veterans Day is _____ on November 11.

3. Children wear _____ on Halloween.

4. We had a Halloween _____ on October 31.

5. Soldiers in the U.S. Army wear _____.

Word Bank

holidays
uniforms
celebration
costumes
observed

WORDS 11–20

▶ Use the Word Bank to label each picture.

Word Bank

flowers
parade
soldiers
fireworks
candy

6. _____

7. _____

8. _____

9. _____

10. _____

4. Develop Language

USING *IN*, *AT*, OR *ON*	
Use	**To talk about**
in	months, years *I was born in July.*
on	days, dates *I was born on Monday.*
at	time *I was born at 4:00 P.M.*

▶ Complete the sentences with *in*, *at*, or *on*.

11. The parade starts _____ 1:00 P.M.

12. Veterans Day is _____ Thursday.

13. Independence Day is _____ July.

14. Halloween is always _____ October 31.

15. Valentine's Day is _____ February.

51 Our Nation's Symbols

Big Idea Our nation's symbols represent the ideas of our country.

1. Look and Explore

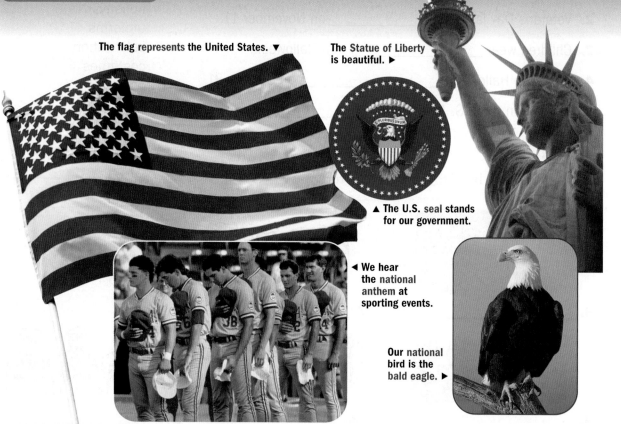

The flag represents the United States. ▼

The Statue of Liberty is beautiful. ►

▲ The U.S. seal stands for our government.

◄ We hear the national anthem at sporting events.

Our national bird is the bald eagle. ►

2. Listen and Talk

WORDS 1–10

1. Many **symbols** represent the United States.
2. **Forefathers** founded this country.
3. The United States was **founded** in 1776.
4. The flag **represents** the United States.
5. We sing the national **anthem** at sports games.
6. The U.S. **seal** stands for the government.
7. The **Statue of Liberty** is beautiful.
8. We say the **Pledge of Allegiance** at school.
9. Soldiers **salute** the flag.
10. Our national bird is the **bald eagle.**

WORDS 11–20

11. Our flag's **colors** are red, white, and blue.
12. The flag is a symbol of **independence.**
13. The 50 **stars** represent the 50 states.
14. The 13 **stripes** represent the original colonies.
15. The flag **hangs** on government buildings.
16. The **patriotic** students love the United States.
17. The bald eagle is our **national** bird.
18. We make a **pledge** to the flag.
19. Americans are **proud** of their country.
20. A symbol **reminds** us of our history.

3. Read and Write

WORDS 1-10

▶ Use the Word Bank to write the word that has the same meaning as the underlined word or words.

1. People use different <u>signs</u> to represent their country. _____

2. Thomas Jefferson and George Washington are <u>men who led this country to independence</u>. _____

3. These forefathers <u>started</u> the United States of America. _____

4. The U.S. flag <u>stands for</u> freedom. _____

5. "The Star-Spangled Banner" is our national <u>patriotic song</u>. _____

Word Bank

represents
symbols
founded
forefathers
anthem

WORDS 11-20

▶ Use the Word Bank to write the word that fits each clue.

6. showing love of your country _____

7. relating to the country _____

8. a promise, an agreement _____

9. the ability to do what you want to do _____

10. makes you remember _____

Word Bank

reminds
independence
pledge
national
patriotic

4. Develop Language

▶ Complete the sentences with the *s* form of the verb.

S FORM TO PRESENT TENSE

Add	To tell about
s to most verbs	1 noun *The flag waves in the wind.*

11. Pam _____ the anthem. (sing)

12. The bald eagle _____ power. (represent)

13. A flag _____ in the classroom. (hang)

14. A soldier _____ the flag. (salute)

15. A symbol _____ us of our country. (remind)

Parts of Speech

Big Idea Sentences have different parts of speech.

1. Look and Explore

Sentences have different parts of speech.

article · verb · preposition · conjunction · interjection

The dogs jumped rapidly over the fence, but they didn't catch the fast cat. Wow!

noun · adverb · pronoun · adjective

2. Listen and Talk

WORDS 1–10

1. Words can be different **parts of speech**.
2. A **noun** names a person, place, thing, or idea.
3. *Jumped* is an action **verb**.
4. *Rapidly* is an **adverb** that describes the verb.
5. Use an **article** to introduce a noun.
6. *Over* is a **preposition** that goes before a noun.
7. A **conjunction** joins sentence parts.
8. A **pronoun** replaces a noun.
9. An **adjective** describes a noun.
10. An **interjection** sometimes shows surprise.

WORDS 11–20

11. The noun *dogs* **names** a kind of animal.
12. An **action** is something that you do.
13. The adverb **describes** the action.
14. An article, such as *the*, **precedes** the noun.
15. The conjunction *but* **joins** two sentence parts.
16. An interjection is said with **excitement**.
17. The pronoun *they* **replaces** the word *dogs*.
18. The dogs **chased** the cats.
19. They jumped **rapidly.**
20. Did they **catch** the fast cat?

3. Read and Write

WORDS 1–10

▶ Use the Word Bank to complete each sentence.

1. _____ are the basic kinds of words in the English language.

2. A _____ shows the relationship between a noun and another word.

3. A _____ joins two sentence parts.

4. A _____ replaces a noun.

5. An _____ expresses an emotion.

Word Bank

pronoun
parts of speech
interjection
conjunction
preposition

WORDS 11–20

▶ Use the Word Bank to write the word that matches the definition.

6. gives a name to something _____

7. gives information about something _____

8. goes before something else _____

9. takes the place of something else _____

10. brings something together _____

Word Bank

replaces
precedes
names
describes
joins

4. Develop Language

USING IN OR AT FOR PLACES

Use	To talk about
in	enclosed places *The cat is in the kitchen.*
at	a certain point *The cousins are at school.*

▶ Complete the sentences with *in* or *at*.

11. My father is _____ work.

12. The teacher is _____ the bus.

13. The students are _____ the classroom.

14. The children are _____ school.

15. I live _____ Texas.

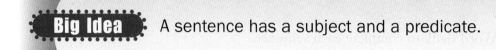

Big Idea A sentence has a subject and a predicate.

1. Look and Explore

A sentence has a subject and a predicate. A predicate includes a verb.

gymnast

simple sentence

The gymnast flips in the air.
subject · predicate

She lands on the mat.

2. Listen and Talk

WORDS 1–10

1. A **sentence** is a group of words.
2. It **consists** of a subject and a predicate.
3. The **subject** is what does the action.
4. The **predicate** is what the subject does.
5. A **phrase** doesn't include a subject and a verb.
6. The words in a phrase are **related**.
7. **Look** for a subject and a verb in each sentence.
8. A **simple sentence** has one idea.
9. A **compound sentence** joins two ideas.
10. A predicate **includes** a verb.

WORDS 11–20

11. Learn to **identify** the parts of a sentence.
12. A **complete sentence** has a subject and a verb.
13. An **incomplete** sentence is missing something.
14. The *gymnast* is the subject of the sentence.
15. *Jumps* and *flips* are both actions.
16. A conjunction **links** together two ideas.
17. The gymnast *lands* on the mat.
18. She **receives** a medal.
19. Too many simple sentences can be **dull**.
20. Longer sentences can be more **interesting**.

3. Read and Write

WORDS 1-10

▶ Use the Word Bank to complete the paragraphs.

Not every group of words is a _____. A
                                                1.
sentence _____ of a subject and a predicate. It
              2.
_____ both of these things.
        3.

A _____ is a group of related words. To be
         4.
sure the words make a sentence, _____ for a
                                              5.
subject and a verb and for it to express a complete thought.

Word Bank

includes
phrase
look
sentence
consists

WORDS 11-20

▶ Use the Word Bank to write the word that fits each definition.

6. to be able to know what something is   _____

7. gets something   _____

8. not exciting   _____

9. exciting enough to pay attention to   _____

10. joins together   _____

Word Bank

links
receives
interesting
identify
dull

4. Develop Language

SENTENCE PARTS

Examples with no predicate
Alice
a friend from school

Examples with no subject
practices every day.
is on my bus.

▶ Decide what is missing from each sentence part. Write
NP (no predicate) or NS (no subject) after each phrase.

11. His address _____

12. doesn't know what time it is _____

13. flips in the air _____

14. The gymnast _____

15. is interesting _____

Big Idea Phrasal verbs have special meanings.

1. Look and Explore

Phrasal verbs **are** formed by **a verb and another word.**

2. Listen and Talk

WORDS 1–10

1. People use **phrasal verbs** every day.
2. They are **formed by** a verb and another word.
3. Together, the words have a **unique** meaning.
4. The verbs are **followed by** another word.
5. Many phrasal verbs can be **separated.**
6. Pronouns can **go between** them.
7. You should be **able** to use phrasal verbs.
8. Soon you'll **recognize** phrasal verbs.
9. People use phrasal verbs **all the time.**
10. Try to use them **once in a while.**

WORDS 11–20

11. **Take out** your pen and write your name.
12. **Put away** your books.
13. **Pick up** the piece of paper you dropped.
14. **Put down** the pencil.
15. **Turn on** the lights.
16. **Turn off** the computer.
17. **Sit down** on the chair.
18. **Stand up** in front of the class.
19. **Hand in** your homework.
20. **Hand out** the papers to the students.

▶ Use the Word Bank to complete each sentence.

1. The phrasal verb *stand up* is _____ a verb and another word.

2. The verb *hand* can be _____ either *in* or *out*.

3. Pronouns *it* and *them* often _____ the verb and the other word.

4. Some phrasal verbs, like *sit down,* can't be _____.

5. Do you _____ these phrasal verbs?

Word Bank

followed by
go between
formed by
separated
recognize

▶ Use the Word Bank to complete each sentence.

6. _____ the test papers to the students.

7. _____ and get in line for lunch.

8. _____ on the sofa.

9. _____ your cellular phone.

10. _____ your homework to your teacher.

Word Bank

sit down
hand out
hand in
stand up
turn off

4. Develop Language

IT AND THEM

Use	To replace
it	singular nouns *Take out your pencil.* *Take it out.*
them	plural nouns *Put down your books.* *Put them down.*

▶ Complete each sentence using *it* or *them.*

11. Put your book away. Put _____ away.

12. Turn off the lights. Turn _____ off.

13. Hand in the assignment. Hand _____ in.

14. Hand out the papers. Hand _____ out.

15. Pick up your jacket. Pick _____ up.

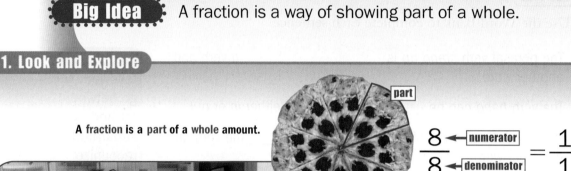

Big Idea A fraction is a way of showing part of a whole.

1. Look and Explore

A fraction is a part of a whole amount.

▲ Slice the pizza into eight pieces.

part

$$\frac{8}{8} \leftarrow \text{numerator} \atop \leftarrow \text{denominator} = \frac{1}{1}$$

whole

pieces

$$\frac{4}{8} = \frac{1}{2}$$ one half

$$\frac{2}{8} = \frac{1}{4}$$ one fourth

$$\frac{1}{8}$$ one eighth

2. Listen and Talk

WORDS 1–10

1. A **fraction** is a part of a whole amount.
2. The **denominator** is the number of parts.
3. The **numerator** tells how many equal parts.
4. The numerator is the **top** number.
5. The denominator is the **bottom** number.
6. $\frac{2}{3}$ and $\frac{4}{6}$ are **equivalent fractions.**
7. We **reduce** fractions to make them easier.
8. $\frac{2}{3}$ is the **simplest form** of $\frac{4}{6}$.
9. Find **common** factors of both numbers.
10. $\frac{8}{8}$ is a **whole** amount.

WORDS 11–20

11. A whole amount is a **complete** set.
12. **Slice** the pizza into 8 pieces.
13. The **pizza** has 8 parts.
14. Each **part** is a fraction of the whole.
15. How many **pieces** of pizza is $\frac{2}{8}$?
16. $\frac{4}{8}$ of the pizza is **one half** ($\frac{1}{2}$).
17. One of 3 slices is **one third** ($\frac{1}{3}$).
18. One slice out of 4 is **one fourth** ($\frac{1}{4}$).
19. **One eighth** ($\frac{1}{8}$) is 1 of 8 slices.
20. **One tenth** ($\frac{1}{10}$) is 1 out of 10.

3. Read and Write

WORDS 1–10

▶ Use the Word Bank to complete each sentence.

1. The denominator is the _____ number.

2. The _____ pizza has eight pieces.

3. 9 is a _____ factor of 18 and 27.

4. The _____ number is called the numerator.

5. You can _____ $\frac{3}{9}$ to $\frac{1}{3}$.

Word Bank

bottom
reduce
top
whole
common

WORDS 11–20

▶ Use the Word Bank to label each fraction.

6. $\frac{4}{8} = \frac{1}{2}$ _____

7. $\frac{3}{9} = \frac{1}{3}$ _____

8. $\frac{4}{12} = \frac{1}{4}$ _____

9. $\frac{2}{16} = \frac{1}{8}$ _____

10. $\frac{2}{20} = \frac{1}{10}$ _____

Word Bank

one eighth
one tenth
one half
one fourth
one third

4. Develop Language

▶ Write the fractions in words.

SAYING FRACTIONS

Rule	Number
Say the numerator like a number.	11, 12, 13
Use ordinal numbers to say the denominator.	eleventh twelfth thirteenth
If the numerator is greater than 1, add an s to the ordinal number.	fourteenths fifteenths

11. $\frac{4}{14}$ _____

12. $\frac{3}{11}$ _____

13. $\frac{1}{12}$ _____

14. $\frac{2}{10}$ _____

15. $\frac{1}{15}$ _____

56 Decimals

Decimal numbers show parts of a whole.

1. Look and Explore

We use decimals to show parts of a whole.

Compare the runners' times. ▶

	Runners' Times in seconds
1st	7.74
2nd	7.75
3rd	7.76

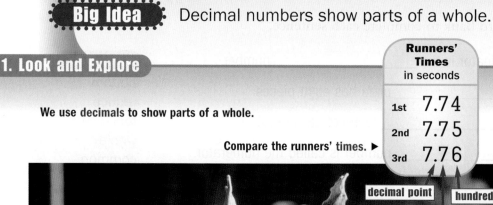

decimal point — hundredths — tenths

2. Listen and Talk

WORDS 1–10

1. We use **decimals** to show parts of a minute.
2. The **decimal point** comes after the ones place.
3. A decimal point is a **dot**.
4. Tenths and hundredths are **decimal places**.
5. A **time clock** shows hundredths of a second.
6. 0.7 shows seven **tenths**.
7. Seventy-five **hundredths** is written as 0.75.
8. Put the times **in order** from least to greatest.
9. **Line up** the decimals to compare numbers.
10. Make a **comparison** of the times.

WORDS 11–20

11. The runners ran in a **race**.
12. Compare the runners' **times**.
13. Which of the **runners** ran the fastest?
14. The **slowest** time is the greatest number.
15. The **fastest** time was 7.74 seconds.
16. 7.76 is **higher** than 7.74.
17. 7.74 is **lower** than 7.75.
18. 7.74 is a **record** time for Donovan.
19. Donovan **sprints** quickly.
20. Donovan crossed the **finish line** first.

3. Read and Write

WORDS 1–10

▶ Use the Word Bank to complete each sentence.

1. 1.25 and 2.46 are examples of _____ .

2. A decimal point looks like a _____ .

3. A _____ shows hundredths of a second.

4. To make a _____ between two numbers, line up the decimal points.

5. Make sure the decimal points _____ with each other.

Word Bank

decimals
line up
time clock
comparison
dot

WORDS 11–20

▶ Use the Word Bank to complete the story.

School Runner Wins Race

Three students ran a _____ on Saturday. The
6.

first person to cross the _____ was Tanique Harrison.
7.

She ran the race in the _____ time, so she was the
8.

winner. It is a new school _____ ! Congratulations to
9.

our school's _____ !
10.

Word Bank

race
fastest
record
runners
finish line

4. Develop Language

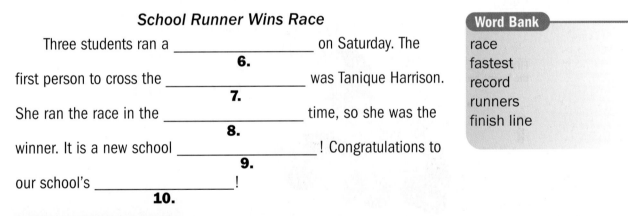

SAYING DECIMALS

Decimal	How to say it
7.75	Read a decimal point as *and*. *seven and seventy-five hundredths*
7.5	*seven and five tenths*
7.51	*seven and fifty-one hundredths*

▶ Write the numbers the way you would say them out loud.

11. 3.5 _____

12. 2.20 _____

13. 1.19 _____

14. 6.18 _____

15. 7.3 _____

Percents

Big Idea You can convert decimals and fractions to percents.

1. Look and Explore

It is easy to **convert fractions and decimals** to percents.

shaded

◄ **Ten percent of the** grid **is shaded.**

grid

$$\frac{10}{100} = .10 = 10\%$$

▲ **Fifty percent of the students** got a **hundred percent.**

Fifteen percent of the beans are black. ►

Write an equivalent fraction with a denominator of 100.

$$\frac{3}{20} \Rightarrow \frac{15}{100} = 15\%$$

convert

2. Listen and Talk

WORDS 1–10

1. A **percent** is part of a whole.
2. Percent means part **per** hundred.
3. A percent names a **portion** of 100.
4. A **percent symbol** follows a percent.
5. The **grid** shows 100 boxes.
6. The **ratio** is 10 shaded boxes to 100 boxes.
7. It is easy to **convert** fractions and decimals.
8. You need to **rewrite** the fraction.
9. Write an **equivalent** fraction.
10. You **shift** the position of the decimal point.

WORDS 11–20

11. Ten percent of the grid is **shaded.**
12. **Determine** the ratio of green to white boxes.
13. The decimal **moves over** two places.
14. A percent sign **follows** the number.
15. The decimal .10 is the **same** as 10%.
16. They are not **different** at all.
17. Teachers often show **grades** as percents.
18. The student got a **hundred** percent.
19. **Fifty** percent of the students got 100%.
20. **Fifteen** percent of the beans are red.

3. Read and Write

WORDS 1–10

▶ Use the Word Bank to complete each sentence.

1. Manuel got 98 _____ on his homework.

2. A _____ of the beans are black.

3. Enrique studies English two hours _____ day.

4. You need to _____ $\frac{50}{100}$ as $\frac{1}{2}$.

5. You must _____ the decimal point over two places.

Word Bank

per
percent
shift
portion
rewrite

WORDS 11–20

▶ Use the Word Bank to write the word that has the same meaning.

6. changes position   _____

7. find out   _____

8. goes after   _____

9. like each other   _____

10. not the same   _____

Word Bank

different
moves over
follows
same
determine

4. Develop Language

USING HAS/HAVE TO

Singular	Plural
has	**have**
He has to convert the fraction.	They have to draw a grid.

▶ Complete the sentences with *has* or *have*. Then underline the verb that follows it.

11. We _____ to convert the decimal.

12. She _____ to move the decimal point.

13. Jan _____ to rewrite the fraction.

14. The students _____ to study.

15. They _____ to review percents.

58 Water Cycle

Big Idea The water cycle has four main stages.

1. Look and Explore

The sun turns water into vapor. It rises into the air. ▶

◀ Raindrops form in clouds.

evaporation

condensation

collection

precipitation

Water collects in puddles on the ground. ▶

◀ The water falls to the ground as raindrops.

2. Listen and Talk

WORDS 1–10

1. A **cycle** is a set of events that repeat.
2. Earth's **water** goes through a cycle.
3. The water cycle has four main **stages**.
4. The first stage is **evaporation**.
5. **Condensation** is the second stage.
6. The third stage is **precipitation**.
7. The last stage is **collection**.
8. The sun turns water into **vapor**.
9. Condensation happens in **clouds**.
10. The cycle **repeats** itself.

WORDS 11–20

11. Water **turns into** a vapor.
12. Vapor **rises** into the air.
13. **Dew** forms on plants and grass at night.
14. The vapor forms clouds in the **sky**.
15. Drops of rain **form** in clouds.
16. Water **falls** to the earth as rain or snow.
17. The water falls to the ground as **raindrops**.
18. **Snowflakes** are made of water.
19. The **ground** takes in water.
20. Water collects in **puddles** on the ground.

3. Read and Write

WORDS 1–10

▶ Use the Word Bank to write the word that matches the definition.

1. a set of events that happen again and again _____

2. steps _____

3. very small drops of water _____

4. a collection of vapor in the sky _____

5. happens again _____

Word Bank

clouds
cycle
repeats
vapor
stages

WORDS 11–20

▶ Use the Word Bank to label the pictures.

6. _____

7. _____

8. _____

9. _____

10. _____

Word Bank

raindrops
snowflakes
ground
puddles
sky

4. Develop Language

REGULAR AND IRREGULAR PAST TENSE

	Present tense	Past tense
Regular	turn	**turned**
	change	**changed**
	form	**formed**
Irregular	fall	**fell**
	rise	**rose**

▶ Complete the sentences with the past tense form of the verbs.

11. The water _____ vapor. (turns into)

12. The raindrop _____ in the clouds. (forms)

13. The cloud _____ shape. (changes)

14. The water _____ from the clouds. (falls)

15. Vapor _____ into the sky. (rises)

59 Ecosystems

Big Idea Living things interact in an ecosystem.

1. Look and Explore

A rain forest has many living things.

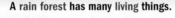

rain forest

plant life

species

▲ All living things interact in an ecosystem.

2. Listen and Talk

WORDS 1–10

1. An ecosystem is a **system** of life.
2. A **rain forest** has many living things.
3. All living things are part of the **environment**.
4. There are many different **species** together.
5. **Humans** are part of the ecosystem, too.
6. All living things **interact** in an ecosystem.
7. **Animals** depend on other living things.
8. Some **insects** depend on one type of tree.
9. They need each other to **survive**.
10. **Plant life** depends on the sun.

WORDS 11–20

11. Living things are **connected** for survival.
12. People **cut down** rain forests.
13. They use the trees for **lumber**.
14. **Logging** can destroy rain forests.
15. Logging **destroys** the environment.
16. Animals **depend on** one another to survive.
17. Many **living** things interact in a rain forest.
18. The government tries to **preserve** the land.
19. Some animals are becoming **extinct**.
20. Other animals are **endangered**.

3. Read and Write

WORDS 1–10

▶ Use the Word Bank to complete each sentence.

1. A group of things that interact is called a _____.

2. The land and everything living on it makes up the
_____.

3. Plant life, animals, insects, and humans all _____
with one another.

4. A rain forest has millions of different plant and animal
_____.

5. Living things depend on one another to _____.

Word Bank

environment
system
survive
interact
species

WORDS 11–20

▶ Use the Word Bank to complete the paragraph.

We humans _____ the environment for survival.
6.
Many materials we need to live come from the ecosystem. Some

living things, like gorillas, are _____. If we continue
7.
to cut down trees, they may become _____. Too
8.
much logging _____ the rain forests. Learn how you
9.
can help _____ the ecosystem.
10.

Word Bank

destroys
endangered
depend on
preserve
extinct

4. Develop Language

VERBS AND NOUNS

Verb	Noun
connect	**connection**
interact	**interaction**
preserve	**preservation**
extinct	**extinction**
destroy	**destruction**

▶ Complete the sentences with the noun form.

11. An ecosystem shows the _____ of living
things. (connect)

12. Survival depends on _____. (interact)

13. Some animals face _____. (extinct)

14. There is _____ of the rain forest. (destruct)

15. Learn about _____. (preserve)

60 The Solar System

1. Look and Explore

Our solar system has nine planets. ▶

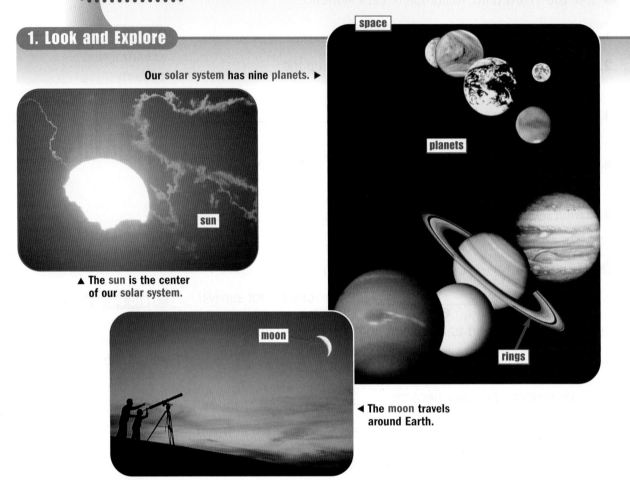

space

planets

sun

rings

▲ The sun is the center
of our solar system.

moon

◀ The moon travels
around Earth.

2. Listen and Talk

WORDS 1–10

1. Earth belongs to a **solar system.**
2. Our solar system has nine **planets.**
3. Earth **rotates** every twenty-four hours.
4. It takes one year to **revolve** around the sun.
5. Earth follows an **orbit.**
6. The sun is a powerful **star.**
7. There are over a **billion** stars in the universe.
8. Energy from the sun **sustains** life.
9. **Comets** are traveling balls of ice.
10. A **satellite** travels through space.

WORDS 11–20

11. The **sun** is the center of our solar system.
12. The **moon** travels around Earth.
13. Earth **spins** in place once a day.
14. The planets follow a **path** around the sun.
15. Stars **shine** in the sky.
16. The sun **gives off** light and heat.
17. It's very dark in outer **space.**
18. There are **rings** around the planet Saturn.
19. A planet is a large **object** in the sky.
20. Some planets are balls of **gases.**

3. Read and Write

WORDS 1–10

▶ Use the Word Bank to complete the crossword puzzle.

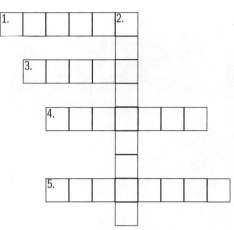

ACROSS

1. balls of ice traveling in space

3. a path

4. the number 1,000,000,000

5. maintains, makes life possible

DOWN

2. an object that moves around a planet

Word Bank

comets
orbit
sustains
billion
satellite

WORDS 11–20

▶ Use the Word Bank to write the word that has the same meaning as the underlined word or words.

6. Our planet <u>rotates</u> once every 24 hours. _____

7. The planets follow a <u>route</u> around the sun. _____

8. Stars <u>give off light</u> in the sky. _____

9. A planet is a large <u>thing</u> in the sky. _____

10. A <u>small planet</u> revolves around Earth. _____

Word Bank

moon
path
shine
spins
object

4. Develop Language

THERE IS/ARE

Singular	Plural
there is	there are
There is a sun in the solar system.	**There are** stars in the sky.

▶ Complete the sentences with *There is* or *There are*.

11. _____ a satellite that travels around Earth.

12. _____ comets traveling in space.

13. _____ rings around Saturn.

14. _____ planets made of gases.

15. _____ a star called the sun.

American People

Big Idea America is a land of immigrants.

1. Look and Explore

My ancestors came from Haiti.

America is a land of immigrants. ▶

Different races bring diversity to America. ▼

▲ **Some Americans** descended **from Europeans.**

2. Listen and Talk

WORDS 1–10

1. America is a land of **immigrants.**
2. People of many **races** come to America.
3. Her **ancestors** came from Haiti.
4. Some Americans **descended** from Europeans.
5. Are there **differences** in customs?
6. Are there any **similarities?**
7. Different races bring **diversity** to America.
8. **Prejudice** hurts people, and it is wrong.
9. Fairness is an **ideal** Americans share.
10. Shared ideals bring **unity.**

WORDS 11–20

11. What is your **native** country?
12. People here come from many **nations.**
13. Native Americans were the **original** people.
14. What is your country of **origin?**
15. Many Americans are a **mixture** of races.
16. Every country has its own **flag.**
17. Newcomers **adapt** to new ways of life.
18. Some people **hold on** to old customs.
19. **Latinos** share Latin American customs.
20. **African Americans** descended from Africans.

3. Read and Write

WORDS 1–10

▶ Use the Word Bank to write the correct word that matches the definition.

1. perfect idea that many people share _____

2. an unfair opinion of other people's race, culture, or religion _____

3. differences of race, culture, religion, and ways of doing things _____

4. people who move to a new country _____

5. came from _____

Word Bank

diversity
ideal
descended
prejudice
immigrants

WORDS 11–20

▶ Use the Word Bank to complete the sentences.

6. _____ have African ancestors.

7. Some _____ come from South America.

8. Cambodia is Lie's country of _____.

9. Native Americans were the _____ Americans.

10. Rachel is a _____ of Irish and German.

Word Bank

mixture
African Americans
Latinos
original
origin

4. Develop Language

NATIONALITIES

Korea ⟶ Korean
Mexico ⟶ Mexican
Germany ⟶ German
Bosnia ⟶ Bosnian
Japan ⟶ Japanese
England ⟶ English
France ⟶ French
China ⟶ Chinese
Poland ⟶ Polish

▶ Complete each sentence with the country or nationality.

11. Mexican people come from _____.

12. _____ are from Germany.

13. People from _____ are called Bosnians.

14. _____ people come from Japan.

15. Where are _____ people from? They are from Korea.

American Regions

Big Idea The United States is made up of many regions.

1. Look and Explore

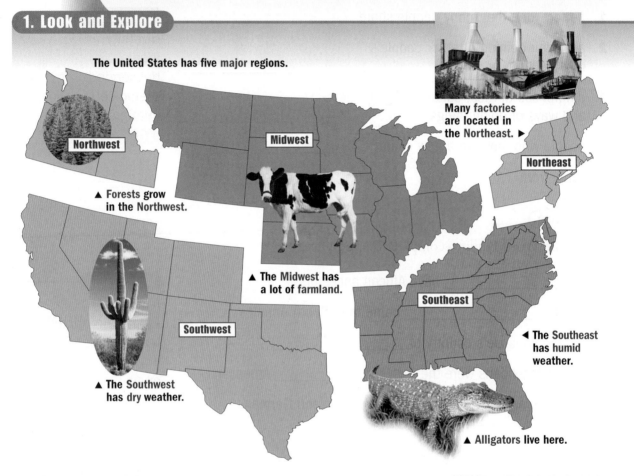

The United States has five **major regions**.

Northwest

Midwest

Many factories are located in the Northeast. ▶

Northeast

▲ Forests grow in the Northwest.

▲ The Midwest has a lot of farmland.

Southeast

Southwest

◀ The Southeast has humid weather.

▲ The Southwest has dry weather.

▲ Alligators live here.

2. Listen and Talk

WORDS 1–10

1. A **region** has many similar features.
2. America has five **major** regions.
3. A region has **features** in common.
4. **For example,** Midwestern states have farmland.
5. The **Northeast** gets a lot of snow.
6. The **Southeast** has humid weather.
7. The **Midwest** is famous for its farmland.
8. The **Northwest** has many forests.
9. The **Southwest** has dry weather.
10. The **climate** is the usual weather in a place.

WORDS 11–20

11. The Northwest has a lot of **rainfall.**
12. Southwestern states are **dry.**
13. The Midwest has **extreme** weather.
14. Summers are **humid** in the Southeast.
15. The weather is usually **mild** in Los Angeles.
16. The Midwest has a lot of **farmland.**
17. Many **factories** are located in the Northeast.
18. A **cactus** plant grows in the Southwest.
19. **Alligators** live in Florida.
20. **Forests** grow in the Northwest.

3. Read and Write

WORDS 1–10

▶ Use the Word Bank to complete the report.

There are five _____ regions in the United

1.

States. Wisconsin is a state in the Midwest. This _____

2.

is known for its farmland.

Wisconsin shares some _____ with other states

3.

in the Midwest. _____, Iowa and Illinois have a lot

4.

of farmland, too. They also have the same _____.

5.

Word Bank

region
major
features
for example
climate

WORDS 11–20

▶ Use the Word Bank to label the pictures.

Word Bank

cactus
forests
factories
farmland
alligators

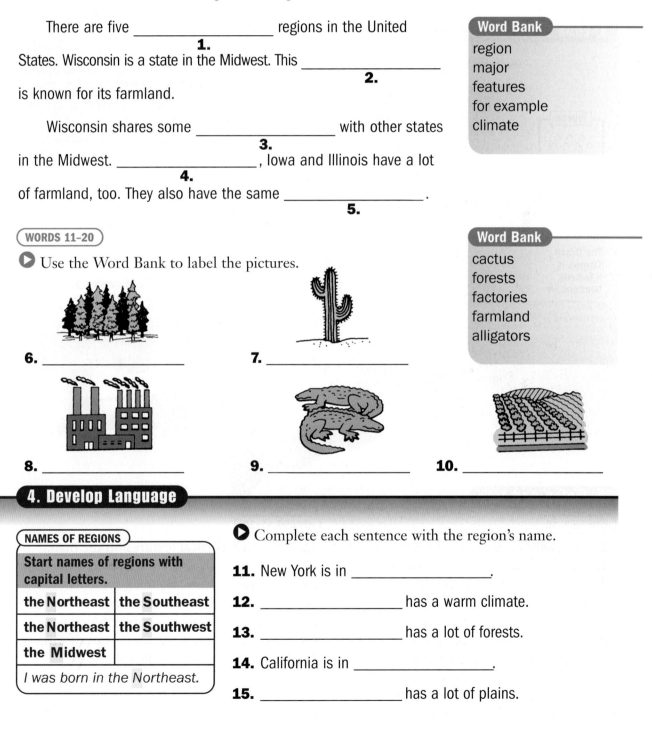

6. _____

7. _____

8. _____

9. _____

10. _____

4. Develop Language

NAMES OF REGIONS

Start names of regions with capital letters.	
the Northeast	the Southeast
the Northeast	the Southwest
the Midwest	
I was born in the Northeast.	

▶ Complete each sentence with the region's name.

11. New York is in _____.

12. _____ has a warm climate.

13. _____ has a lot of forests.

14. California is in _____.

15. _____ has a lot of plains.

63 U.S. Geography

Learn about the physical features of the United States.

1. Look and Explore

The United States borders two countries.

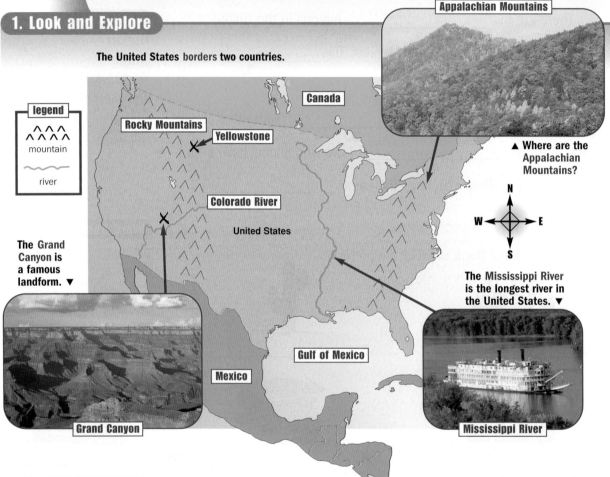

Appalachian Mountains

Canada

legend

^^^
mountain

~~~
river

Rocky Mountains

Yellowstone

Colorado River

United States

▲ Where are the Appalachian Mountains?

N
W ←✦→ E
S

The Grand Canyon is a famous landform. ▼

The Mississippi River is the longest river in the United States. ▼

Gulf of Mexico

Mexico

Grand Canyon

Mississippi River

2. Listen and Talk

WORDS 1–10

1. **Geography** is the study of Earth's surface.
2. The United States **borders** two countries.
3. It borders **Canada** to the north.
4. **Mexico** is south of the United States.
5. America also borders the **Gulf of Mexico.**
6. Locate the **Rocky Mountains** on the map.
7. Where are the **Appalachian Mountains?**
8. How many mountain **chains** are shown?
9. The **Mississippi River** is a long river.
10. Where does the **Colorado River** flow?

WORDS 11–20

11. Study the **physical** features on the map.
12. The Colorado River is **labeled** on the map.
13. The **legend** shows the map symbols.
14. Mountains are **shown** with jagged lines.
15. Rivers are **drawn** with curved blue lines.
16. The **Grand Canyon** is a famous landform.
17. What are some other **landforms?**
18. The United States has many **national parks.**
19. Some states, **such as** California, have parks.
20. **Yellowstone** National Park is beautiful.

3. Read and Write

WORDS 1–10

▶ Use the Word Bank to answer each question.

1. What is the study of Earth's surface? _____

2. What is the longest U.S. river? _____

3. What country is south of the
United States? _____

4. What country is north of the
United States? _____

5. Which mountain chain runs through
the west? _____

Word Bank

geography
Canada
Mississippi River
Mexico
Rocky Mountains

WORDS 11–20

▶ Use the Word Bank to complete the paragraph.

Earth's surface is covered with landforms, _____
                                                              6.
mountains. Mapmakers use special symbols to show the

_____ features. These features are
            7.

_____ on the map. The _____
            8.   9.

explains the symbols. In some legends, mountains are

_____ with upside-down *Vs*.
            10.

Word Bank

drawn
such as
labeled
physical
legend

4. Develop Language

PASSIVE VERB FORMS	
Active verb	**Passive form**
show	is/are **shown**
teach	is/are **taught**
make	is/are **made**
draw	is/are **drawn**
label	is/are **labeled**

▶ Complete the sentences using the passive form of the verb.

11. Mountains _____ on the map. (show)

12. The land features _____. (label)

13. U.S. geography _____ in Social Studies. (teach)

14. Maps _____ with the help of geographers. (make)

15. The maps _____ very carefully. (draw)

Big Idea Learn how to look up words in a dictionary.

1. Look and Explore

Look up **new words** in a **dictionary**.

guide words

Guide words help you find the word. ▶

h hug–hungry

hug (verb) to hold closely: *My mother hugs me every day.*
Plural Form: hugs

plural form

huge (adj.) of great size: *The* Titanic *was a huge ship.*
Synonym: large
Antonym: tiny

example

entry

hungry (adj.) a need or desire for food: *We were hungry before lunch.*

definition

How do you define *huge*?

▲ **Look at the word's entry.**

2. Listen and Talk

WORDS 1–10

1. Look up new words in a **dictionary**.
2. How do you **define** *huge*?
3. **Guide words** help you find words.
4. Look at the word's **entry**.
5. Some words have more than one **definition**.
6. A **synonym** is a word with the same meaning.
7. An **antonym** is the word's opposite.
8. What is the **opposite** of *huge*?
9. The **plural form** of *hug* is *hugs*.
10. **Past tense** forms of verbs are listed.

WORDS 11–20

11. You can **look up** words in the dictionary.
12. A dictionary gives a **meaning** of a word.
13. Entry words are in **bold**.
14. The plural forms of nouns are **given**.
15. The words are **listed** from A to Z.
16. **Scan** the words to find the one you need.
17. Read the word in the **example**.
18. An example is the word **used** in a sentence.
19. Words are **divided into** syllables.
20. What kind of a word is *huge*?

3. Read and Write

WORDS 1–10

▶ Use the Word Bank to complete each sentence.

1. You can look up words in a _____.

2. The word _____ means *give the meaning of a word*.

3. A _____ of the word *huge* is *large*.

4. An _____ of the word *huge* is *tiny*.

5. _____ means as *different as possible*.

Word Bank

define
dictionary
synonym
antonym
opposite

WORDS 11–20

▶ Use the Word Bank to complete the paragraph.

When I read, I always _____ words I don't
6.
understand. First, I look at the guide words _____
7.
on the top of the page. Next, I _____ the page
8.
to find the word I need. Then, I find out the word's

_____ . Finally, I read the example. The example
9.
tells me how the word is _____ .
10.

Word Bank

meaning
listed
used
scan
look up

4. Develop Language

ASKING QUESTIONS WITH *DO/DOES*

How	**do**	I you we they	use a dictionary?
	does	he she it	

▶ Complete the questions with *do* or *does*. Then answer the questions aloud.

11. How _____ you spell your last name?

12. What _____ *antonym* mean?

13. What _____ *synonym* mean?

14. How _____ you spell *bold?*

15. What _____ *huge* mean?

Big Idea Learn to find resources in a library.

1. Look and Explore

A library has a large **collection** of books.

librarian

Use the catalog to search **for** a book. ▶

Go to the shelves **to** find it. ▶

Use a library card **to** check out the book. ▶

2. Listen and Talk

WORDS 1–10

1. A library has a large **collection** of books.
2. The **librarian** works in the library.
3. You can use the computer **catalog**.
4. Use the catalog to **search** for a book.
5. **Enter** the title of the book.
6. You can search by the name of the **author**.
7. Every book has a **call number**.
8. You can also search the books by **subject**.
9. A library has **encyclopedias**.
10. It has other **reference** books you can use.

WORDS 11–20

11. You can **borrow** a book for a short time.
12. Go to the **shelves** to find it.
13. The library will **loan** you the book.
14. You need to **check out** the book first.
15. Use a **library card** to check out the book.
16. When is the book's **due date**?
17. Remember to **return** it when you are done.
18. Look at all the maps in the **atlas**.
19. You can read the **newspaper**.
20. You can search for a **magazine**.

3. Read and Write

WORDS 1–10

▶ Use the Word Bank to complete the paragraphs.

Mr. Morton works as a _____ at the school. The
1.
library has a large _____ of books, newspapers, and
2.
magazines. The librarian can help you _____ for a
3.
book or any information you might need.

Use a _____ book if you need to find
4.
information quickly. The _____ hold a lot of
5.
information about many subjects.

Word Bank

search
collection
encyclopedias
reference
librarian

WORDS 11–20

▶ Use the Word Bank to write the word that matches the definition.

6. to use your library card to borrow books _____

7. to use something and then give it back _____

8. to let someone use something
for a short time _____

9. the date by when you need to
return the book _____

10. to give back _____

Word Bank

check out
loan
due date
return
borrow

4. Develop Language

SHORT ANSWERS WITH CAN

Question
Can you borrow books at the library?
Positive answer
Yes, you can.
Negative answer
No, you can't.

▶ Answer the questions with *Yes, you can* or *No, you can't.*

11. Can you buy library books? _____

12. Can you find books on shelves? _____

13. Can you borrow books without
a library card? _____

14. Can you find articles in a magazine? _____

15. Can you use an encyclopedia? _____

66 Using the Internet

Big Idea Learn to use the Internet to find information.

1. Look and Explore

The Internet offers a lot of information.

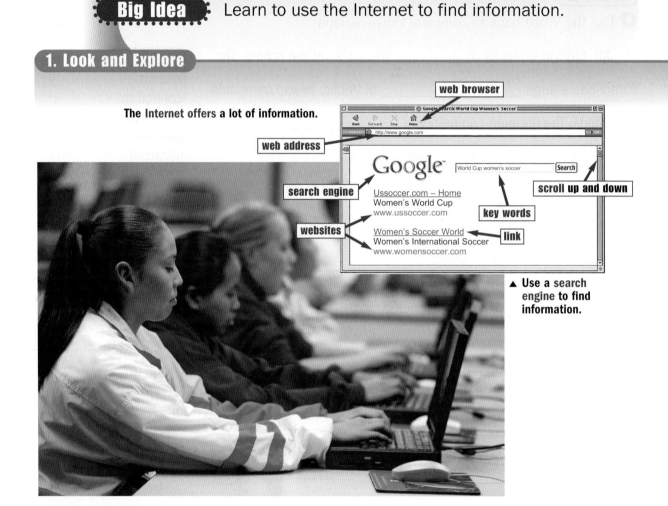

web browser

web address

search engine

websites

key words

scroll up and down

link

▲ Use a search engine to find information.

2. Listen and Talk

WORDS 1–10

1. The **Internet** is a network of information.
2. The Internet is often called the **Web**.
3. **WWW** stands for World Wide Web.
4. Open a **web browser** to get online.
5. You can enter the **web address**.
6. Use a **search engine** to find information.
7. Enter the **key words** *World Cup* and *soccer*.
8. There are many soccer **websites** to visit.
9. **Scroll** up and down to view a web page.
10. Click a **link** to go to another page.

WORDS 11–20

11. Let's **surf** the Web.
12. The Internet **offers** a lot of information.
13. You can **browse** for information on soccer.
14. Click the search **button** to begin.
15. Use **caution** on the web.
16. Pick a website that is **well known**.
17. You shouldn't **rely on** all websites.
18. Always get a parent's **permission**.
19. Don't **give out** your password to anyone.
20. Keep your personal information **private**.

3. Read and Write

WORDS 1–10

▶ Use the Word Bank to complete each sentence.

1. The _____ is also called the Web.

2. The _____ is used all over the world.

3. _____ stands for World Wide Web.

4. You use a _____ to get online.

5. Places on the Internet are called _____ .

Word Bank

websites
Web
Internet
WWW
web browser

WORDS 11–20

▶ Use the Word Bank to write the word that has the same meaning as the underlined word or words.

6. You must use <u>great care to avoid danger</u> when browsing the Internet. _____

7. Pick a website that is <u>popular</u>. _____

8. You shouldn't <u>depend on</u> some of the information on websites. _____

9. Never <u>offer</u> your password to a stranger. _____

10. Keep your personal information <u>secret</u>. _____

Word Bank

rely on
caution
private
give out
well known

4. Develop Language

IMPERATIVES

Positive = verb
Surf *the web.*
Negative = *Don't* + verb
***Don't* give** *out your password.*

▶ Write the words to make imperative statements.

11. words./Enter/key _____

12. page./Scroll/the/down _____

13. the/link./Click _____

14. out/Don't/give/password./your

_____

15. Web./on/Use/caution/the _____

Big Idea We can measure length and distance.

1. Look and Explore

We can measure length and distance.

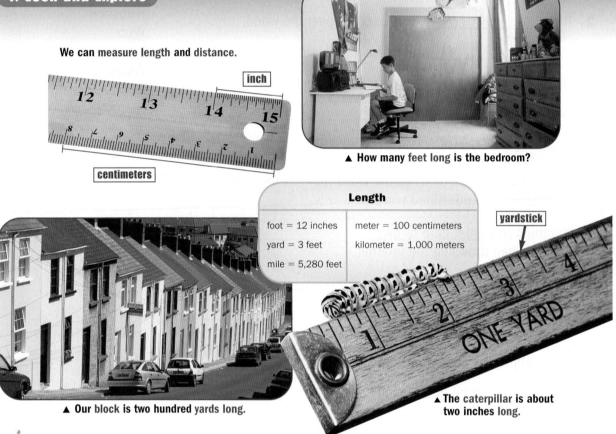

▲ How many feet long is the bedroom?

Length

foot = 12 inches	meter = 100 centimeters
yard = 3 feet	kilometer = 1,000 meters
mile = 5,280 feet	

inch

centimeters

yardstick

▲ Our block is two hundred yards long.

▲ The caterpillar is about two inches long.

2. Listen and Talk

WORDS 1–10

1. **Length** tells how long something is.
2. An **inch** is a small unit of length.
3. A **foot** is 12 inches.
4. How many **feet** are between each corner?
5. How many **yards** are in a mile?
6. A **meter** is a little longer than a yard.
7. A **mile** is 5,280 feet.
8. A **kilometer** is 1,000 meters.
9. There are 100 **centimeters** in a meter.
10. There are 1,000 **millimeters** in a meter.

WORDS 11–20

11. We **measure** things to find their length.
12. We measure the **distance** between points.
13. We can measure things with a **ruler.**
14. The **caterpillar** is about two inches long.
15. The **yardstick** is one yard long.
16. A meter is **longer** than a yard.
17. An inch is **shorter** than a foot.
18. Use a **tape measure** for long distances.
19. How **long** is the classroom wall?
20. Our **block** is two hundred yards long.

3. Read and Write

(WORDS 1–10)

▶ Use the Word Bank to write the average length of each item.

1. the length of a pencil tip   5 _____

2. the length of a pencil   8 _____

3. the length of a desk   1 _____

4. the length of a football field   100 _____

5. the length of a street   1 _____

Word Bank

millimeters
yards
centimeters
kilometer
meter

(WORDS 11–20)

▶ Use the Word Bank to label the pictures.

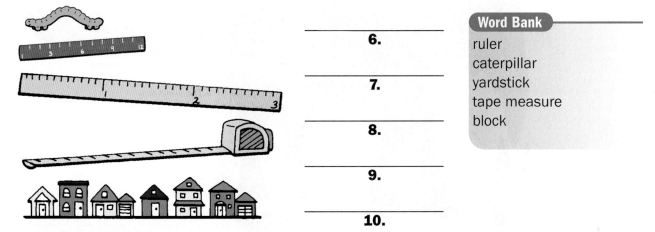

_____ **6.**

_____ **7.**

_____ **8.**

_____ **9.**

_____ **10.**

Word Bank

ruler
caterpillar
yardstick
tape measure
block

4. Develop Language

COMPARATIVE VS. SUPERLATIVE	
Add	**To compare**
er to adjectives	2 things *The <u>pencil</u> is short**er** than the <u>ruler</u>.*
est to adjectives	3 or more things *Henry is the short**est** student of all.*

▶ Add *er* or *est* to the adjective to complete each sentence.

11. The pencil is _____ than the pen. (long)

12. I live on the _____ street in the city. (long)

13. My sister is _____ than I am. (short)

14. Sears Tower is one of the _____ buildings. (tall)

15. I am _____ than my teacher. (tall)

68 Weight and Mass

Big Idea We can measure the weight and mass of objects.

1. Look and Explore

We can measure the **weight** of objects.

Weight	Mass
ounce	**gram**
pound = 16 ounces	kilogram = 1,000 grams
ton = 2,000 pounds	metric ton = 1,000 kilograms

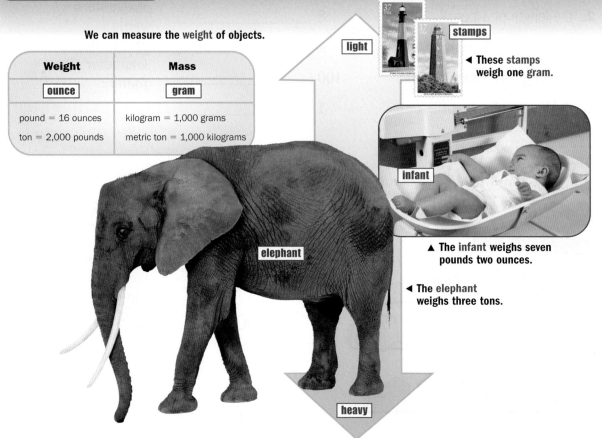

stamps

light

◄ These **stamps** weigh one **gram**.

infant

elephant

▲ The **infant** weighs seven pounds two ounces.

◄ The **elephant** weighs three tons.

heavy

2. Listen and Talk

WORDS 1–10

1. **Weight** tells how heavy something is.
2. We can use a **scale** to measure weight.
3. A **balance** is one kind of scale.
4. An **ounce** is a small unit of weight.
5. A **pound** is 16 ounces.
6. A **ton** is 2,000 pounds.
7. The **mass** of something also tells its weight.
8. A **gram** is a very small unit of mass.
9. A **kilogram** is 1,000 grams.
10. A **metric ton** is 1,000 kilograms.

WORDS 11–20

11. How much does each object **weigh**?
12. An elephant is **heavy**.
13. A feather is very **light**.
14. The **elephant** weighs three tons.
15. These **stamps** weigh one gram.
16. The **infant** weighs seven pounds two ounces.
17. The baby is **heavier** than the stamps.
18. The baby is **lighter** than the elephant.
19. The **size** of an object doesn't show its weight.
20. Some **really** big objects are light.

3. Read and Write

WORDS 1–10

▶ Use the Word Bank to complete the paragraph.

Measuring the _____ is one way to see how
1.

heavy something is. The total _____ of an object
2.

also tells its weight. A piece of paper has a mass of about

one _____. A book has a mass of about one
3.

_____. A car has a mass of over one
4.

_____.
5.

Word Bank

mass
kilogram
metric ton
gram
weight

WORDS 11–20

▶ Use the Word Bank to complete the crossword puzzle.

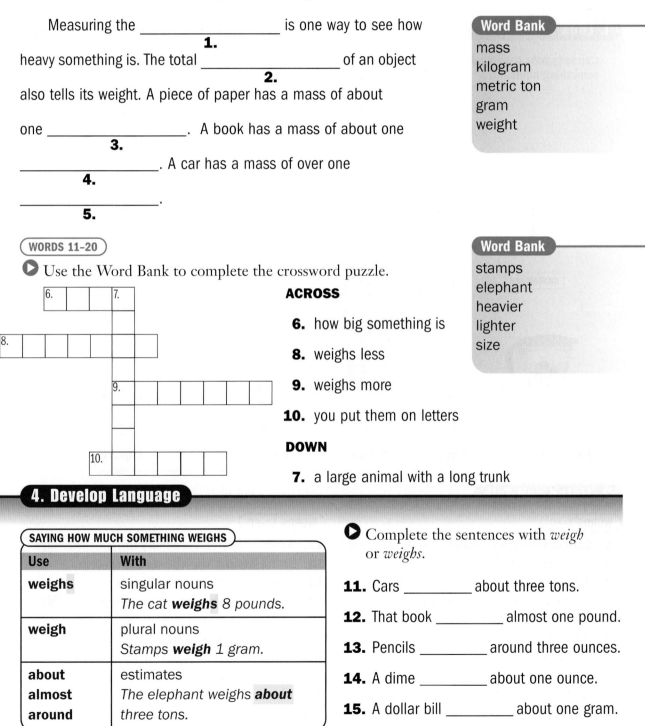

ACROSS

6. how big something is

8. weighs less

9. weighs more

10. you put them on letters

DOWN

7. a large animal with a long trunk

Word Bank

stamps
elephant
heavier
lighter
size

4. Develop Language

SAYING HOW MUCH SOMETHING WEIGHS

Use	With
weighs	singular nouns The cat **weighs** 8 pounds.
weigh	plural nouns Stamps **weigh** 1 gram.
about **almost** **around**	estimates The elephant weighs **about** three tons.

▶ Complete the sentences with *weigh* or *weighs*.

11. Cars _____ about three tons.

12. That book _____ almost one pound.

13. Pencils _____ around three ounces.

14. A dime _____ about one ounce.

15. A dollar bill _____ about one gram.

> **Big Idea** Capacity is a measure of how much a container can hold.

1. Look and Explore

Capacity **tells how much something** holds.

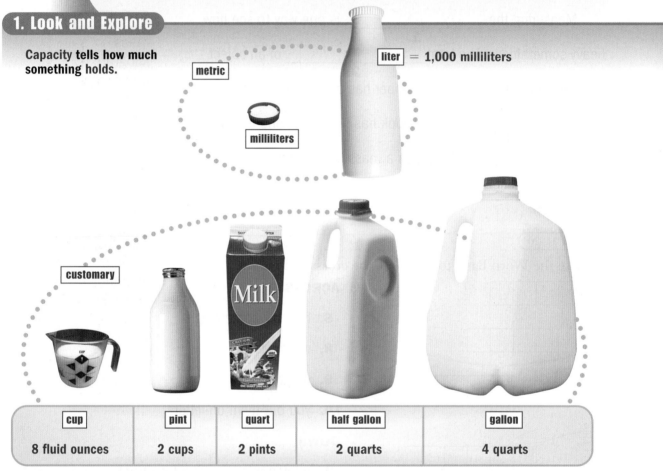

liter = 1,000 milliliters

metric

milliliters

customary

Milk

cup	pint	quart	half gallon	gallon
8 fluid ounces	2 cups	2 pints	2 quarts	4 quarts

2. Listen and Talk

WORDS 1–10

1. **Capacity** tells how much something holds.
2. Cups and gallons are **units** of capacity.
3. A **fluid ounce** is equal to 2 tablespoons.
4. A **cup** (c) holds 8 fluid ounces.
5. 2 cups make a **pint** (pt).
6. A **quart** (qt) is 2 pints.
7. 2 quarts is one **half gallon** ($\frac{1}{2}$ gal).
8. A **gallon** (gal) is 4 quarts.
9. A **liter** (L) holds a little more than a quart.
10. There are 1,000 **milliliters** (ml) in a liter.

WORDS 11–20

11. Americans use **customary** units of measure.
12. Some people use the **metric** system.
13. Some containers hold **liquids**.
14. Capacity is the amount a container **holds**.
15. This cup **contains** milk.
16. **Empty** the cup of milk.
17. **Fill** the measuring cup with milk.
18. We use a **measuring cup** for recipes.
19. There are 3 teaspoons in a **tablespoon**.
20. Use the **teaspoon** to measure the milk.

3. Read and Write

▶ Use the Word Bank to complete the paragraph.

The amount of liquid a container holds is called its

_____ . There are two types of _____ ,
    1.   **2.**
customary and metric. American people measure gasoline by the

_____ . People who live in other parts of the world,
    3.
such as Europe, buy gas by the _____ . A liter is one
                                            4.
thousand _____ .
                5.

Word Bank
milliliters
units
capacity
gallon
liter

▶ Use the Word Bank to label each picture.

Word Bank
empty
measuring cup
fill
tablespoon
teaspoon

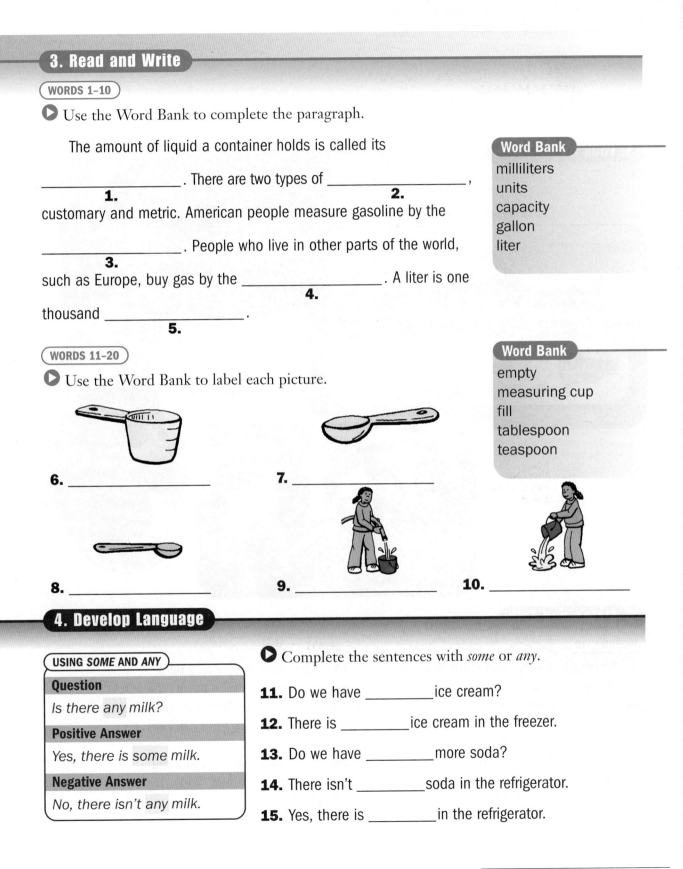

6. _____

7. _____

8. _____

9. _____

10. _____

4. Develop Language

USING *SOME* AND *ANY*

Question
Is there any milk?
Positive Answer
Yes, there is some milk.
Negative Answer
No, there isn't any milk.

▶ Complete the sentences with *some* or *any*.

11. Do we have _____ ice cream?

12. There is _____ ice cream in the freezer.

13. Do we have _____ more soda?

14. There isn't _____ soda in the refrigerator.

15. Yes, there is _____ in the refrigerator.

Big Idea Farmers grow crops and raise animals.

1. Look and Explore

Farming gives you many things you use. ▼

barn

beef | dairy | leather | wool

▲ Farmers harvest their crops.

They grow vegetables and grains. ▶

They raise cattle for milk and meat. ▶

2. Listen and Talk

WORDS 1–10

1. **Farming** is a very important industry.
2. **Farmers** live and work on a farm.
3. Farmers **harvest** their crops.
4. They grow vegetables and **grains.**
5. Farmers raise **livestock,** like pigs and cows.
6. Some people eat the **meat** of animals.
7. **Fabric** is made from the wool of sheep.
8. **Dairy** products, like butter, come from cows.
9. A **herd** of cattle lives on the farm.
10. Farmers raise **cattle** for milk and meat.

WORDS 11–20

11. The animals live in a **barn.**
12. The farmers feed **hay** to the cattle.
13. The children **feed** the cows in the morning.
14. Some farmers raise **chickens,** too.
15. **Beef** comes from a cow.
16. Does **pork** come from a pig?
17. **Rice** grows in wet fields.
18. **Leather** is used for clothing and shoes.
19. Bread is made from **wheat.**
20. **Wool** comes from sheep.

3. Read and Write

WORDS 1–10

▶ Use the Word Bank to complete the paragraph.

I live on a farm, so _____ is a way of life for my

1.

family and me. My mother and father are _____ .

2.

We grow corn and wheat. We all work hard to prepare for the

_____ . We also raise livestock. There are

3.

_____ and pigs on our farm. It is my job to feed hay

4.

to the _____ of cows every morning.

5.

Word Bank

farmers
harvest
farming
herd
cattle

WORDS 11–20

▶ Use the Word Bank to complete each sentence.

6. A hamburger is _____ from a cow.

7. _____ is a grain that grows in a wet field.

8. Some shoes are made of _____ that comes
from cows.

9. Bread is made of flour that comes from grains, like
_____ and corn.

10. _____ comes from sheep.

Word Bank

wool
wheat
leather
beef
rice

4. Develop Language

USING *IS* OR *ARE*

Singular	Plural
What is	**What are**
What is bread made of?	**What are** your shoes made of?

▶ Complete the questions with *is* or *are*. Then answer the questions aloud.

11. What _____ a baseball glove made of?

12. What _____ hamburgers made of?

13. What _____ bacon made of?

14. What _____ dairy products made of?

15. What _____ flour made of?

71 Pollution

Big Idea Pollution harms the environment.

1. Look and Explore

Pollution is bad for the environment.

The **exhaust** from cars causes smog. ▶

exhaust

Smog makes the air dirty. ▼

smog

▲ **Toxins** can harm people and animals.

Chemicals pollute the water. ▼

2. Listen and Talk

WORDS 1–10

1. **Pollution** is bad for the environment.
2. Martina remembers not to **litter.**
3. Sam puts **trash** in a garbage can.
4. You can see **smog** in the air in some cities.
5. Smog comes from the **exhaust** of cars.
6. Exhaust is **released** from machines.
7. Some **chemicals** in our water can hurt us.
8. **Toxins** are bad chemicals.
9. They **pollute** our air, water, and land.
10. Toxins can **harm** our lakes and rivers.

WORDS 11–20

11. Remember to pick up your **garbage.**
12. Don't toss **wrappers** on the ground.
13. **Toss** trash in its proper place.
14. Pollution makes the soil **dirty.**
15. Chemicals pollute our **land.**
16. Toxins can **ruin** our water supply.
17. Smog pollutes the **air** we breathe.
18. **Smoke** from exhaust looks black in the sky.
19. Factory smoke **fouls** the air.
20. Try to keep our air and water **clean.**

3. Read and Write

WORDS 1–10

▶ Use the Word Bank to complete each sentence.

1. Bad chemicals that can hurt us are called _____.

2. _____ makes our air, land, and water dirty.

3. Mexico City and Los Angeles have a lot of _____.

4. Exhaust is _____ into the air by cars and trucks.

5. Pollution can _____ Earth's resources.

Word Bank
released
toxins
smog
pollution
harm

WORDS 11–20

▶ Use the Word Bank to complete the chart.

Ways you can help stop pollution:
☑ Don't throw food _____ on the ground. **6.**
☑ _____ garbage into the garbage can. **7.**
☑ Pick up the _____ you see on the ground. **8.**
☑ Help keep your school grounds _____. **9.**
☑ Ride a bike or walk because exhaust from cars makes the air _____. **10.**

Word Bank
dirty
clean
garbage
toss
wrappers

4. Develop Language

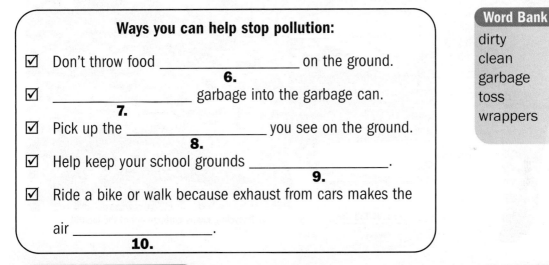

USING IT OR THEY

Use	To tell about
it	1 thing _Smog_ is in the air. _It_ looks black.
they	more than 1 thing _Chemicals_ spill into lakes. _They_ pollute our water.

▶ Complete each sentence with _It_ or _They_.

11. _____ harms Earth's resources. (pollution)

12. _____ cover food. (wrappers)

13. _____ belongs in the trash can. (trash)

14. _____ can make people sick. (toxins)

15. _____ release exhaust. (cars)

Big Idea Learn what materials can be recycled.

1. Look and Explore

We recycle **things** we are done using.

glass

landfill

GLASS BOTTLES
THIS BIN CONTAINS 20% RECYCLED PLASTIC

tin   aluminum   plastic

recycle

ALUMINUM AND TIN CANS
PLASTIC BOTTLES
THIS BIN CONTAINS 20% RECYCLED PLASTIC

paper

recycling bin
NEWSPAPERS
MAGAZINES
THIS BIN CONTAINS 20% RECYCLED PLASTIC

▲ Recycling keeps garbage out of the landfill.

2. Listen and Talk

WORDS 1–10

1. We don't **throw away** everything we use.
2. Some **materials** can be used again.
3. We **recycle** things we are done using.
4. You can **reuse** glass and plastic.
5. Recycling keeps garbage out of a **landfill.**
6. Some bottles are made of **plastic.**
7. Other bottles are made of **glass.**
8. Polly collects **aluminum** soda cans.
9. Soup cans are often made of **tin.**
10. We can reuse some **paper** products.

WORDS 11–20

11. Not all trash belongs in the **garbage can.**
12. Some of it belongs in the **recycling bin.**
13. Many **containers** can be recycled.
14. Plastic shopping **bags** can be reused.
15. Pasta sauce **jars** are made of glass.
16. Let's save the aluminum **cans.**
17. **Boxes** can be used for other things.
18. Some materials are **valuable.**
19. Glass **bottles** are worth money.
20. Let's collect the **deposit.**

3. Read and Write

WORDS 1–10

▶ Use the Word Bank to write the word that matches the definition.

1. what things are made of   _____

2. to not throw away   _____

3. to use again   _____

4. where garbage goes   _____

5. to put something in the garbage can _____

Word Bank

recycle
throw away
reuse
landfill
materials

WORDS 11–20

▶ Use the Word Bank to complete the chart.

Container	Material	Description
_____ 6.	aluminum	soft metal, used to hold soda
_____ 7.	paper or plastic	to carry groceries
_____ 8.	cardboard	used to move things
_____ 9.	glass or plastic	have necks
_____ 10.	glass or plastic	have lids

Word Bank

bags
jars
cans
boxes
bottles

4. Develop Language

ABLE WORDS

Verb	Adjective
reuse	**reusable**
recycle	**recyclable**
value	**valuable**

▶ Complete each sentence with the adjective form of the verb.

11. Bottles are _____. (reuse)

12. Newspapers are _____. (recycle)

13. Bottles are _____. (value)

14. Aluminum cans are _____. (recycle)

15. Some resources are _____. (reuse)

School Readiness

73 Native Americans

Big Idea Native Americans settled North America. They used the resources of the land.

1. Look and Explore

village

wigwams

◄ Long ago, Native Americans lived in villages.

The Plains Indians lived in tipis. ►

hides

buffalo

bow

▲ Some Native Americans hunted buffalo.

ceremony

feathers

Today, they still have a ceremony to give thanks. ►

moccasins

2. Listen and Talk

WORDS 1–10

1. Native Americans **settled** North America.
2. Native Americans are also called **Indians**.
3. Native Americans **belong to** tribes.
4. They lived together in **tribes**.
5. The Plains Indians lived in **tipis**.
6. Some Native Americans lived in **wigwams**.
7. Every tribe has a **chief**.
8. They have a **ceremony** to give thanks.
9. They used the **resources** of the land.
10. The Plains Indians hunted **buffalo**.

WORDS 11–20

11. Native Americans lived in **villages**.
12. They are **members** of a tribe.
13. Native Americans honor **nature**.
14. They wear **feathers** to honor their religion.
15. They **hunted** animals for meat and hides.
16. They **gathered** wild fruits and vegetables.
17. Native Americans wore **moccasins** on their feet.
18. Native Americans used **clay** to make pots.
19. They used **hides** to make tipis.
20. Some hunted buffalo with a **bow** and arrow.

WORDS 1–10

▶ Use the Word Bank to write the word that has the same meaning as the underlined words.

1. <u>Native Americans</u> were the first people of America.

_____

2. They <u>started living</u> in Canada and the United States.

_____

3. Native Americans used the country's <u>land, water, and animals</u>.

_____

4. Native American people belong to <u>cultural groups</u>.

_____

5. They <u>are members of</u> a tribe.

_____

Word Bank

tribes
settled
resources
Indians
belong to

WORDS 11–20

▶ Use the Word Bank to complete the chart.

Item:	How they use them:
6. _____	to honor their religion
7. _____	to hunt
8. _____	to make tipis
9. _____	to make pots
10. _____	to wear on their feet

Word Bank

hides
clay
bow
moccasins
feathers

4. Develop Language

PAST TENSE VERBS

Present	Past
live	**lived**
hunt	**hunted**
belong	**belonged**
gather	**gathered**
honor	**honored**

▶ Complete the sentences with the past tense of the verb.

11. Native Americans _____ in villages. (live)

12. They _____ buffalo for food. (hunt)

13. Native Americans _____ to tribes. (belong)

14. They _____ fruits and vegetables. (gather)

15. Native Americans _____ the land. (honor)

74

European Settlers

 **Big Idea** European settlers came to North America for many reasons.

1. Look and Explore

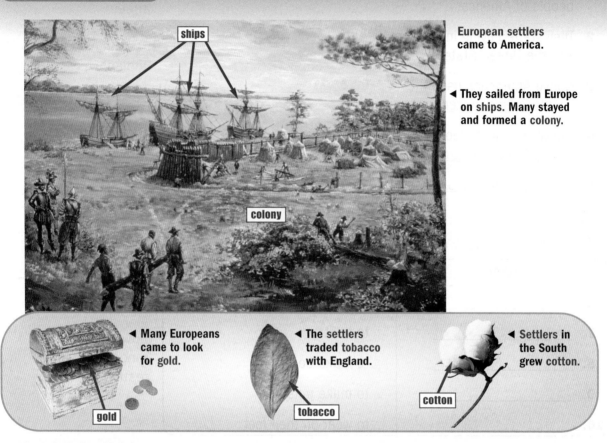

European settlers came to America.

◀ They sailed from Europe on **ships**. Many stayed and formed a **colony**.

ships

colony

◀ **Many Europeans came to look for gold.**

gold

◀ **The settlers traded tobacco with England.**

tobacco

◀ **Settlers in the South grew cotton.**

cotton

2. Listen and Talk

WORDS 1–10

1. **European** settlers came to America.
2. They sailed from Europe on **ships**.
3. The **settlers** came for different reasons.
4. Some wanted to be free from British **control**.
5. Many Europeans came to look for **gold**.
6. They wanted to practice their own **religion**.
7. They wanted to **worship** in their own way.
8. Many people stayed and formed a **colony**.
9. Settlers in the South grew **cotton**.
10. They traded **tobacco** with England.

WORDS 11–20

11. They **traded** with the Indians.
12. Many people settled **along** the East Coast.
13. They traded **fur** for other goods.
14. Some came for the **chance** of a better life.
15. **Slaves** were brought from Africa to work.
16. Settlers **forced** the slaves to work.
17. Many slaves tried to **escape**.
18. They wanted to be **free**.
19. **Poor** Europeans came to find work.
20. They wanted to get **rich**.

3. Read and Write

WORDS 1–10

▶ Use the Word Bank to complete each sentence.

1. People from Europe are _____.

2. Many left to get away from British _____.

3. Some _____ came for religious freedom.

4. They wanted to _____ in their own way.

5. In North America, they were free to practice their own _____.

Word Bank

worship
settlers
control
religion
European

WORDS 11–20

▶ Use the Word Bank to complete the paragraph.

European settlers came to America for the _____
6.
of a better life. _____ were brought from their homes
7.
in Africa to work in America. Settlers _____ them to
8.
work on their plantations. It was a hard life for slaves. Many of them tried
to _____ . They wanted to be _____.
9. **10.**

Word Bank

free
chance
forced
escape
slaves

4. Develop Language

PAST TENSE QUESTIONS WITH *DID*

Question = *did* + present tense verb
What did the settlers trade with the Indians?
Answer = past tense verb
They traded furs.

▶ Complete the questions with the present tense form of the verb. Then answer each question aloud.

11. What did the settlers _____? (traded)

12. Where did many people _____? (settled)

13. Where did Europeans _____? (went)

14. What did settlers _____ to do? (tried)

15. Why did settlers _____ to America? (came)

75 Pilgrims

Big Idea The Pilgrims came to America from Europe. They crossed the Atlantic Ocean. They met Native Americans.

1. Look and Explore

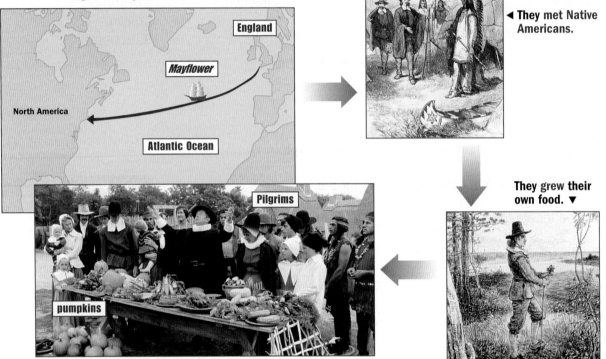

The Pilgrims came to North America from England. They crossed the Atlantic Ocean. ▼

England

Mayflower

North America

Atlantic Ocean

Native Americans

◄ They met Native Americans.

They grew their own food. ▼

Pilgrims

pumpkins

▲ The Pilgrims had a feast to give thanks. It was the first Thanksgiving Day.

2. Listen and Talk

WORDS 1–10

1. The **Pilgrims** came to North America.
2. They came, or **migrated,** from England.
3. The Pilgrims came from **England**.
4. The Pilgrims crossed the **Atlantic Ocean**.
5. Their boat was called the *Mayflower*.
6. The Pilgrims met **Native Americans**.
7. They planted **seeds** in the spring.
8. The Pilgrims grew **crops,** such as corn.
9. Their feast was the first **Thanksgiving Day**.
10. We **celebrate** this holiday every year.

WORDS 11–20

11. The Pilgrims **met** Native Americans.
12. The Pilgrims **farmed** the land.
13. They **planted** crops, like corn and squash.
14. They **grew** their own food.
15. They **invited** Native Americans.
16. Together, they **shared** the food.
17. The Pilgrims had a **feast** to give thanks.
18. They ate vegetables, such as **corn**.
19. The Pilgrims grew **pumpkins**.
20. We now eat **turkey** on Thanksgiving Day.

3. Read and Write

WORDS 1–10

▶ Use the Word Bank to complete each sentence.

1. Pilgrims _____ from England.

2. They planted _____ in the spring.

3. The Pilgrims grew _____ like corn.

4. Their feast was the first _____.

5. We _____ this holiday every year.

Word Bank

crops
Thanksgiving Day
celebrate
migrated
seeds

WORDS 11–20

▶ Use the Word Bank to complete the paragraph.

The Pilgrims _____ Native Americans. They
　　　　　　　　　　6.
_____ crops. After the harvest, they had a
　　　7.
_____. The Pilgrims _____ the
　　　8.　　　　　　　　　　　　　　　**9.**
Native Americans to the feast. The Pilgrims and Native Americans

_____ the food.
　　10.

Word Bank

shared
invited
met
planted
feast

4. Develop Language

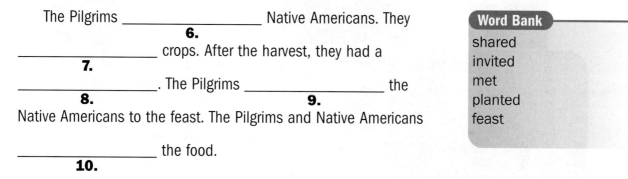

REGULAR AND IRREGULAR PAST TENSE

	Present	Past
Regular	plant	**planted**
	farm	**farmed**
	share	**shared**
Irregular	meet	**met**
	grow	**grew**

▶ Complete the sentences using the past tense of the verb.

11. The Pilgrims _____ the Native Americans. (meet)

12. They _____ seeds in the spring. (plant)

13. The Pilgrims _____ the land. (farm)

14. They _____ their own food. (grow)

15. They _____ the food. (share)

76 Sounds and Syllables

Big Idea — Learning the sounds and syllables of words helps you pronounce them.

1. Look and Explore

Some words have similar sounds.

syllables

syl/la/ble

Words have sounds and syllables.

◄ Jill learns how to pronounce words.

◄ dog

◄ frog

▲ *Frog* and *dog* have the same ending sound.

tree ►

◄ *Tree* and *trail* have the same beginning sound.

◄ trail

2. Listen and Talk

WORDS 1–10

1. Jill learns how to **pronounce** words.
2. Some words have **similar** sounds.
3. *Tree* and *trail* have the same **beginning** sound.
4. *Frog* and *dog* have the same **ending** sound.
5. Look for common sound **patterns**.
6. Some words have many **syllables**.
7. **Pronunciation** has five syllables.
8. **Separate** the sounds slowly in your head.
9. Then combine them with your **tongue**.
10. Finally, say the word **aloud**.

WORDS 11–20

11. Letters are the **basis** of the English language.
12. Jill learns to **sound out** words.
13. She uses her **voice** to speak.
14. Jill says each sound **slowly** at first.
15. Then she says the word **quickly**.
16. Jill says each sound **clearly**.
17. **Take apart** words into separate sounds.
18. **Put together** sounds to make a word.
19. Raise your voice to speak **loudly**.
20. Lower your voice to speak **softly**.

3. Read and Write

WORDS 1–10

▶ Say each word's syllables. Then write the word.

1. sim • i • lar _____

2. a • loud _____

3. pat • terns _____

4. pro • nun • ci • a • tion _____

5. pro • nounce _____

Word Bank

similar
aloud
patterns
pronunciation
pronounce

WORDS 11–20

▶ Use the Word Bank to complete the paragraph.

Saying new English words can be hard. Here's what I do: First,

I _____ a word. Then, I _____ each
    6.   **7.**

syllable slowly. Next, I _____ the sounds quickly.
                              8.

Finally, I use my _____ to say the word aloud. I try
                        9.

to say every word _____.
                        10.

Word Bank

take apart
put together
clearly
voice
sound out

4. Develop Language

ADJECTIVES AND ADVERBS

Adjective	Adverb
slow	**slowly**
quick	**quickly**
clear	**clearly**
soft	**softly**
loud	**loudly**

▶ Complete each sentence by changing the adjective to an adverb.

11. Junko pronounces words _____. (clear)

12. Our teacher speaks _____. (slow)

13. Amanda says her name _____. (quick)

14. Lupé and Janet talk _____. (loud)

15. The librarian speaks _____. (soft)

Singular and Plural

 **Big Idea** Nouns have singular and plural forms. Some plural forms are irregular.

1. Look and Explore

Singular **means** *one*.
Plural **means** *more than one*.

bushes
foxes

Plural Spelling Rules

	Singular	Plural
Add *s* to most regular nouns.	girl book pencil	girls books pencils
Add *es* to words ending in *ch*, *sh*, *s*, and *x*.	lunch bush dress fox	lunches bushes dresses foxes
Irregular nouns have special plural forms.	foot child deer	feet children deer

children ▼

ladies ▼

lunches

dresses

2. Listen and Talk

WORDS 1–10

1. **Singular** means *one*.
2. **Plural** means *more than one*.
3. **Spelling** rules help you make plurals.
4. Most nouns have **regular** plural forms.
5. We **form** most plural nouns by adding *s*.
6. **Attach** *es* to some words.
7. Some nouns have **irregular** plural forms.
8. You need to **memorize** irregular plural forms.
9. The noun *lady* **becomes** *ladies* as a plural.
10. Write *ies* **instead** of *y* in *ladies*.

WORDS 11–20

11. Irregular plural nouns have **unusual** forms.
12. There are two **foxes** in the yard.
13. The foxes are behind the **bushes**.
14. The ladies are wearing **dresses**.
15. The children are eating their **lunches**.
16. Some plural forms are **completely** different.
17. What are the ladies wearing on their **feet**?
18. Is anybody wearing **glasses**?
19. Some plural forms **stay** the same.
20. There are three **deer** behind the bushes.

3. Read and Write

▶ Use the Word Bank to write the word that matches the definition.

1. the order of letters for a word _____

2. to connect one thing to something else _____

3. to remember something exactly _____

4. in place of something _____

5. comes to be something different _____

Word Bank

attach
instead of
becomes
memorize
spelling

▶ Use the Word Bank to write the word that belongs to each group of words.

6. *x* words	boxes, taxes,	_____
7. *sh* words	dishes, wishes,	_____
8. *ss* words	classes, kisses,	_____
9. *ch* words	benches, inches,	_____
10. irregular nouns	children, feet,	_____

Word Bank

bushes
foxes
deer
dresses
lunches

4. Develop Language

USING *THERE IS/ARE*

Use	To tell about
There is a **There is an**	one person or thing *There is an egg on the table.*
There are **+ number**	more than one person or thing *There are dogs in the yard.*

▶ Complete each sentence with *is* or *are*.

11. There _____ a baby in the park.

12. There _____ three deer in the yard.

13. There _____ a dress in the closet.

14. There _____ glasses on the table.

15. There _____ a lady in the office.

 Idioms

Big Idea Idioms are common expressions in English. We use them in informal speaking.

1. Look and Explore

Idioms **are everyday expressions.**

▲ **The teacher told us to hit the books.**

If you mess around, you'll be in hot water. ▶

We are busy as bees. ▼

2. Listen and Talk

WORDS 1–10

1. **Idioms** are common in every language.
2. An idiom is an everyday **expression.**
3. Idioms are used in **informal** speaking.
4. Informal words are called **slang.**
5. Slang is not **formal** speaking.
6. What are some idioms in your **language?**
7. Idioms do not **mean** what they say.
8. You need to **interpret** their meanings.
9. Idioms are very **common** in English.
10. You will **encounter** idioms often.

WORDS 11–20

11. **Pipe down** when the teacher is talking.
12. The students are **busy as bees.**
13. I think learning English is a **piece of cake.**
14. We're **in the same boat.**
15. The teacher told us to **hit the books.**
16. Don't **throw in the towel** before you try.
17. You need to **buckle down** and study.
18. Don't **mess around** when the teacher talks.
19. If you do, you will **be in hot water.**
20. Could you please **give me a hand?**

(WORDS 1–10)

► Use the Word Bank to complete the paragraph.

Learning _____ can be a pain in the neck! They

  1.

do not _____ what they say. Idioms are very

  2.

_____ in English. Can you _____

  3.   **4.**

what "pain in the neck" means? It's an _____ for

  5.

something that is annoying and not easy to do.

Word Bank

interpret
mean
common
idioms
expression

(WORDS 11–20)

► Use the Word Bank to write the idioms that have the same meaning as the underlined words.

6. The students are <u>working hard</u>.   _____

7. You need to <u>study hard</u> if you want to
do well on the test.   _____

8. The teacher gets mad when you
<u>behave badly</u>.   _____

9. Mia and Ming will <u>be in trouble</u> for
passing notes in class.   _____

10. Could you please <u>help me</u>?   _____

Word Bank

hit the books
busy as bees
give me a hand
mess around
be in hot water

4. Develop Language

OBJECT PRONOUNS

Use object pronouns after a verb.			
Give me a hand.			
Singular		**Plural**	
I	**me**	we	**us**
you	**you**	you	**you**
he	**him**		
she	**her**	they	**them**
it	**it**		

► Complete each sentence with the correct object pronoun.

11. Give _____ a hand with the dishes. (Alex and Udranka)

12. Could you give _____ a hand? (Lee and I)

13. I could give _____ a hand with your homework. (you)

14. Give _____ a hand. (Alicia)

15. Please give _____ a hand. (I)

Big Idea — You estimate a sum when you don't need an exact amount.

1. Look and Explore

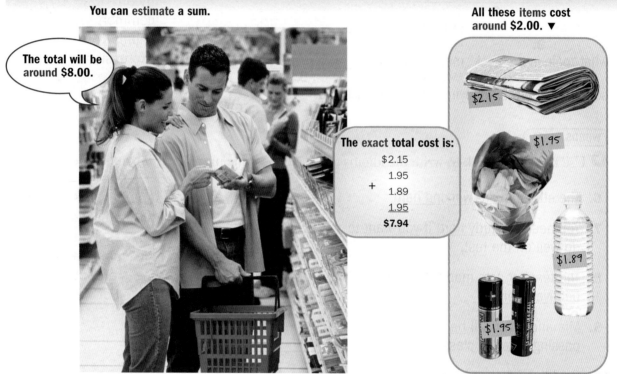

You can estimate a sum.

All these items cost around $2.00. ▼

The total will be around $8.00.

The exact total cost is:
$2.15
1.95
+ 1.89
1.95
$7.94

$2.15

$1.95

$1.89

$1.95

▲ Julia estimates how much the items will cost.

2. Listen and Talk

WORDS 1–10

1. You can **compute** sums in your head.
2. Use **mental math** to make an estimate.
3. You can **estimate** a sum.
4. Estimate when you don't need to be **exact**.
5. **Compatible** numbers are easy to add.
6. Add **front-end digits** to get an estimate.
7. Their sum is less than the exact **amount**.
8. Julia's estimate is **accurate**.
9. She has enough money to buy the **items**.
10. She decides **whether** she can afford them.

WORDS 11–20

11. You don't always need a **calculator**.
12. An estimate is not **quite** exact.
13. You can compute numbers **mentally**.
14. All the items are **around** $2.00.
15. The total is **approximately** $8.00.
16. It is **actually** $7.94.
17. An estimate is a **bit** above or below.
18. Some numbers add more **easily** than others.
19. Julia has **enough** money to buy these items.
20. She estimated the sum **closely**.

3. Read and Write

WORDS 1–10

▶ Use the Word Bank to write the word that fits the definition.

1. to add, subtract, multiply, or divide numbers _____

2. computing numbers in your head _____

3. if _____

4. things _____

5. how much of something there is _____

Word Bank

items
mental math
amount
compute
whether

WORDS 11–20

▶ Use the Word Bank to complete the chart.

Adjective	Adverb
6. easy	_____
7. actual	_____
8. mental	_____
9. approximate	_____
10. close	_____

Word Bank

closely
actually
mentally
approximately
easily

4. Develop Language

QUESTIONS WITH *DO/DOES*	
Use	**To ask about**
Do	plural nouns **Do** calculators compute numbers?
Does	singular nouns **Does** a calculator compute numbers?

▶ Complete each question with *do* or *does*. Then answer them aloud.

11. _____ compatible numbers add easily?

12. _____ you always need to use a calculator?

13. _____ an estimate describe amounts well?

14. _____ they know how to make estimates?

15. _____ all numbers add easily?

Big Idea Multiples and factors help you to understand numbers.

1. Look and Explore

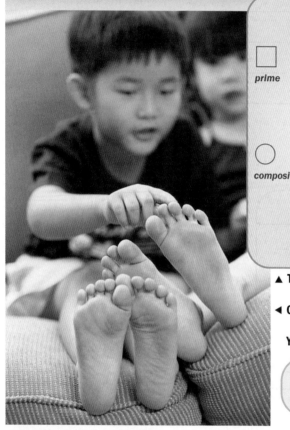

Hundreds Chart

1	2	3	4	5	6	7	8	9	10
11	12	13	14	15	16	17	18	19	20
21	22	23	24	25	26	27	28	29	30
31	32	33	34	35	36	37	38	39	40
41	42	43	44	45	46	47	48	49	50
51	52	53	54	55	56	57	58	59	60
61	62	63	64	65	66	67	68	69	70
71	72	73	74	75	76	77	78	79	80
81	82	83	84	85	86	87	88	89	90
91	92	93	94	95	96	97	98	99	100

☐ prime

◯ composite

▲ The prime **numbers** are boxed. The composite **numbers** are circled.

◀ Count your toes by 1s, 2s, and 5s.

You can skip-count your toes by 2s. ▼

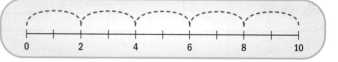

2. Listen and Talk

WORDS 1–10

1. Numbers 1, 2, 5, and 10 are **factors** of 20.
2. A factor divides **evenly** into another number.
3. The number 10 is **divisible** by 5.
4. Numbers 10 and 20 have **common factors.**
5. Numbers 10 and 20 are **multiples** of 2.
6. You can **skip-count** your toes by 2s.
7. Numbers 2 and 5 have **common multiples.**
8. Their **least common multiple** is 10.
9. A **composite** number has more than 2 factors.
10. A **prime** number has only 2 factors.

WORDS 11–20

11. An **even** number has 2 as a factor.
12. An **odd** number is not divisible by 2.
13. The number 5 is divisible by 1 and **itself.**
14. The number 1 is different from **other** numbers.
15. The prime numbers are **boxed.**
16. The composite numbers are **circled.**
17. All the numbers in the first **column** are odd.
18. Say the composite numbers in the first **row.**
19. Your toes can be put into **pairs.**
20. Count your **toes** by 1s, 2s, and 5s.

3. Read and Write

▶ Use the Word Bank to complete the paragraphs.

Lin has 6 sisters. The number 6 is _____ by 2
1.
and by 3, which means they divide _____ into 6. The
2.
numbers 2 and 3 are _____ of 6.
3.

You can _____ by 10s to find their total
4.
number of toes. Together 6 sisters have 60 toes. The number 60 is

a _____ number because it has more than two
5.
factors. Can you find all the factors of 60?

Word Bank

evenly
factors
divisible
composite
skip-count

▶ Use the Word Bank to complete the sentences.

6. The numbers 1, 3, 5, 7, and 9 are _____ numbers.

7. The numbers 2, 4, 6, 8, 10, and 12 are _____ numbers.

8. A prime number is divisible only by 1 and _____.

9. Your feet have 10 _____.

10. You can put an even number of things into _____.

Word Bank

pairs
itself
even
odd
toes

4. Develop Language

QUESTIONS WITH *WHAT IS/ARE*	
Use	**To ask about**
What is	1 thing *What is* a prime number?
What are	more than 1 thing *What are* prime numbers?

▶ Complete the sentences with *is* or *are*. Then answer the questions aloud.

11. What _____ a prime number?

12. What _____ the common factors of 10 and 20?

13. What _____ the even numbers between 20 and 30?

14. What _____ the least prime number?

15. What _____ factors?

81 Math Properties

Big Idea Knowing properties can help you find the sum or product of a problem.

1. Look and Explore

$$3 + 2 = 5$$

Distributive Property					
$4 \times (2 + 1) = (4 \times 2) + (4 \times 1)$					
$4 \times$	3	=	8	+	4
12		=	12		

regroup

$$2 + 3 = 5$$

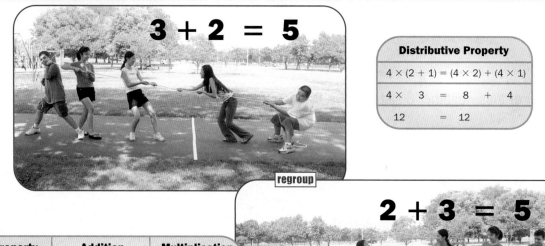

Property	Addition	Multiplication
Commutative	$3 + 2 = 5$ $2 + 3 = 5$	$8 \times 4 = 32$ $4 \times 8 = 32$
Associative	$(6 + 3) + 5 = 14$ $6 + (3 + 5) = 14$	$(5 \times 2) \times 7 = 70$ $5 \times (2 \times 7) = 70$

2. Listen and Talk

WORDS 1–10

1. A **property** is something that is always true.
2. **Addition** is the adding of addends.
3. **Multiplication** is the multiplying of factors.
4. **Apply** these properties to problems.
5. **Commutative** refers to the order of numbers.
6. **Commute** means to go back and forth.
7. **Associative** refers to the grouping of numbers.
8. You **associate** with friends in groups.
9. The **distributive** property makes math easier.
10. You **distribute** things by spreading them out.

WORDS 11–20

11. You can **reorder** addends and factors.
12. Add or multiply the numbers **forward.**
13. You can do the same problems **backward.**
14. **Switch** the order of $7 + 3$.
15. Switching the order doesn't **change** the sum.
16. You can **regroup** addends and factors.
17. Regrouping makes solving problems **easier.**
18. This property lets you **spread out** numbers.
19. Working with numbers **separately** is easier.
20. You can multiply factors **in your head.**

3. Read and Write

WORDS 1–10

▶ Use the Word Bank to write the word that fits each definition.

1. a rule about numbers that is always true _____

2. to put to use _____

3. to go back and forth _____

4. to connect things _____

5. to spread things out _____

Word Bank

commute
apply
associate
distribute
property

WORDS 11–20

▶ Use the Word Bank to write the word that has the same meaning as the underlined words.

6. Changing the order of factors doesn't <u>make</u> the product <u>different</u>. _____

7. Commutative properties let you <u>put</u> addends and factors <u>into different order</u>. _____

8. Associative properties let you <u>change the grouping of</u> addends and factors. _____

9. Using these properties helps to make computing <u>less difficult</u>. _____

10. Working with numbers <u>apart from one another</u> is easier. _____

Word Bank

regroup
reorder
separately
change
easier

4. Develop Language

PRESENT PROGRESSIVE SENTENCES		
Subject	**Be**	**Verb + ing**
I	**am**	
He She It	**is**	commuting.
We You They	**are**	

▶ Complete the sentences with *am*, *is*, or *are*.

11. Bill _____ commuting to work.

12. The students _____ regrouping the addends.

13. Tina _____ distributing the papers.

14. The students _____ associating groups of numbers.

15. Jill _____ applying the Associative Property.

Big Idea The heart and lungs give our bodies the oxygen we need.

1. Look and Explore

Our lungs take in air when we breathe. Air contains oxygen. ▼

Arteries carry blood away from the heart. Veins carry blood to the heart. ▶

heart

◀ The heart pushes blood through the body.

blood vessels

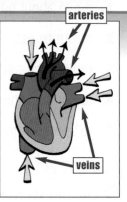
arteries

veins

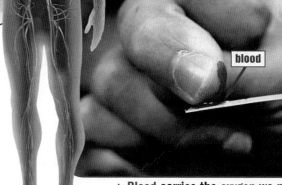

blood

▲ Blood carries the oxygen we need.

pulse

▲ You can feel your pulse on your wrist.

2. Listen and Talk

WORDS 1–10

1. Your body has many **organs**.
2. The **heart** pushes blood through the body.
3. Our **lungs** take in air when we breathe.
4. Your body needs **oxygen**.
5. You **breathe** air to get oxygen.
6. **Blood** carries oxygen through your body.
7. **Arteries** carry blood away from the heart.
8. **Capillaries** carry blood to and from cells.
9. **Veins** carry blood back to the heart.
10. You can take your pulse on your **wrist**.

WORDS 11–20

11. The heart is like a **pump** in your chest.
12. Blood **flows** through arteries and veins.
13. Blood **vessels** are like pipes that carry blood.
14. Arteries and veins are like tiny **tubes**.
15. The heart **beats** all the time.
16. You can measure your heart **rate**, or pulse.
17. It **increases** when you exercise.
18. Your pulse **decreases** when you rest.
19. You can feel your **pulse** through your skin.
20. Can you feel your **heartbeat**?

3. Read and Write

WORDS 1–10

▶ Use the Word Bank to answer the questions.

1. What is the air that your body needs? _____

2. What carries oxygen? _____

3. What carries blood away from the heart? _____

4. What carries blood to and from cells? _____

5. What carries blood back to the heart? _____

Word Bank
blood
veins
arteries
capillaries
oxygen

WORDS 11–20

▶ Use the Word Bank to complete the story.

I went to the doctor's office last week. Dr. Chan used a

machine to measure my heart _____. She said it
                                        6.

_____ when I run and play. My heart rate
        7.

_____ when I sleep or watch TV. You can feel your
        8.

own _____. Just put your hand over your heart.
            9.

You can feel your _____ on your wrist, too.
                        10.

Word Bank
pulse
rate
increases
decreases
heartbeat

4. Develop Language

VERBS

| **State of being verb: be** |
| Blood *is* inside your body. |
| Arteries *are* like tubes. |

| **Action verbs** |
| Blood *flows* through your body. |
| Arteries *carry* blood away from the heart. |

▶ Complete each sentence with the correct form of the verb.

11. The heart _____ blood. (push)

12. The heart _____ all the time. (beat)

13. Blood _____ through veins. (flow)

14. Capillaries _____ blood to cells. (carry)

15. The heart _____ like a pump. (be)

83 How We Use Food

Big Idea Your stomach digests food. Food gives your body nutrients.

1. Look and Explore

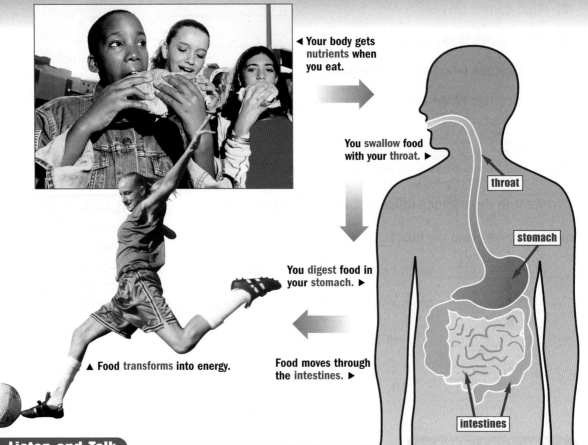

◄ Your body gets nutrients when you eat.

You swallow food with your throat. ►

throat

stomach

You digest food in your stomach. ►

Food moves through the intestines. ►

intestines

▲ Food transforms into energy.

2. Listen and Talk

WORDS 1–10

1. Your body gets **nutrients** from food.
2. You put food in your **mouth.**
3. You **chew** food in your mouth.
4. Then you **swallow** the food.
5. You swallow food with your **throat.**
6. The food goes into your **stomach.**
7. You **digest** food in your stomach.
8. Stomach **acids** break down food.
9. The food moves through the **intestines.**
10. The intestines **absorb** nutrients.

WORDS 11–20

11. You **bite** with your teeth.
12. Your teeth **break down** food.
13. The **bits** of food get smaller and smaller.
14. Food **transforms** into energy.
15. Your body takes **useful** nutrients from food.
16. The part that is left over is **waste.**
17. Waste is **useless** to your body.
18. Your body **gets rid of** waste.
19. Food **travels** through your body.
20. Waste **winds up** leaving your body.

3. Read and Write

WORDS 1–10

▶ Use the Word Bank to complete each sentence.

1. _____ the pizza in your mouth.

2. _____ the small pieces of food.

3. You _____ the food in your stomach.

4. _____ come from the food.

5. Your intestines _____ the food nutrients.

Word Bank
absorb
swallow
chew
digest
nutrients

WORDS 11–20

▶ Use the Word Bank to write the word that fits each clue.

6. parts of something _____

7. able to be used _____

8. unable to be used _____

9. things that can't be used _____

10. moves from one place to another _____

Word Bank
useful
bits
travels
waste
useless

4. Develop Language

SUBJECT/VERB AGREEMENT

Singular noun

My body gets the nutrients from food.

Plural noun

Our bodies get the nutrients from food.

▶ Complete each sentence with the correct form of the verb.

11. They _____ the food carefully. (chew)

12. He _____ a piece of pizza. (swallow)

13. It _____ to the stomach. (move)

14. She _____ fruits and vegetables. (eat)

15. The intestines _____ nutrients. (absorb)

How We React

Big Idea The brain and nerves in your body control your actions.

1. Look and Explore

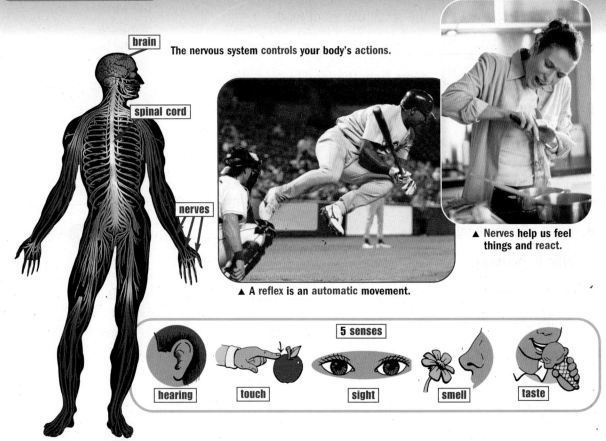

brain

The nervous system controls your body's actions.

spinal cord

nerves

▲ Nerves help us feel things and react.

▲ A reflex is an automatic movement.

5 senses

hearing | touch | sight | smell | taste

2. Listen and Talk

WORDS 1–10

1. The nervous system **controls** your actions.
2. **Nerves** help us feel things.
3. A **sensation** is what your body feels.
4. This feeling travels like a **current** in the body.
5. The **brain** receives this information.
6. The brain **translates** it into actions.
7. Nerve cells are called **neurons**.
8. The **spinal cord** helps you move.
9. The spinal cord is in your **backbone**.
10. The baseball player had a **reflex**.

WORDS 11–20

11. Your body has five **senses**.
12. You **taste** things with your tongue.
13. Your hands give you the sense of **touch**.
14. Eyes give you **sight**.
15. Your ears give you **hearing**.
16. Your nose gives you the sense of **smell**.
17. Your brain controls your body's **reactions**.
18. Some of your actions are **automatic**.
19. How do you **react** when you fall?
20. A doctor tests your reflexes with a **hammer**.

3. Read and Write

▶ Use the Word Bank to complete each question.

1. What _____ your actions? (the nervous system)

2. What moves like a _____? (sensations)

3. What _____ information? (the brain)

4. What is a _____? (an automatic movement)

5. What is a _____? (what your body feels)

Word Bank

current
controls
reflex
sensation
translates

▶ Use the Word Bank to label each picture.

Word Bank

sight
taste
smell
hearing
touch

6. _____

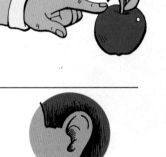

7. _____

8. _____

9. _____

10. _____

4. Develop Language

USED FOR/USED TO	
Use	**To describe**
used to	base verb forms *A hammer is* used to *test reflexes.*
used for	*ing* verb forms *A hammer is* used for *testing reflexes.*

▶ Complete the sentences with *used to* or *used for*.

11. Your eyes are _____ see.

12. Your tongue is _____ tasting.

13. Your ears are _____ hear.

14. Your nose is _____ smelling.

15. Your hands are _____ touch.

Unit 28 • BODY SYSTEMS 209

85 Making Laws

Big Idea The legislative branch makes laws. The Senate and the House of Representatives make up Congress.

1. Look and Explore

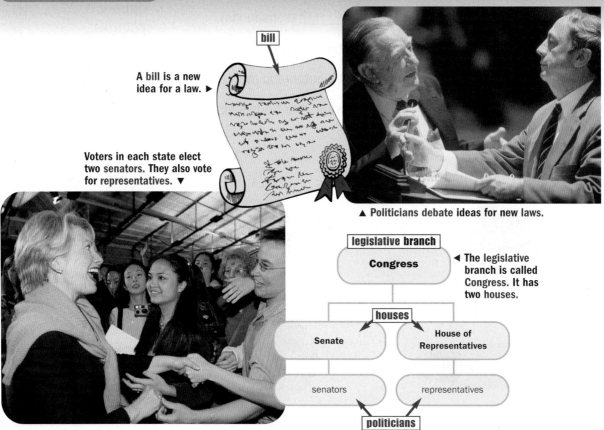

bill

A bill is a new idea for a law. ▶

Voters in each state elect two senators. They also vote for representatives. ▼

▲ Politicians debate ideas for new laws.

legislative branch

Congress

◀ The legislative branch is called Congress. It has two houses.

houses

Senate

House of Representatives

senators

representatives

politicians

2. Listen and Talk

WORDS 1–10

1. The U.S. government has three **branches**.
2. The **legislative** branch makes laws.
3. It is also called **Congress**.
4. Congress has two **houses**.
5. One house is called the **Senate**.
6. The other is the **House of Representatives**.
7. Voters in each state elect two **senators**.
8. They also vote for **representatives**.
9. A **bill** is a new idea for a law.
10. Politicians **debate** ideas for new laws.

WORDS 11–20

11. Senators vote to **pass** a bill.
12. Sometimes they **reject** a bill.
13. Laws are **necessary** rules.
14. **Society** needs laws to work well.
15. **Laws** keep Americans safe.
16. **Without** laws, society would be dangerous.
17. People in government are **politicians**.
18. They make **political** decisions.
19. They make **agreements** about laws.
20. They often **disagree** with one another.

3. Read and Write

WORDS 1–10

▶ Use the Word Bank to write the word that fits each clue.

1. the U.S. government has three of these _____

2. the branch that makes laws _____

3. the legislative branch is also called this _____

4. senators and representatives write this _____

5. senators and representatives
do this to bills _____

Word Bank

debate
bill
legislative
branches
Congress

WORDS 11–20

▶ Use the Word Bank to choose the word that belongs to each group of words.

6. community, group of people, _____

7. senators, representatives, _____

8. to not pass, to refuse, _____

9. not agree, argue, _____

10. rules, _____

Word Bank

reject
laws
disagree
society
politicians

4. Develop Language

NEGATIVE SHORT ANSWERS

Subject	Be
I	**am not**
he she it	is not = **isn't**
we you they	are not = **aren't**

▶ Complete each sentence with *am not*, *isn't*, or *aren't*.

11. Are laws always obeyed? No, they _____.

12. Is the legislative branch also called the Senate?
No, it _____.

13. Are you a senator? No, I _____.

14. Are all bills passed? No, they _____.

15. Is the Senate a branch of government? No, it _____.

The President

The executive branch carries out the laws. The president is the head of the executive branch.

1. Look and Explore

The **president** leads the **executive branch.** ▼

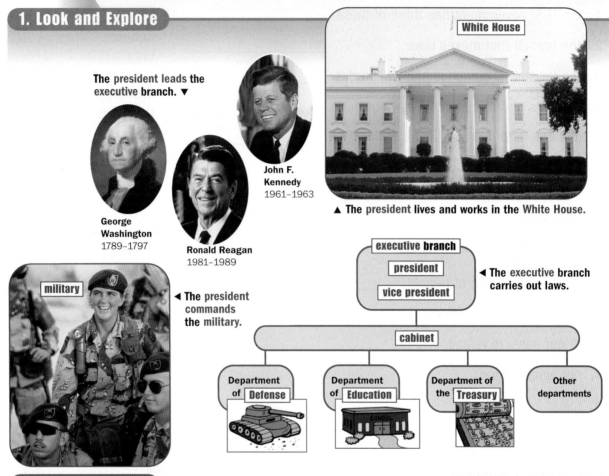

George **Washington** 1789–1797

Ronald Reagan 1981–1989

John F. **Kennedy** 1961–1963

White House

▲ The **president** lives and works in the **White House.**

◄ The **president commands** the **military.**

military

executive **branch**

president

vice president

◄ The **executive branch** carries out laws.

cabinet

Department of **Defense**

Department of **Education**

Department of the **Treasury**

Other **departments**

2. Listen and Talk

WORDS 1–10

1. The **executive** branch carries out laws.
2. The **president** is the leader of this country.
3. The president works in the **White House.**
4. The **vice president** helps the president.
5. A **cabinet** of people work for the president.
6. Many **departments** make up the cabinet.
7. The Dept. of **Education** helps schools.
8. The Dept. of the **Treasury** manages money.
9. The Dept. of **Defense** controls the military.
10. The **military** includes the Army and Navy.

WORDS 11–20

11. The executive branch **leads** the government.
12. The cabinet is a group of **advisers.**
13. The cabinet **manages** the country.
14. The president is the **commander** in chief.
15. The president **commands** the military.
16. The president **serves** the people.
17. The people **elect** the president.
18. The president's **term** is four years.
19. The president belongs to a political **party.**
20. A political party has a **policy.**

3. Read and Write

WORDS 1–10

▶ Use the Word Bank to write the short answer to the questions.

1. Which branch does the president belong to? _____

2. Who is the leader of the country? _____

3. Who helps the president lead? _____

4. Where does the president live? _____

5. What is the group of people that advise the president? _____

Word Bank

White House
vice president
executive
president
cabinet

WORDS 11–20

▶ Use the Word Bank to write the word that can replace the underlined words.

6. The president <u>works for</u> the people. _____

7. The people <u>vote for</u> the president. _____

8. The U.S. president's <u>time in office</u> is 4 years. _____

9. A political party shares a <u>common plan</u>. _____

10. A president belongs to a <u>political group</u>. _____

Word Bank

elect
party
policy
serves
term

4. Develop Language

WHO, WHERE, AND WHAT

Use	To ask about
Who	people *Who* lives in the White House?
Where	places *Where* is the White House?
What	things *What* is the White House?

▶ Complete the questions with *who*, *where*, or *what*. Then answer them aloud.

11. _____ advises the president?

12. _____ is the cabinet?

13. _____ does the president live?

14. _____ is the president now?

15. _____ is a term?

Big Idea The judicial branch interprets the law.

1. Look and Explore

Constitution

◄ Laws are based on the Constitution.

Criminals **are** people who commit **crimes.** ►

People go to **court** for a **trial.** ▼

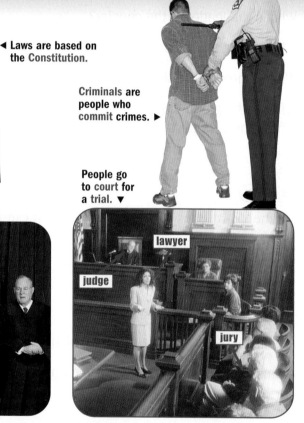

lawyer

judge

jury

The **Supreme Court** is the highest court. ▼

justices

2. Listen and Talk

WORDS 1–10

1. U.S. laws are based on the **Constitution.**
2. The **judicial** branch interprets the law.
3. The highest court is the **Supreme Court.**
4. The U.S. Supreme Court has 9 **justices.**
5. The **Chief Justice** is the leader.
6. People who do illegal things go to **court.**
7. A **lawyer** advises people about the law.
8. The **judge** decides who is guilty.
9. Sometimes a **jury** of people decide.
10. **Criminals** are people who commit crimes.

WORDS 11–20

11. A **justice** system treats people fairly.
12. If you **commit** a serious crime, you get a trial.
13. A **trial** is held in court.
14. Lawyers **represent** people on trial.
15. Doing something **illegal** can send you to jail.
16. A person is **innocent** until proven guilty.
17. He or she has to be proven **guilty.**
18. A judge makes sure the trial is **fair.**
19. Some guilty people go to **jail.**
20. Others have to pay a different **penalty.**

3. Read and Write

WORDS 1–10

▶ Use the Word Bank to write the word that answers the question.

1. Which branch of the government interpret the law? _____

2. What is the highest court in the judicial system? _____

3. What is the leader of the Supreme Court called? _____

4. Who advises people about the law? _____

5. Who decides if a person is guilty or innocent? _____

Word Bank

judge
Chief Justice
judicial
Supreme Court
lawyer

WORDS 11–20

▶ Use the Word Bank to write the word that fits each clue.

6. did not commit the crime _____

7. did commit the crime _____

8. some criminals are sent here _____

9. a fine _____

10. what we expect a judge to be _____

Word Bank

fair
jail
guilty
penalty
innocent

4. Develop Language

QUESTIONS WITH *DO/DOES*	
Use	**To ask about**
does	singular nouns *What does a lawyer do?*
do	plural nouns *Who do lawyers represent?*

▶ Complete each question with *do* or *does*. Then answer them aloud.

11. What _____ the Constitution guarantee to criminals?

12. Why _____ people break the law?

13. Where _____ guilty people go?

14. What _____ the Chief Justice do?

15. What _____ you call someone who is guilty?

Big Idea All sentences need a punctuation mark.
Punctuation marks are signs for the reader.

1. Look and Explore

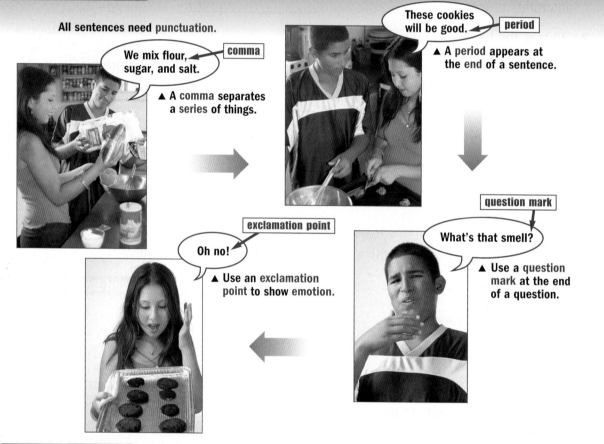

All sentences need punctuation.

We mix flour, sugar, and salt. **comma**

▲ A **comma** separates a series of things.

These cookies will be good. **period**

▲ A **period** appears at the end of a sentence.

question mark

What's that smell?

▲ Use a question mark at the end of a question.

exclamation point

Oh no!

▲ Use an exclamation point to show emotion.

2. Listen and Talk

WORDS 1–10

1. All sentences need **punctuation**.
2. A **period** tells you to stop at the end.
3. Use an **exclamation point** to show emotion.
4. Use a **question mark** at the end of a question.
5. **Quotation marks** show someone is speaking.
6. A **comma** separates words in a series.
7. **Capitalize** the first letter of a new sentence.
8. Punctuation marks **inform** the reader.
9. The *N* in *Nancy* is an **uppercase** letter.
10. The other letters are **lowercase** letters.

WORDS 11–20

11. Punctuation **marks** are signs for the reader.
12. **Signs** tell people what to do.
13. A list, or **series** of things, needs commas.
14. **Titles**, like *Mr.* and *Mrs.*, take capital letters.
15. **Begin** first and last names with capital letters.
16. Put a period at the **end** of a statement.
17. Questions **require** a question mark.
18. "Oh no!" said Nancy, with **emotion**.
19. Use quotation marks to **report** what is said.
20. Put a comma between each **thing** in a list.

WORDS 1–10

▶ Use the Word Bank to write the word that fits each clue.

1. what all kinds of sentences need   _____

2. what you do to the first letter of a name   _____

3. what punctuation marks do   _____

4. in big letters, such as *A*, *B*, and *C*   _____

5. in small letters, such as *a*, *b*, and *c*   _____

Word Bank

capitalize
uppercase
inform
lowercase
punctuation

WORDS 11–20

▶ Use the Word Bank to write the word that has the same meaning as the underlined word or words.

6. Questions <u>need</u> question marks.   _____

7. Quotation marks are used to <u>tell</u> what is said.   _____

8. An exclamation point is used to show a <u>strong feeling</u>.   _____

9. <u>Marks</u> tell people what to do.   _____

10. Put a comma between each <u>item</u> in a list.   _____

Word Bank

thing
report
signs
require
emotion

4. Develop Language

PUNCTUATION MARKS

Mark	Use
period **.**	to end a statement
question mark **?**	to end a question
exclamation point **!**	to show emotion
comma **,**	to separate a series of words
quotation marks **" "**	to show someone is speaking

▶ Complete each sentence with the correct punctuation mark.

11. What is your teacher's name ☐

12. Stop talking ☐

13. ☐ I'm trying to study, ☐ Angeline said.

14. Sharon ☐ Jo ☐ and I are at the library.

15. They are studying for an important exam ☐

89 Kinds of Sentences

Big Idea There are four kinds of sentences. Each kind of sentence has a different purpose.

1. Look and Explore

A declarative **sentence** makes a statement. ▶

I can score a goal.

Will Carlos score a goal?

▲ An **interrogative** sentence asks a question.

Imperative sentences tell us what to do. ▼

Score a goal.

It's a goal!

▲ Exclamatory sentences show strong feelings.

2. Listen and Talk

WORDS 1–10

1. There are four **kinds** of sentences.
2. We **classify** sentences into four groups.
3. Each group has a different **role**.
4. **Declarative** sentences make a statement.
5. An **interrogative** sentence asks a question.
6. **Imperative** sentences tell us what to do.
7. **Exclamatory** sentences show strong feelings.
8. A sentence expresses a **thought**.
9. We use sentences to **communicate**.
10. Use a sentence to give your **opinion**.

WORDS 11–20

11. The players listen to the **command**.
12. Julio asked a **question**.
13. "Will we win this game?" he **asked**.
14. "Carlos plays soccer" is a **statement**.
15. "Goal!" is an **exclamation**.
16. The coach **demanded** we win the game.
17. "We love soccer," the players **declared**.
18. The coach **told** the players what to do.
19. A fan **wondered** whether Carlos would score.
20. What **type** of sentence is this one?

WORDS 1–10

▶ Use the Word Bank to complete the chart.

Sentence	Kind	_____ 1.
Soccer is exciting.	_____ 2.	make something known
Is soccer exciting?	_____ 3.	ask a question
I love soccer!	_____ 4.	show emotion
Pass the ball to me.	_____ 5.	tell someone what to do

Word Bank

imperative
interrogative
role
declarative
exclamatory

WORDS 11–20

▶ Use the Word Bank to complete the story.

"Our teacher is so strict," Rosie _____.
                                        6.
"Yesterday, he _____ us to do 10 pages of
                      7.
homework. Then he _____ if we had any questions.
                            8.
He _____ that we finish it by tomorrow. We have to
        9.
follow his _____."
                  10.

Word Bank

command
told
asked
declared
demanded

4. Develop Language

COMMANDS

Things you should do

Kick the ball.

Play hard.

Win.

Things you should not do

Don't worry.

Don't be nervous.

Don't lose.

▶ Write the words in the correct order to make a command.

11. (chew/Don't/gum.) _____

12. (sit/down./Please) _____

13. (teacher./Listen/to/the) _____

14. (your/hand./Raise) _____

15. (page/to/Turn/96.) _____

 **Reading a Paragraph**

> **Big Idea** Paragraphs have different parts to help organize ideas.

1. Look and Explore

A paragraph **is made of** sentences.

A paragraph **has different** elements. ▼

topic sentence

A topic sentence gives the main idea. ▶

body

The body gives more information. ▶

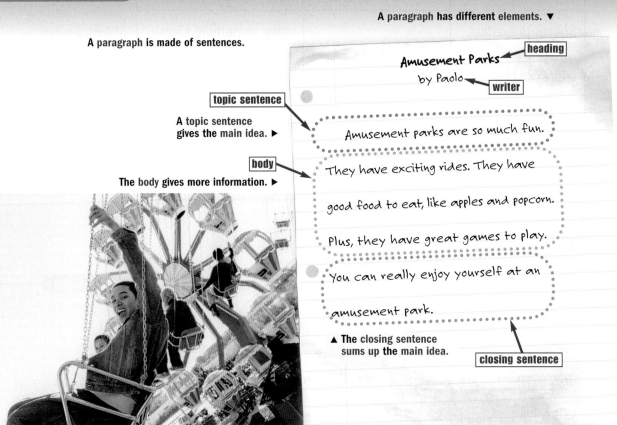

Amusement Parks ← heading
by Paolo ← **writer**

Amusement parks are so much fun.

They have exciting rides. They have good food to eat, like apples and popcorn. Plus, they have great games to play.

You can really enjoy yourself at an amusement park.

▲ The closing sentence **sums up the** main idea.

closing sentence

2. Listen and Talk

WORDS 1–10

1. A **paragraph** is made up of sentences.
2. Paragraphs have different **elements**.
3. The **heading** gives you the subject.
4. What is the **topic** of Paolo's paragraph?
5. The **topic sentence** states the main idea.
6. The **main idea** is what the writer thinks.
7. The **body** gives more information.
8. Paolo gives **details** about amusement parks.
9. The **closing sentence** ends the paragraph.
10. Paolo is the **writer** of the paragraph.

WORDS 11–20

11. Paolo informs the **reader** about the topic.
12. He writes about the **essential** information.
13. Paragraphs are **split** into sentences.
14. Paolo organizes his **ideas** before writing.
15. He communicates his **interest** in the topic.
16. The first sentence is the most **important** idea.
17. It **introduces** the main idea to the reader.
18. Paolo **supports** his main idea well.
19. The closing sentence **sums up** the main idea.
20. It **states** what the body was all about.

3. Read and Write

WORDS 1–10

▶ Use the Word Bank to write the word that fits each clue.

1. pieces of something   _____

2. a group of related sentences   _____

3. more information about something   _____

4. what the writer is saying about the topic _____

5. what the paragraph is about   _____

Word Bank

topic
details
elements
main idea
paragraph

WORDS 11–20

▶ Use the Word Bank to complete the paragraph.

Paragraphs are usually _____ into three main
                                    6.
parts. Each part helps the _____ understand the
                                    7.
paragraph. The topic sentence usually gives the most

_____ idea. The body _____ the
          8.   **9.**
main idea. The closing sentence usually _____
                                                10.
the main idea.

Word Bank

important
split
supports
reader
sums up

4. Develop Language

SUBJECT/VERB AGREEMENT

Singular Noun

A writer *informs* readers.

Plural Noun

Writers inform readers.

▶ Complete each sentence with the correct form of the verb.

11. Writers _____ ideas into paragraphs. (organize)

12. Paolo _____ his ideas. (support)

13. Jack and Sami _____ good paragraphs. (write)

14. Most paragraphs _____ one main idea. (have)

15. A writer _____ the main idea. (summarize)

91 Word Problems

Big Idea Having a strategy or method helps to make solving word problems easier.

1. Look and Explore

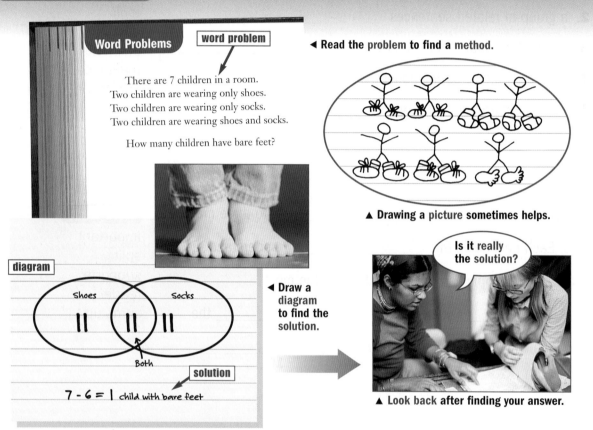

Word Problems

word problem

There are 7 children in a room.
Two children are wearing only shoes.
Two children are wearing only socks.
Two children are wearing shoes and socks.

How many children have bare feet?

diagram

Shoes   Socks

Both

solution

7 − 6 = 1 child with bare feet

◀ Read the **problem** to find a **method**.

▲ Drawing a **picture** sometimes helps.

◀ Draw a **diagram** to find the **solution**.

Is it really the solution?

▲ **Look back** after finding your answer.

2. Listen and Talk

WORDS 1–10

1. We need a plan to solve a **word problem**.
2. How will you solve the **problem?**
3. There are many ways to find the **solution**.
4. Read the problem to select a **method**.
5. You need to **select** a method to solve it.
6. Word problems **provide** a lot of information.
7. Sometimes you can **simplify** the problem.
8. Drawing a **picture** sometimes helps.
9. Draw a **diagram** to find the solution.
10. Make sure your answer is **reasonable**.

WORDS 11–20

11. Word problems may seem **confusing**.
12. Which information is **known?**
13. Some information is **needed**.
14. You can **ignore** the unneeded information.
15. Use the method to **discover** the answer.
16. **Look back** after finding your answer.
17. Is it **really** the solution?
18. Your first try **might** not be correct.
19. Don't **give up** after one try.
20. You can always try **another** method.

3. Read and Write

WORDS 1–10

▶ Use the Word Bank to write the word that fits each definition.

1. in math, something you need to solve _____

2. an answer to a math problem _____

3. to make easier _____

4. to give _____

5. to choose _____

Word Bank
select
provide
solution
problem
simplify

WORDS 11–20

▶ Use the Word Bank to write the word that has the opposite meaning.

6. pay attention to ≠ _____

7. unneeded ≠ _____

8. easy to understand ≠ _____

9. unknown ≠ _____

10. try ≠ _____

Word Bank
give up
confusing
ignore
needed
known

4. Develop Language

USING SHOULD/SHOULDN'T	
Use	**With**
should	*yes* statements You **should** read story problems carefully.
shouldn't	*no* statements You **shouldn't** read them quickly.

▶ Complete each sentence with *should* or *shouldn't*.

11. You _____ look up words you don't understand.

12. You _____ make a diagram when possible.

13. You _____ skip words you don't know.

14. You _____ look back at the question.

15. You _____ give up.

Signed Numbers

Big Idea Positive numbers show amounts greater than zero. Negative numbers are less than zero.

1. Look and Explore

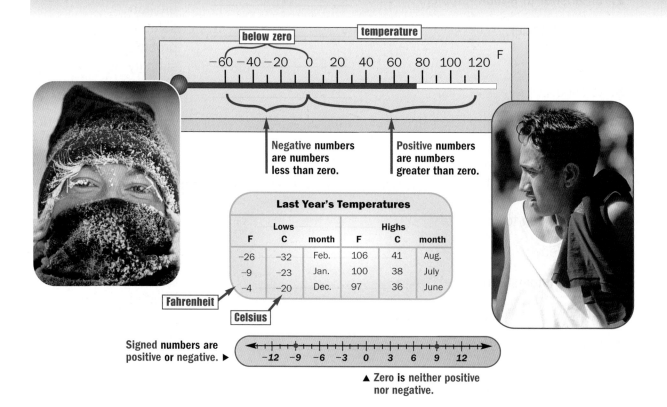

Last Year's Temperatures					
Lows			Highs		
F	C	month	F	C	month
−26	−32	Feb.	106	41	Aug.
−9	−23	Jan.	100	38	July
−4	−20	Dec.	97	36	June

Fahrenheit

Celsius

Signed **numbers** are positive or negative. ▶

▲ Zero **is** neither positive nor negative.

2. Listen and Talk

WORDS 1–10

1. **Positive** numbers are greater than zero.
2. **Negative** numbers are less than zero.
3. A negative number takes a **negative sign.**
4. **Integers** are positive and negative numbers.
5. **Zero** is an integer, too.
6. **Signed** numbers are positive or negative.
7. What is the **outdoor** temperature?
8. We use degrees to tell the **temperature.**
9. The temperature was 97° **Fahrenheit** (F).
10. 97° F is equal to 36° **Celsius** (C).

WORDS 11–20

11. Positive numbers are **written** without a sign.
12. A signed number is **either** positive or negative.
13. We use *either* and *or* to give 2 **choices.**
14. Zero is **neither** positive nor negative.
15. It is neither positive **nor** negative.
16. The **initials** *F* or *C* go after *degrees.*
17. −12° is read as *12 degrees **below zero.***
18. What was the **hottest** temperature last year?
19. What was the **coldest** temperature this year?
20. Have you **ever** experienced −10° F?

3. Read and Write

WORDS 1–10

▶ Use the Word Bank to complete the paragraphs.

Thermometers show the indoor and _____

1.

temperatures. People all over the world use _____

2.

to describe the temperature. In the United States, Americans use

the _____ scale.

3.

A _____ goes before temperatures below zero.

4.

What's the coldest _____ you have ever experienced?

5.

Word Bank

Celsius
outdoor
negative sign
temperature
Fahrenheit

WORDS 11–20

▶ Use the Word Bank to complete each sentence.

6. Negative numbers are _____ with negative signs.

7. In true/false questions, you only have two _____.

8. What is the coldest temperature _____ recorded?

9. One of the _____ days last year was 106° F.

10. One of the _____ days was −26° F.

Word Bank

hottest
written
coldest
ever
choices

4. Develop Language

USING OR AND NOR

Use	With
or	**either** to name 2 positive choices It is <u>either</u> hot or cold.
nor	**neither** to name 2 negative choices It is <u>neither</u> hot nor cold.

▶ Complete the sentences with *or* or *nor*.

11. Write either F _____ C after degrees.

12. 60° F is neither too hot _____ too cold.

13. I can live in either the city _____ the country.

14. Neither she _____ he knows the answer.

15. The answer is either true _____ false.

> **Big Idea**
>
> Equations show how numbers are related.
> An equation is one kind of math sentence.

1. Look and Explore

Vincent owns 20 baseball cards. Vincent and his brother Tom own 60 baseball cards altogether. How many baseball cards does Tom own?

How many baseball cards do you have, Tom?

20 = number of Vincent's baseball cards

T = number of Tom's baseball cards

equation

$$20 + T = 60$$
$$T = 60 - 20$$
$$T = 40$$

variable

Tom owns 40 baseball cards.

substitute

$$20 + \cancel{T} = 60$$
$$40$$

▲ Make sure your answer is correct.

2. Listen and Talk

WORDS 1–10

1. In **algebra,** equations are number sentences.
2. You write **equations** to solve problems.
3. **20 + T** is an **expression.**
4. An expression may include **operations.**
5. Expressions are made of parts called **terms.**
6. A **variable** is something that changes.
7. T is the **missing addend** in the equation.
8. You need to find the **quantity** of T.
9. In the equation, **60 is equal to 20 + T.**
10. T is the **unknown quantity.**

WORDS 11–20

11. Something that **varies** changes a lot.
12. A variable is not **constant.**
13. An equation shows how numbers are **related.**
14. Vincent **owns** 20 baseball cards.
15. His brother owns a **certain** number of cards.
16. **Assign** a name to the unknown quantity.
17. T stands for Tom's baseball **cards.**
18. They own 60 baseball cards **altogether.**
19. Make **sure** your answer is correct.
20. **Substitute** your answer for the variable.

3. Read and Write

WORDS 1–10

▶ Use the Word Bank to write the word that fits each clue.

1. a kind of math that uses variables to express how numbers are related _____

2. something that changes _____

3. number or amount of something _____

4. another way to say *equals* _____

5. some math sentences _____

Word Bank

quantity
variable
equations
is equal to
algebra

WORDS 11–20

▶ Use the Word Bank to write the word that has the same meaning as the underlined word or words.

6. The weather <u>changes often</u>. _____

7. Vincent and Tom have a <u>specific</u> number of baseball cards. _____

8. One brother <u>possesses</u> 20 baseball cards. _____

9. Vincent and Tom own 60 baseball cards <u>in all</u>. _____

10. An equation shows how numbers <u>are connected</u>. _____

Word Bank

certain
altogether
related
varies
owns

4. Develop Language

USING *A* OR *AN*

Use *a* to name:

a noun that begins with a consonant sound

A <u>variable</u> is something that changes.

Use *an* to name:

a noun that begins with a vowel sound

The weather is an <u>example</u> of a variable.

▶ Complete each sentence with *a* or *an*.

11. _____ expression is a part of an equation.

12. _____ variable changes.

13. *T* is _____ unknown quantity.

14. Adding is _____ operation.

15. _____ quantity is a number or amount.

Energy and Food

Big Idea Living things need energy. They get it from food or sunlight.

1. Look and Explore

Plants get energy from sunlight. ▶

producers

Sheep **eat plants. They get energy from grass.** ▼

consumers

decomposers

▲ Mushrooms get energy **from dead plants** and animals.

scavengers

▲ Vultures feed on dead animals.

predators

▲ Wolves **hunt** and eat sheep. They get energy **from meat.**

2. Listen and Talk

WORDS 1–10

1. **Plants** get energy from the sun.
2. **Vultures** feed on other animals.
3. **Sheep** get energy from the grass they eat.
4. **Wolves** get energy from the sheep's meat.
5. **Producers** make their own food.
6. **Consumers** eat other organisms.
7. **Decomposers** get energy from dead material.
8. **Predators** hunt and eat animals.
9. **Scavengers** feed on dead animals.
10. **Mushrooms** are decomposers.

WORDS 11–20

11. All living things are **organisms**.
12. Every organism belongs to the **food chain**.
13. Organisms need **energy** to live.
14. The **sunlight** gives energy to plant life.
15. A wolf is a **hunter**.
16. A sheep is a wolf's **prey**.
17. Wolves are **meat-eaters**.
18. Sheep are **plant-eaters**.
19. Some living things **feed on** each other.
20. Plants **produce** their own food.

3. Read and Write

WORDS 1-10

▶ Use the Word Bank to answer the questions.

1. What organisms make their own food?

_____

2. Which organisms eat other organisms?

_____

3. Which group do mushrooms belong to?

_____

4. What living things feed on dead animals?

_____

5. Which organisms are hunters? _____

Word Bank

consumers
producers
decomposers
scavengers
predators

WORDS 11-20

▶ Say each word and copy it to complete the questions. Then answer the questions aloud.

6. hunter   Is a wolf a _____?

7. prey   What is a wolf's _____?

8. energy   What provides _____ for plants?

9. meat-eaters   What other organisms are _____?

10. plant-eaters Are humans _____?

Word Bank

energy
prey
meat-eaters
plant-eaters
hunter

4. Develop Language

▶ Complete each sentence with the plural of the word.

IRREGULAR PLURALS

Singular	Plural
sheep	**sheep**
wolf	**wolves**
mouse	**mice**
fish	**fish**
deer	**deer**

11. _____ feed on sheep. (wolf)

12. _____ live on farms. (sheep)

13. Wolves also eat _____. (mouse)

14. Some fish eat other _____. (fish)

15. _____ are consumers. (deer)

95 Growing Up

Big Idea   Living things go through life stages from birth to death.

1. Look and Explore

Human beings **go through a life cycle.**

The first stage is birth. ▼   ▼ Your body **develops** during **childhood.**

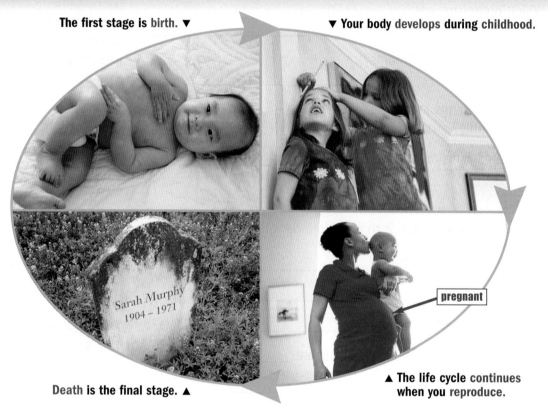

pregnant

Death **is the final stage.** ▲

▲ The life cycle **continues** when you **reproduce.**

2. Listen and Talk

WORDS 1–10

1. **Human beings** go through a life cycle.
2. The first stage is **birth.**
3. You grow up during your **childhood.**
4. Your body **develops** as you get older.
5. A young person enters **adulthood.**
6. Some males and females **reproduce.**
7. A woman grows when she is **pregnant.**
8. **Motherhood** is taking care of children.
9. Moms and dads take part in **parenting.**
10. **Death** is the final stage of life.

WORDS 11–20

11. We enter life as **babies.**
12. Parents take care of their **children.**
13. We **grow up** during our childhood.
14. Parents **raise** their children.
15. Children grow into **teenagers.**
16. Teenagers grow into **adults.**
17. Every human **dies** one day.
18. With reproduction, the life cycle **continues.**
19. A woman is also called a **female.**
20. A man is also called a **male.**

3. Read and Write

WORDS 1-10

▶ Use the Word Bank to complete the paragraph.

Like _____ , animals go through a life cycle, too.
1.

Most penguins _____ once every year. After a
2.

female penguin becomes _____ , she lays an egg.
3.

The male penguin helps the female during _____ .
4.

After the baby penguin _____ into an adult, it
5.

reproduces. The life cycle continues.

Word Bank

pregnant
human beings
motherhood
develops
reproduce

WORDS 11-20

▶ Use the Word Bank to write the word that fits each clue.

6. starts again, goes on   _____

7. to become an adult   _____

8. what parents do for their children   _____

9. woman   _____

10. man   _____

Word Bank

female
raise
male
grow up
continues

4. Develop Language

ORDER WORDS	
Use	**To list**
First	the 1st stage (only) *First,* you are born.
Next	2nd, 3rd, . . . stages *Next,* you grow up.
Finally	the last stage (only) *Finally,* you die.

▶ Write the word *First, Next,* or *Finally* to show the order of the life cycle.

11. _____ , Lim was an infant.

12. _____ , Lim was a child.

13. _____ , Lim became a teenager.

14. _____ , Lim was an adult.

15. _____ , Lim died when she was 88.

Big Idea All living things are made up of cells. All cells have similar parts.

1. Look and Explore

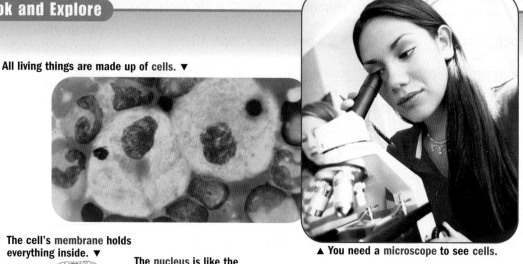

All living things are made up of cells. ▼

▲ You need a microscope to see cells.

The cell's membrane holds everything inside. ▼

membrane

The nucleus is like the cell's brain. ▼

Cells have other parts called organelles. ▼

DNA controls the action of the cells. ▼

DNA

nucleus

cytoplasm

▲ Cytoplasm holds everything in place.

organelles

2. Listen and Talk

WORDS 1–10

1. All living things are made up of tiny **cells.**
2. You need a **microscope** to see a cell.
3. Organisms made of one cell are **unicellular.**
4. Organisms with many cells are **multicellular.**
5. Cells have tiny organs called **organelles.**
6. **Cytoplasm** holds everything in place.
7. The **nucleus** is like the cell's brain.
8. The nucleus contains DNA **molecules.**
9. **DNA** controls the action of the cell.
10. The **membrane** holds everything inside.

WORDS 11–20

11. Cells are **tiny.**
12. The **function** of the cell is to continue life.
13. Some cells are **simple.**
14. Other cells are more **complex.**
15. Some organisms are made up of **single** cells.
16. Multicellular organisms have **multiple** cells.
17. A **cell wall** protects a plant cell.
18. Cytoplasm is like **jelly** inside the membrane.
19. DNA molecules are shaped like a **ladder.**
20. Organelles make the cell work **properly.**

3. Read and Write

WORDS 1-10

▶ Use the Word Bank to answer the questions.

1. What do you need to see cells? _____

2. What is the cell's brain? _____

3. What is an organism with many cells called? _____

4. What are all living things made of? _____

5. What is an organism with one cell called? _____

Word Bank

unicellular
cells
microscope
multicellular
nucleus

WORDS 11-20

▶ Use the Word Bank to complete each sentence.

6. A plant cell has a _____.

7. DNA molecules look like a _____.

8. Cytoplasm is like _____.

9. Organelles are like _____ organs.

10. A cell's _____ is to continue life.

Word Bank

ladder
cell wall
tiny
jelly
function

4. Develop Language

IS AND ARE

Use	To tell about
is	singular nouns *The nucleus is the cell's brain.*
are	plural nouns *Organisms are unicelluar or multicellular.*

▶ Complete each sentence with *is* or *are*.

11. Cells _____ tiny.

12. The membrane _____ like a wall.

13. The nucleus _____ important to the cell.

14. All living things _____ made up of cells.

15. DNA molecules _____ in the nucleus.

Buying and Selling

| Big Idea | Business is the buying and selling of goods and services. |

1. Look and Explore

Business is the buying and selling of things.

▲ Goods are things made by a person.

▲ Consumers have a demand for goods.

◀ Businesses have a supply of goods.

▲ A service is work a customer pays for.

2. Listen and Talk

WORDS 1–10

1. **Business** is the buying and selling of things.
2. A **customer** buys goods and services.
3. **Goods** are things made by people.
4. A **service** is work customers pay for.
5. People buy and sell goods in a **market**.
6. An **employee** works for a company.
7. A **salesperson** sells goods to customers.
8. **Labor** is the work employees do.
9. Companies **advertise** to sell products.
10. The service **industry** employs many people.

WORDS 11–20

11. A car company **employs** my dad.
12. My father earns an hourly **wage**.
13. My father **earns** $11.00 an hour.
14. What **company** does he work for?
15. It is a company that **manufactures** cars.
16. The **demand** for cars is great.
17. The United States has a good **supply** of labor.
18. Companies make **ads** to sell their products.
19. I saw a car **commercial** on television.
20. Some people are **unemployed**.

3. Read and Write

WORDS 1-10

▶ Use the Word Bank to complete the sentences.

1. _____ is the buying and selling of things for money.

2. People go to a _____ to buy and sell goods.

3. An _____ works for a company.

4. Companies _____ on television.

5. The auto _____ sells a lot of cars every year.

Word Bank

industry
advertise
market
business
employee

WORDS 11-20

▶ Use the Word Bank to complete the story.

My father works for a clothing _____. His
                                        6.
company _____ clothing for women and children.
              7.
Before he got the job, he was _____ for two years.
                                        8.
It was difficult for my family because he didn't earn much money.

Now, he _____ a good _____. Our
              9.   **10.**
family is so proud of him.

Word Bank

wage
earns
company
manufactures
unemployed

4. Develop Language

ASKING *WHAT DOES/DO* QUESTIONS	
Use	**To ask about**
What does	singular nouns *What does a customer buy?*
What do	plural nouns *What do employees work for?*

▶ Write *do* or *does* to complete the questions. Then answer them aloud.

11. What _____ ads advertise?

12. What _____ salespeople sell?

13. What _____ a factory make?

14. What _____ companies advertise?

15. What _____ an employee earn?

Geography

Big Idea Geography is the study of Earth's surface. Earth is divided into four hemispheres.

1. Look and Explore

Geography is the study of Earth's surface.

The equator divides Earth into north and south. ▶

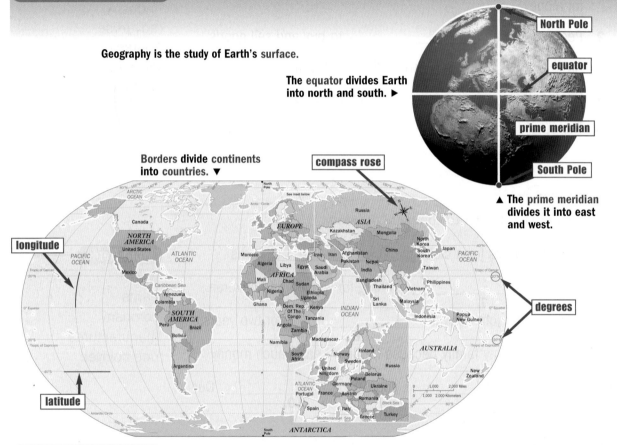

Borders divide continents into countries. ▼

compass rose

North Pole

equator

prime meridian

South Pole

▲ The prime meridian divides it into east and west.

longitude

latitude

degrees

2. Listen and Talk

WORDS 1–10

1. Earth is divided into four **hemispheres**.
2. The **Northern** Hemisphere is the north half.
3. The **Southern** Hemisphere is the south half.
4. The **Western** Hemisphere is the west half.
5. The **Eastern** Hemisphere is the east half.
6. We use **degrees** (°) to locate places.
7. The **equator** is a line around Earth's middle.
8. It is zero degrees **latitude** north and south.
9. The **prime meridian** divides Earth, too.
10. It is zero degrees **longitude** west and east.

WORDS 11–20

11. Land and water cover Earth's **surface**.
12. A **globe** is like a ball with a map on it.
13. Hemispheres are **halves**.
14. Earth has seven **continents**.
15. Continents are divided into **countries**.
16. **Borders** are lines between countries.
17. A **map** shows places on the earth.
18. A **compass rose** gives directions on a map.
19. The **North Pole** is on the top of the globe.
20. The **South Pole** is on the bottom.

3. Read and Write

WORDS 1–10

▶ Use the Word Bank to answer the questions.

1. What is located at 0° latitude
(north and south)?   _____

2. What is located at 0° longitude
(east and west)?   _____

3. What is the distance from north to
south called?   _____

4. What is the distance east to west called?   _____

5. What are used to give an exact location? _____

Word Bank

prime meridian
latitude
degrees
longitude
equator

WORDS 11–20

▶ Use the Word Bank to complete each sentence.

6. Water covers 70 percent of Earth's _____.

7. Asia, South America, and Australia are _____.

8. The United States, Canada, and Mexico are
_____ in North America.

9. The _____ is located in Antarctica.

10. The equator and prime meridian divide the world into
two _____.

Word Bank

halves
surface
continents
South Pole
countries

4. Develop Language

USING *A* OR *THE*	
Use	**To talk about**
a	a common item (non-specific) *A map shows Earth's surface.*
the	a specific item (only one) *The equator is an imaginary line.*

▶ Complete each sentence with *a* or *the*.

11. _____ Prime Meridian is located at 0° longitude.

12. _____ globe is round.

13. Brazil is one of _____ biggest countries.

14. _____ map is flat.

15. _____ North Pole is located in the Arctic Ocean.

99 Being American

Big Idea America has a democracy. The citizens have rights and responsibilities.

1. Look and Explore

Citizens **have** rights **and** responsibilities.

citizens

Voting **is an important right.** ▶

▲ Citizens **help to improve** their community.

ADOPT A HIGHWAY
LITTER CONTROL
NEXT 2 MILES

Some freedoms Americans have

religion   speech   press

LET US END THE VIOLENCE

▲ We enjoy **freedom** of religion, free **speech**, and free **press**.

2. Listen and Talk

WORDS 1–10

1. America has a system of **democracy**.
2. Citizens have **rights** in the United States.
3. The government **guarantees** these rights.
4. American **citizens** have the right to vote.
5. Americans have the **freedom** of religion.
6. Free **speech** is a right people have.
7. The Constitution protects a free **press**.
8. **Voting** is an important right.
9. By voting, we choose the people who **govern**.
10. New citizens must **register** to vote.

WORDS 11–20

11. Citizens also have **responsibilities**.
12. They have a **duty** to do things.
13. Americans must **obey** the law.
14. U.S. citizens have to pay **taxes** every year.
15. We should **respect** other people's rights.
16. We ought to respect the freedoms of **others**.
17. Citizens must be **loyal** to their country.
18. We help to **improve** their community.
19. We **participate** in democracy by voting.
20. We **choose** our leaders in a democracy.

3. Read and Write

WORDS 1-10

▶ Use the Word Bank to answer the questions.

1. What kind of system does America have? _____

2. What are guaranteed by law? _____

3. What must new citizens do before voting? _____

4. What do leaders do? They _____ the people.

5. What does the government do with our rights?
It _____ them.

Word Bank

govern
democracy
register
guarantees
rights

WORDS 11-20

▶ Use the Word Bank to complete the paragraph.

American citizens have some _____ to their
                                                6.
country. They _____ in democracy by voting. Citizens
                          7.
should _____ the laws of the country they live in.
                  8.
People who earn money must pay _____ every year.
                                                        9.
Everyone has the same rights in America. A citizen ought to respect

the rights of _____ .
                          10.

Word Bank

others
taxes
responsibilities
obey
participate

4. Develop Language

USING *HAVE* AND *HAS*

Singular		Plural	
I	**have**	we	**have**
you	**have**	you	**have**
he			
she	**has**	they	**have**
it			

▶ Complete the sentences with *have* or *has*.

11. The United States _____ laws.

12. American citizens _____ responsibilities.

13. Our country _____ freedom of the press.

14. A citizen _____ the right to vote.

15. Citizens _____ a duty to their country.

100 Reading Process

Big Idea — The reading process helps you understand what you read.

1. Look and Explore

My purpose is to enjoy an exciting story.

1 ◄ Set a purpose.

2 ◄ Preview the text.

3 Read the text. As you do, **connect** to the text and take notes. ►

4 ◄ **Reflect** on what you read.

5 ◄ Reread the parts you don't understand.

2. Listen and Talk

WORDS 1–10

1. The reading process helps you read **text**.
2. The **process** has five steps to follow.
3. Before reading, get ready for the **task**.
4. Use the **knowledge** you already have.
5. First, set a **purpose** for reading.
6. Then, **preview** the text.
7. Next, **connect** to the text while you read.
8. Take **notes** to remember the facts.
9. After reading, **reflect** on what you read.
10. **Reread** any parts you didn't understand.

WORDS 11–20

11. These steps help you **prepare** to read.
12. What do you **expect** to learn about?
13. It's easy to **forget** what you read.
14. The process helps you **remember** facts.
15. Remember your **reason** for reading it.
16. **During** reading, connect to the text.
17. Take notes **while** reading the text.
18. Then **review** your notes.
19. Try to **explain** what you read to a friend.
20. Connect it to your own **life.**

3. Read and Write

WORDS 1–10

▶ Use the Word Bank to write the word that fits each clue.

1. things you know   _____

2. written words   _____

3. something with steps   _____

4. something you need to do   _____

5. things you write in a notebook   _____

Word Bank

process
task
notes
knowledge
text

WORDS 11–20

▶ Use the Word Bank to complete the chart.

Synonyms	Antonyms
_____ = while **6.**	_____ ≠ remember **8.**
_____ = purpose **7.**	preview ≠ _____ **9.**
	_____ ≠ forget **10.**

Word Bank

review
reason
during
forget
remember

4. Develop Language

USING *SHOULD/SHOULDN'T*

Use	With
should	*yes* statements *You should take notes while reading.*
shouldn't	*no* statements *You shouldn't talk while reading.*

▶ Complete the sentences with *should* or *shouldn't*.

11. You _____ read each word carefully.

12. You _____ chew gum in class.

13. You _____ connect to the text.

14. You _____ write in your textbook.

15. You _____ remember what you read.

5 Steps to Writing

 Follow the five steps of the writing process to make writing easier.

1. Look and Explore

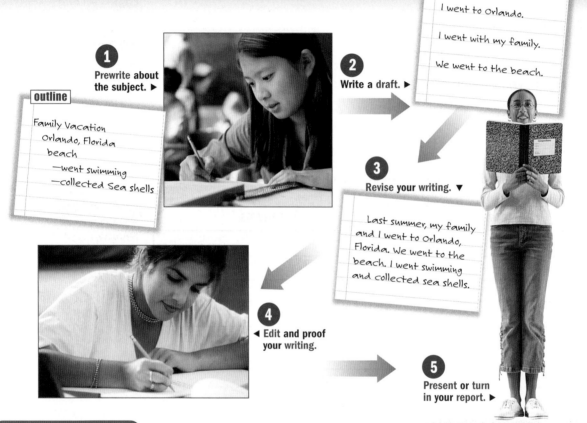

1 Prewrite **about the subject.** ▶

outline

Family Vacation
  Orlando, Florida
  beach
    —went swimming
    —collected sea shells

2 Write a draft. ▶

I went to Orlando.

I went with my family.

We went to the beach.

3 Revise **your writing.** ▼

Last summer, my family and I went to Orlando, Florida. We went to the beach. I went swimming and collected sea shells.

4 ◀ Edit **and proof your writing.**

5 Present **or turn in your report.** ▶

2. Listen and Talk

WORDS 1–10

1. Carmen needs to write a **report** for class.
2. She follows the five steps of **writing.**
3. First, **prewrite** before you start writing.
4. Make an **outline** of your ideas.
5. An outline helps you **organize** your ideas.
6. Second, write a **draft.**
7. Third, **revise** your first draft.
8. Fourth, **edit** and proof your work.
9. Fifth, you're ready to **present** your work.
10. Carmen gives a great **presentation.**

WORDS 11–20

11. It is easy to make **mistakes.**
12. A draft is a first **attempt** at writing.
13. We **correct** mistakes when we edit.
14. Make sure you **spelled** the words correctly.
15. **Indent** the start of each paragraph.
16. Find any words spelled **incorrectly.**
17. Check to see you used correct **grammar.**
18. Use good **handwriting.**
19. When you're done, make a clean **copy.**
20. Then you're ready to **turn in** your report.

3. Read and Write

▶ Use the Word Bank to write the word that fits each clue.

1. You write this for class. _____

2. You use a pencil or pen to do this. _____

3. You make this to organize your ideas. _____

4. You do this to put your ideas in order. _____

5. You may give this when you are finished with the writing steps. _____

Word Bank

writing
report
presentation
outline
organize

▶ Use the Word Bank to answer the questions in the checklist.

Before you hand in your report, ask yourself these questions:

✔ Did you make any spelling _____ ?
   6.

✔ Are all your words _____ correctly?
   7.

✔ Did you _____ all your mistakes?
   8.

✔ Did you use good _____ ?
   9.

✔ Did you _____ every paragraph?
   10.

Word Bank

spelled
mistakes
correct
indent
grammar

4. Develop Language

UPPERCASE LETTERS

Use uppercase letters to
Begin sentences
Write names of people and places
Write titles (Ms., Mrs., Mr.)
My report about Cuba was corrected by Mrs. Handy.

▶ Circle the letter or letters in each sentence that should be capitalized.

11. she always corrects my spelling mistakes.

12. he uses a red pen to add punctuation.

13. I am writing a speech about bolivia.

14. first, I have to make an outline.

15. I called my speech "Living in south america."

102

Reading a Story

Big Idea Stories have parts in common.

1. Look and Explore

Fiction is based on the imagination.

title

King Midas and the Golden Touch

King Midas was a greedy king who lived in a palace. He wanted to be the richest man in the world.

He made a wish. His wish came true. Everything he touched turned to gold! But it was a bad wish.

King Midas couldn't eat because the food he touched turned to gold. He hugged his daughter, and she turned to gold. That was very sad.

A **myth** is an imaginary story about the past. ▶

characters

◀ The people in a story are characters. ▼

setting

plot

The **plot** is what happens in the story. ▼

▲ The **setting** shows when and where the story happens.

2. Listen and Talk

WORDS 1–10

1. **Fiction** is based on the imagination.
2. The **title** is the name of the story.
3. The people in the story are its **characters**.
4. The **setting** is where the story happens.
5. The **plot** is what happens in the story.
6. A story describes a series of **events**.
7. The message in the story is its **theme**.
8. All stories have an **ending**.
9. The **myth** of King Midas is old.
10. A **story** sometimes has a lesson.

WORDS 11–20

11. King Midas is the **main** character.
12. The king was **greedy**.
13. King Midas made a **wish**.
14. Everything he **touched** turned to gold.
15. He **hugged** his daughter.
16. He **turned** his daughter to gold.
17. King Midas **learned** a lesson.
18. This story is **imaginary**.
19. Fiction is not **real**.
20. The story teaches a **lesson** about greed.

3. Read and Write

WORDS 1–10

▶ Use the Word Bank to write the word that fits each clue.

1. a story not based on true events _____

2. the people in a story _____

3. a very old story _____

4. the story's message _____

5. things that happen _____

Word Bank

myth
events
fiction
theme
characters

WORDS 11–20

▶ Use the Word Bank to complete the summary of *King Midas and the Golden Touch*.

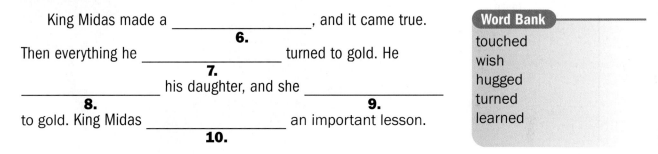

King Midas made a _____, and it came true.
                        6.
Then everything he _____ turned to gold. He
                            7.
_____ his daughter, and she _____
        8.   **9.**
to gold. King Midas _____ an important lesson.
                            10.

Word Bank

touched
wish
hugged
turned
learned

4. Develop Language

WH QUESTIONS

Use	To ask about
What	things *What is the story about?*
Who	people *Who is the main character?*
Where	places *Where does the story take place?*

▶ Complete each sentence with *Who, What,* or *Where*. Then answer them aloud.

11. _____ is the main character?

12. _____ does King Midas live?

13. _____ is the title?

14. _____ wrote *King Midas*?

15. _____ did he wish for?

Big Idea Points and lines help describe basic shapes.

1. Look and Explore

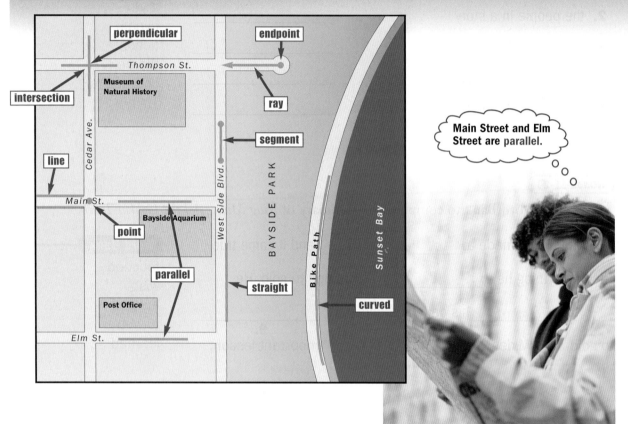

Main Street and Elm Street are **parallel**.

2. Listen and Talk

WORDS 1–10

1. A **point** is an exact location in space.
2. A **line** is a path of points that goes on forever.
3. A **ray** is part of a line.
4. A ray has one **endpoint**.
5. A **segment** has two endpoints.
6. **Parallel** lines never meet.
7. **Intersecting** lines meet at one point.
8. **Perpendicular** lines form square corners.
9. A **horizontal** line goes straight across.
10. A **vertical** line goes up and down.

WORDS 11–20

11. A line goes in a straight **direction.**
12. Parallel lines never **intersect.**
13. Intersecting lines **cross** at one point.
14. A line **goes on** in both directions.
15. A point has an exact **place.**
16. A ray goes on **forever** in one direction.
17. Lines, rays, and segments are **straight.**
18. The letter *C* is **curved.**
19. An **intersection** is where two lines cross.
20. A **corner** forms where two lines meet.

3. Read and Write

WORDS 1-10

▶ Use the Word Bank to complete each sentence.

1. Lines in a plane that never cross are _____ lines.

2. Lines that meet at a point are _____ lines.

3. Lines that form a square corner are _____.

4. Lines that go up and down are _____ lines.

5. Lines that go straight across are _____ lines.

Word Bank

horizontal
parallel
intersecting
vertical
perpendicular

WORDS 11-20

▶ Use the Word Bank to complete the conversation.

6. *Beth:* Can I help you find a _____ on the map?

7. *Crista:* Yes, I am looking for the post office at the _____ of Elm Street and Cedar Avenue.

8. *Beth:* That's easy. Walk _____ up Cedar Avenue.

9. *Crista:* Do I _____ Elm Street?

10. *Beth:* Yes, it's right on the _____.

Word Bank

straight
place
cross
intersection
corner

4. Develop Language

ADJECTIVES

Adjectives appear

after am/is/are
The street is <u>straight</u>.

before nouns `noun`
Main is a <u>straight</u> street.

▶ Put each sentence in the correct order.

11. line./is/It/straight/a _____

12. is/The/curved./road _____

13. is/curved/road./a/It _____

14. a/Walk/line./straight/in _____

15. is/Wells/Street/curved. _____

104 Angles and Circles

Big Idea

You can measure the degrees of an angle.
You can find the parts of a circle.

1. Look and Explore

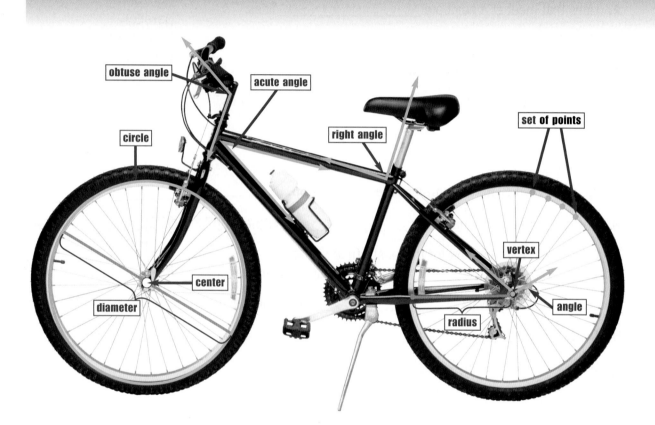

obtuse angle

acute angle

set of points

circle

right angle

center

vertex

diameter

angle

radius

2. Listen and Talk

WORDS 1–10

1. Two rays and an endpoint form an **angle.**
2. The endpoint is the angle's **vertex.**
3. You can find the **measure** of an angle.
4. A **right angle** has a measure of 90°.
5. An **acute angle** has a measure of less than 90°.
6. A **straight angle** has a measure of 180°.
7. An **obtuse angle** is between 90° and 180°.
8. The **center** of a circle is its middle point.
9. A **radius** is a segment from the circle's center.
10. A **diameter** passes through its center.

WORDS 11–20

11. The wheel of a bicycle is a perfect **circle.**
12. A circle is a **set** of points.
13. There is equal **space** from the center.
14. A diameter **passes** through the center.
15. A diameter is **twice** as long as a radius.
16. It's hard to draw a perfect circle **by hand.**
17. Sam **draws** a circle using a piece of string.
18. You can use a **compass** to draw a circle.
19. Use the **edge** of a book to identify angles.
20. The corner is a **perfect** right angle.

3. Read and Write

WORDS 1–10

▶ Use the Word Bank to complete each sentence.

1. The _____ of a right angle is 90°.

2. An _____ has two rays that share an endpoint.

3. The _____ is a point that is the same distance from all points on a circle.

4. A line segment from the center of a circle to a point on the circle is called the _____.

5. A circle's _____ passes through its center.

Word Bank

angle
center
radius
measure
diameter

WORDS 11–20

▶ Use the Word Bank to complete the paragraph.

When Ralph _____ a circle, it looks crooked.
6.
Have you ever tried to draw a circle _____ ?
7.
It's impossible to draw a _____ circle. That's
8.
why people use a tool called a _____. You can
9.
make a compass with a piece of string and two pencils. Try to draw

your own perfect _____.
10.

Word Bank

by hand
perfect
circle
compass
draws

4. Develop Language

POSSESSIVE NOUNS

Use	Form by
To show a noun owns something	Adding ('s) after noun
An angle's vertex is its endpoint.	

▶ Complete the sentences with the correct possessive noun.

11. A _____ center is in its middle. (circle)

12. An acute _____ measure is less than 90°. (angle)

13. _____ bicycle has many angles and circles. (Phil)

14. The _____ wheels are circles. (bike)

15. His _____ bike has bigger wheels. (father)

Polygons

Big Idea	Polygons are closed figures made up of line segments.

1. Look and Explore

square

rectangle

pentagon

You can find shapes everywhere you look.

hexagon

Polygon	Number of Sides
triangle	3
quadrilateral	4
pentagon	5
hexagon	6
octagon	8

2. Listen and Talk

WORDS 1–10

1. A **polygon** is a shape.
2. A **plane** goes on forever in all directions.
3. A **plane figure** is a shape that lies flat.
4. A polygon is a shape made of **line segments**.
5. A **rectangle** has two pairs of equal sides.
6. A rectangle is a **parallelogram**, too.
7. A **quadrilateral** has 4 sides.
8. A **pentagon** has 5 sides.
9. A **hexagon** has 6 sides.
10. An **octagon** has 8 sides.

WORDS 11–20

11. Not all **shapes** are polygons.
12. A circle also **lies** on a flat surface.
13. A plane **extends** in all directions.
14. How many **sides** does an octagon have?
15. A polygon is a **closed** figure.
16. It does not have an **opening**.
17. A **square** has 4 sides equal in length.
18. A **triangle** has 3 sides.
19. A square is a **familiar** figure.
20. How are a square and a rectangle **alike?**

3. Read and Write

WORDS 1–10

▶ Use the Word Bank to complete each sentence.

1. A rectangle is an example of a _____ .

2. A _____ is a closed plane figure.

3. An octagon is made of 8 _____ .

4. A _____ is flat and goes on forever in every direction.

5. A quadrilateral is a _____ with 4 sides.

Word Bank

plane figure
line segments
parallelogram
plane
polygon

WORDS 11–20

▶ Use the Word Bank to write the word that fits each definition.

6. a polygon with 4 equal sides   _____

7. a polygon with 3 sides and 3 endpoints   _____

8. a way to enter, like a door or window   _____

9. opposite of open   _____

10. reaches over an area   _____

Word Bank

square
closed
triangle
extends
opening

4. Develop Language

USING *HAVE* OR *HAS*	
Use	**With**
has	singular subjects A <u>rectangle</u> has 4 sides.
have	plural subjects <u>Rectangles</u> have 4 sides.

▶ Complete each sentence with *have* or *has*.

11. A hexagon _____ 6 sides.

12. Squares _____ 4 sides.

13. An octagon _____ 8 sides.

14. Quadrilaterals _____ 4 sides.

15. Pentagons _____ 5 sides.

Big Idea Machines can help us do work and make our lives easier.

1. Look and Explore

Machines **help us do work.**

▲ **Wheels help us move things.**

▲ A **lever helps us lift objects.**

▲ We use **force** to **move heavy things.**

▲ We use a **pulley** to **raise** and **lower** heavy **loads.**

◀ **Gears make things go.**

2. Listen and Talk

WORDS 1–10

1. We use **machines** to help us do work.
2. Machines help us **move** heavy things.
3. **Force** makes things move.
4. Some **loads** are too heavy to move by hand.
5. We **apply** force to move them.
6. A hammer has a **lever** to lift nails.
7. A **pulley** raises and lowers loads.
8. **Wheels** help us move things.
9. **Gears** are wheels with teeth.
10. A truck puts the load in **motion**.

WORDS 11–20

11. He uses the hammer to **lift** the nail.
12. They use the pulley to **lower** the load.
13. They can **raise** the load with a pulley, too.
14. Wheels help us **push** heavy objects.
15. The truck **transports** heavy loads.
16. A truck has a **motor** to move the gears.
17. The gears **speed up** the truck's wheels.
18. They can also **slow down** the truck's wheels.
19. The truck can **carry** a heavy load.
20. The load is **too** heavy to lift by hand.

3. Read and Write

WORDS 1–10

▶ Use the Word Bank to complete each sentence.

1. People use washing _____ to wash clothes.

2. We use a bottle opener to _____ force to a bottle cap.

3. When you ride on a bus, you are in _____.

4. The wheels on a skateboard make it _____ quickly.

5. A hammer helps you apply _____ to a nail.

Word Bank

apply
force
machines
motion
move

WORDS 11–20

▶ Use the Word Bank to find the word that fits each clue.

6. what you say to the driver of a car that is moving too fast _____

7. what you say to the driver of a car when you are late _____

8. what you use a backpack for _____

9. more than is wanted _____

10. a car has this, but a bicycle does not _____

Word Bank

speed up
slow down
too
motor
carry

4. Develop Language

TOO

Use too

in place of *also*
Levers are machines.
Pulleys are machines, too.

to mean more than is needed or wanted
The load is too heavy to lift by hand.

▶ Complete each sentence with *too*.

11. Paul studies English. I study English, _____.

12. The books are _____ heavy to lift.

13. Trucks have motors. Cars have motors, _____.

14. Wheels move. Gears move, _____.

15. The car is moving _____ fast.

Big Idea Energy comes in different forms. Some energy sources are renewable. Others are nonrenewable.

1. Look and Explore

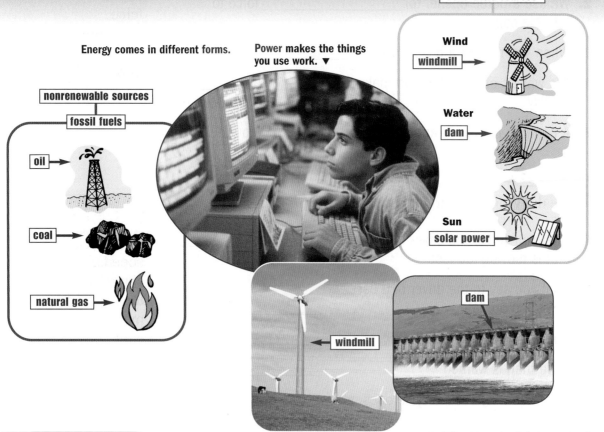

Energy comes in different forms.

Power makes the things you use work. ▼

renewable sources

Wind
windmill

Water
dam

Sun
solar power

nonrenewable sources
fossil fuels

oil

coal

natural gas

windmill

dam

2. Listen and Talk

WORDS 1–10

1. We have different **sources** of energy.
2. Some forms of energy are **renewable**.
3. Other forms of energy are **nonrenewable**.
4. **Solar power** comes from the sun.
5. A **windmill** turns wind into electricity.
6. A **dam** uses water to make electricity.
7. **Fossil fuels** come from dead plants.
8. **Natural gas** is used for gas stoves.
9. **Coal** is a fossil fuel from the earth.
10. Our **oil** supply is limited.

WORDS 11–20

11. **Power** makes the things you use work.
12. Resources come in different **forms.**
13. Cars **run on** gasoline made from oil.
14. **Appliances** in your home need electricity.
15. Some energy sources make **electricity.**
16. Nonrenewable energy sources are **limited.**
17. They will all be gone **someday.**
18. We will **use up** all the coal one day.
19. Renewable energy sources are **unlimited.**
20. We will never **run out** of wind.

3. Read and Write

▶ Use the Word Bank to find the word that fits each clue.

1. a fossil fuel from dead plants   _____

2. power that comes from the sun   _____

3. a nonrenewable source of energy   _____

4. a thing that changes wind into energy   _____

5. a thing that changes water into energy   _____

Word Bank

dam
windmill
oil
solar power
coal

▶ Use the Word Bank to complete each sentence.

6. Solar, water, and wind energy sources are _____.

7. Natural gas energy sources are _____.

8. The world's coal and oil resources will run out _____.

9. Cars and trucks _____ gasoline.

10. What will we do if we _____ the world's oil?

Word Bank

limited
someday
unlimited
run on
use up

4. Develop Language

ANSWERS TO *IS/ISN'T* QUESTIONS

Positive
Question: *Is wind unlimited?*
Statement: *Yes, it is.*
Negative
Question: *Is oil unlimited?*
Statement: *No, it isn't (is not).*

▶ Complete the sentences using *is* or *isn't*.

11. Is coal renewable? No, it _____.

12. Is wind limited? No, it _____.

13. Is oil a power source? Yes, it _____.

14. Is solar power from the sun? Yes, it _____.

15. Is water a fossil fuel? No, it _____.

 **Big Idea** ▸ Earth is made of different layers.

1. Look and Explore

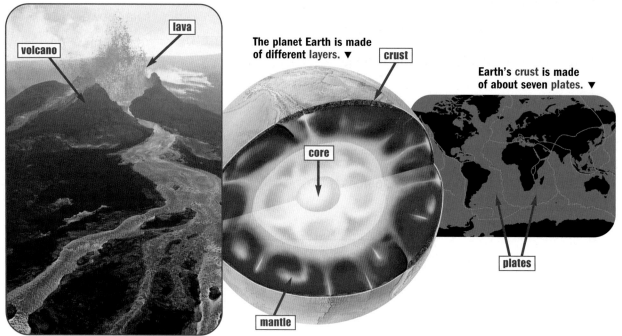

lava

volcano

The planet Earth is made of different layers. ▼

crust

Earth's crust is made of about seven plates. ▼

core

plates

mantle

▲ A volcano is an opening in the crust.

2. Listen and Talk

WORDS 1–10

1. Earth has different **layers**.
2. The **crust** is the layer we live on.
3. The crust is made up of **plates**.
4. A **volcano** is an opening in the crust.
5. **Lava** flows from volcanoes.
6. Beneath the crust is the **mantle**.
7. The mantle is where rocks **melt**.
8. Earth's plates **float** on the mantle.
9. The **core** is a ball of liquid metals.
10. The core is under great **pressure**.

WORDS 11–20

11. The crust is **solid** rock.
12. It is the **outer** layer of Earth.
13. A volcano **lets out** the pressure.
14. Pressure makes a volcano **erupt**.
15. Magma is **liquid** rock inside Earth.
16. Liquid **metals** make up Earth's core.
17. It's even hotter **beneath** the mantle.
18. The **deeper** you go, the hotter it gets.
19. The core is the **deepest** layer.
20. It is Earth's **inner** layer.

3. Read and Write

WORDS 1–10

▶ Use the Word Bank to complete each sentence.

1. The mantle is one of Earth's _____.

2. Some rocks _____ in the mantle.

3. Earth's plates _____ on the mantle's magma.

4. Liquid metals in Earth's core are under _____.

5. Magma is pushed to Earth's surface through a
_____.

Word Bank

volcano
pressure
layers
float
melt

WORDS 11–20

▶ Use the Word Bank to complete the paragraph.

Do you know what makes a volcano _____ ?
6.
_____ Earth's crust is the mantle. The heat is so hot
7.
it melts solid rock into a _____. A volcano is an
8.
opening in Earth's crust that _____ lava. Lava flows
9.
over Earth's _____ layer.
10.

Word Bank

liquid
erupt
outer
beneath
lets out

4. Develop Language

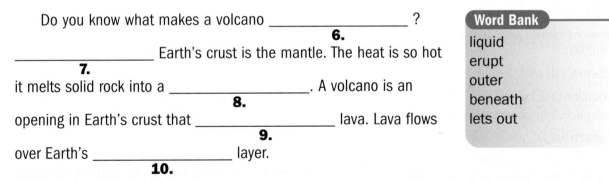

USING *IS* AND *ARE*	
Use	**With**
is	singular subjects *The <u>core</u> is Earth's deepest layer.*
are	plural subjects *<u>Volcanoes</u> are openings in Earth's crust.*

▶ Complete each sentence with *is* or *are*.

11. The crust _____ Earth's outer layer.

12. A volcano _____ an opening in the crust.

13. Plates _____ part of the crust.

14. The core _____ the hottest layer.

15. Liquid metals _____ in the core.

GLOSSARY

Pronunciation Key

ă	pat	ĭ	pit	ôr	**core**	ŭ	**cut**
ā	**pay**	ī	bite	oi	**boy**	ûr	**urge**
âr	**care**	îr	p**ier**	ou	**out**	th	**thin**
ä	father	ŏ	pot	ŏŏ	took	*th*	**th**is
ĕ	pet	ō	toe	ŏŏr	**lure**	zh	vision
ē	be	ô	paw	ōō	b**oot**	ə	about

A

a (ə or ā) *art.* used before a noun to show a single person or thing. **Dolch, GSL** (p. 38)

a lot a large quantity. **GSL** (p. 68)

ABC's *n.* the alphabet. (p. 120)

able (ā′ bəl) *adj.* having the ability to do something. **GSL** (p. 146)

about (ə bout′) *prep.* for. **Dolch, GSL** (p. 96)

above (ə bŭv′) *prep.* in a higher place. **GSL** (p. 90)

absorb (əb sôrb′) *v.* soak up. (p. 206)

accident (ăk′ sĭ dənt) *n.* an event that no one expected to happen. **GSL** (p. 60)

accurate (ăk′ yər ĭt) *adj.* correct. (p. 198)

acid (ăs′ ĭd) *n.* a chemical in your stomach used to break down food. (p. 206)

across (ə krôs′) *prep.* on, at, or from the other side. **GSL** (p. 64)

act (akt) *v.* behave. **GSL** (p. 92)

action (ăk′ shən) *n.* something you do. **GSL** (p. 142)

active (ăk′ tĭv) *adj.* being in motion. **GSL** (p. 132)

activity (ăk tĭv′ ĭ tē) *n.* a thing to do. (p. 84)

actually (ăk′ chōō ə lē) *adv.* in fact. **GSL** (p. 198)

acute angle an angle less than 90 degrees. (p. 248)

ad (ăd) *n.* an advertisement. (p. 234)

adapt (ă dăpt′) *v.* get used to. (p. 160)

add (ăd) *v.* a math function in which you combine 2 or more numbers. **GSL** (p. 74)

addend (ăd′ ĕnd′) *n.* a set of numbers to be added. (p. 74)

addition (ə dĭsh′ ən) *n.* a type of math that combines numbers. (p. 202)

address (ə drĕs′) *n.* where a person lives, as written on mail. **GSL** (p. 42)

adjective (ăj′ ĭk tĭv) *n.* a part of speech that describes a noun. (p. 142)

adult (ə dŭlt′) *n.* a person who is fully grown. (p. 230)

adulthood (a dŭlt′ hŏŏd′) *n.* the state of being an adult. (p. 230)

adverb (ăd′ vûrb) *n.* a part of speech that describes a verb. (p. 142)

advertise (ăd′ vər tīz′) *v.* tell how good a product is in order to sell it. **GSL** (p. 234)

advice (ăd vīs′) *n.* helpful ideas that are told to someone. **GSL** (p. 58)

adviser (ăd vī′ zər) *n.* someone whose job is to give advice. (p. 212)

African American *n.* an American whose ancestors are from Africa. (p. 160)

after (ăf′ tər) *prep.* behind in place or order. **Dolch, GSL** (p. 108)

afternoon (ăf′ tər no͞on′) *n.* the time of day after 12:00 p.m. and before the evening. **GSL** (p. 40)

again (ə gĕn′) *adv.* once more. **Dolch, GSL** (p. 44)

ago (ə gō′) *adv.* in the past. **GSL** (p. 98)

agree (ə grē′) *v.* have the same opinion. **GSL** (p. 96)

agreement (ə grē′ mənt) *n.* a situation in which people have the same opinion about something. (p. 210)

air (âr) *n.* the thing we breathe; oxygen. **GSL** (p. 180)

airplane (âr′ plān′) *n.* a vehicle with two wings that is able to fly. **GSL** (p. 66)

alarm (ə lärm′) *n.* a loud device used to warn people of danger. (p. 82)

algebra (ăl′ jə brə) *n.* a kind of math that uses symbols or letters to show an unknown number. (p. 226)

alike (ə līk′) *adv.* the same or similar. **GSL** (p. 250)

all (ôl) *adj.* the total number of. **Dolch, GSL** (p. 76)

all the time always. (p. 146)

alligator (ăl′ ĭ gā′ tər) *n.* a large reptile that usually lives in a swamp. (p. 162)

allowed (ə loud′) *v.* let happen. **GSL** (p. 106)

almost (ôl′ mōst′) *adv.* nearly. **GSL** (p. 78)

alone (ə lōn′) *adj.* without anyone else. **GSL** (p. 96)

along (ə lông′) *prep.* over the length of. **GSL** (p. 188)

aloud (ə loud′) *adv.* said using your voice. **GSL** (p. 192)

alphabet (ăl′ fə bĕt′) *n.* the letters used to make words. (p. 118)

alphabetical (ăl′ fə bĕt′ ĭ kəl) *adj.* arranged according to the alphabet. (p. 120)

alphabetize (ăl′ fə bĭ tīz′) *v.* put in order according to the alphabet. (p. 120)

also (ôl′ sō) *adv.* too. **GSL** (p. 80)

altogether (ôl tə gĕ*th*′ ər) *adv.* entirely. **GSL** (p. 226)

aluminum (ə lo͞o′ mə nəm) *adj.* made from a common metal used to make many things. (p. 182)

always (ôl wāz) *adv.* at all times. **Dolch, GSL** (p. 70)

A.M. *abbr.* before noon. (p. 100)

am (ăm) *v.* first-person singular present indicative of *be*. **Dolch** (p. 38)

ambulance (ăm′ byə ləns) *n.* a vehicle used to take people to the hospital. (p. 60)

amount (ə mount′) *n.* a sum. **GSL** (p. 198)

ancestor (ăn′ sĕs′ tər) *n.* a relative who lived long before you. (p. 160)

and (ănd) *conj.* along with; as well as. **Dolch, GSL** (p. 42)

angle (ăn gəl) *n.* the figure made by 2 lines meeting at 1 point. **GSL** (p. 248)

angry (ăng′ grē) *adj.* upset; mad. **GSL** (p. 94)

animal (ăn′ ə məl) *n.* a living creature that is not a plant. **GSL** (p. 156)

another (ə nŭ*th*′ ər) *adj.* one more. **GSL** (p. 222)

answer (ăn′ sər) *n.* a solution. **GSL** (p. 74)

anthem (ăn′ thəm) *n.* a song that honors someone or something. (p. 140)

antonym (ăn′ tə nĭm′) *n.* a word with an opposite meaning of another word. (p. 166)

any (ĕn′ ē) *adj.* one, some, or all. **Dolch, GSL** (p. 68)

anyone (ĕn′ē wŭn) *pron.* any person. **GSL** (p. 88)

anything (ĕn′ē thĭng) *pron.* any object or event. **GSL** (p. 88)

apologize (ə pŏl′ ə jīz′) *v.* say you're sorry. (p. 96)

Appalachian Mountains *n.* a mountain range in eastern North America. (p. 164)

appear (ə pîr′) *v.* come into view. **GSL** (p. 120)

appliance (ə plī′ əns) *n.* a machine used in the home for a specific purpose. (p. 254)

apply (ə plī′) **1.** *v.* use. (p. 202) **2.** *v.* put into action. (p. 252) **GSL**

appointment (ə point′ mənt) *n.* an arrangement to meet at a certain time. (p. 58)

approximately (ə prŏk′ sə mĭt lē) *adv.* close to; almost. (p. 198)

apron (ā′ prən) *n.* a cover you wear to stay clean when you are doing something messy. (p. 106)

are (är) *v.* a form of *be.* **Dolch** (p. 38)

area (âr′ ē ə) *n.* a particular space. (p. 112)

argue (är′ gyo͞o) *v.* fight verbally. **GSL** (p. 96)

around (ə round′) **1.** *prep.* to or among places; here and there. (p. 62) **2.** *adv.* about. (p. 198) **Dolch, GSL**

arrange (ə rānj′) *v.* put in order. **GSL** (p. 120)

arrive (ə rīv′) *v.* come. **GSL** (p. 98)

art (ärt) **1.** *adj.* studying drawing, painting, or creating something to look at. (p. 48) **2.** *n.* drawings, paintings, sculptures, or anything people make to look at. (p. 116) **GSL**

arteries (är′ tə rēz) *n.* tubes that carry blood away from the heart to other parts of the body. (p. 204)

article (är′ tĭ kəl) *n.* a part of speech used to indicate nouns. **GSL** (p. 142)

artificial (är′ tə fĭsh′ əl) *adj.* not natural; man-made. **GSL** (p. 130)

artist (är′ tĭst) *n.* a person who creates art (p. 66)

as (ăz) *adv.* equal with. **Dolch, GSL** (p. 58)

ask (ăsk) *v.* present a question to be answered. **Dolch, GSL** (p. 46)

asked (ăskd) *v.* past tense form of *ask.* (p. 218)

aspirin (ăs′ pər ĭn) *n.* a pill people take, often to cure a headache. (p. 58)

assign (ə sīn′) *v.* give; name. (p. 226)

associate (ə sō′ shē āt′) *v.* relate. (p. 202)

associative *adj.* refers to the grouping of numbers. (p. 202)

at (ăt) *prep.* in or near. **Dolch, GSL** (p. 64)

ate (āt) *v.* past tense of *eat.* **Dolch** (p. 52)

athlete (ăth′ lēt′) *n.* a person who plays a sport. (p. 132)

Atlantic Ocean *n.* the ocean that meets the eastern coast of the United States. (p. 190)

atlas (ăt′ ləs) *n.* a book of maps. (p. 168)

attach (ə tăch′) *v.* connect. (p. 194)

attempt (ə tĕmpt′) *n.* a try. **GSL** (p. 242)

attend (ə tĕnd′) *v.* be present for something. **GSL** (p. 48)

attendance (ə tĕn′ dəns) *n.* the number of people who are present. (p. 120)

attention (ə tĕn′ shən) *n.* the act of looking and listening. **GSL** (p. 106)

attic (ăt′ ĭk) *n.* a room at the top of a house often used for storage. (p. 90)

aunt (änt) *n.* the sister of your mother or father. **GSL** (p. 86)

author (ô′ thər) *n.* the writer of a book, story, or article. (p. 168)

automatic (ô′ tə măt′ ĭk) *adj.* reacting in a way without thought. (p. 208)

autumn (ô′ təm) *n.* the season that comes after summer. **GSL** (p. 84)

average (ăv′ ər ĭj) *n.* a number that represents a set of numbers. **GSL** (p. 128)

avoid (ə void′) *v.* stay away from. **GSL** (p. 130)

away (ə wā′) *adv.* from a particular thing or place. **Dolch, GSL** (p. 74)

axis (ăk′ sĭs) *n.* a reference line from which distances or angles are measured. (p. 124)

B

babies (bā′ bēz) *n.* children who were recently born (singular is *baby*). **GSL** (p. 230)

back (băk) *adv.* away from. **GSL** (p. 108)

backbone (băk′ bōn′) *n.* your spine. It contains your spinal cord. (p. 208)

backward (băk′ wərd) *adj.* going towards the back. **GSL** (p. 202)

bacteria (băk tîr′ ē ə) *n.* germs that make people sick. (p. 134)

bag (băg) *n.* a sack to put things in. **GSL** (p. 182)

baking soda *n.* a white powder with many everyday uses, such as cooking. (p. 108)

balance (băl′ əns) *n.* a kind of scale made out of a beam with trays hanging on both sides. **GSL** (p. 174)

bald eagle *n.* a large bird that is a symbol of the United States. (p. 140)

ballot (băl′ ət) *n.* a card or sheet of paper used to vote for something. (p. 126)

bandage (băn′ dĭj) *n.* a strip of material used to cover an injury. (p. 56)

bank (băngk) *n.* the business that holds people's money. **GSL** (p. 64)

bar (bär) *n.* a solid, rectangular block used in graphs. **GSL** (p. 124)

bar graph *n.* a chart that uses bars to measure and compare amounts. (p. 124)

barn (bärn) *n.* a building on a farm used to keep horses and other livestock. (p. 178)

baseball (bās′ bôl′) *n.* a popular team sport using a bat and a ball. (p. 124)

basis (bā′ sĭs) *n.* the main part. **GSL** (p. 192)

bathroom (băth′ rōōm′) *n.* a room with a sink, toilet, and often a bathtub or shower. (p. 46)

be (bē) *v.* remain in a certain state. **Dolch, GSL** (p. 94)

be in hot water an idiom that means be in trouble. (p. 196)

beach (bēch) *n.* the sandy area near a body of water. (p. 112)

beat (bēt) *v.* pulse. **GSL** (p. 204)

beautiful (byōō′ tə fəl) *adj.* very pretty. (p. 86)

because (bĭ kôz′) *conj.* as a result of. **Dolch, GSL** (p. 94)

become (bĭ kŭm′) *v.* turn into. **GSL** (p. 194)

bedroom (bĕd′ rōōm′) *n.* the room in a house where you sleep. **GSL** (p. 90)

beef (bēf) *n.* the meat that comes from cows. (p. 178)

been (bĭn) *v.* past participle of *be*. See *be*. **Dolch** (p. 94)

before (bĭ fôr′) *adv.* earlier in time. **Dolch, GSL** (p. 108)

begin (bĭ gĭn′) *v.* start. **GSL** (p. 216)

beginning (bĭ gĭn′ ĭng) *adj.* starting. **GSL** (p. 192)

behave (bĭ hāv′) *v.* act. **GSL** (p. 106)

behind (bĭ hīnd′) *prep.* in back of. **GSL** (p. 90)

belief (bĭ lēf′) *n.* what someone thinks. **GSL** (p. 116)

belong to be a member of. **GSL** (p. 186)

below (bĭ lō′) *prep.* in a lower place; beneath. **GSL** (p. 90)

below zero any negative number. (p. 224)

belt (bĕlt) *n.* a strip of material used to hold up a person's pants. **GSL** (p. 72)

beneath (bĭ nēth′) *prep.* under. **GSL** (p. 256)

best (bĕst) *adj.* surpassing others in excellence. See *good, well*. **Dolch, GSL** (p. 102)

better (bĕt′ ər) *adj.* more than good. **Dolch, GSL** (p. 58)

between (bǐ twēn′) *adj.* in the middle of two things. **GSL** (p. 64)

bicycle (bī′ sǐk′ əl) *n.* a vehicle with two wheels that you pedal in order to move. **GSL** (p. 62)

big (bǐg) *adj.* large. **Dolch, GSL** (p. 74)

big hand the hand on a clock that shows the minute. (p. 100)

bill (bǐl) **1.** *n.* paper money. (p. 54) **2.** *n.* a document that might become a law. (p. 210) **GSL**

billion (bǐl′ yən) *adj.* a thousand millions. (p. 158)

birth (bûrth) *n.* the act of being born. **GSL** (p. 230)

birthday (bûrth′ dā′) *n.* the annual celebration of the day you were born. (p. 98)

bit (bǐt) *n.* a small amount. **GSL** (p. 198, 206)

bite (bīt) *v.* close your teeth together. **GSL** (p. 206)

bleeding (blē′ dǐng) *v.* losing blood. **GSL** (p. 56)

blend (blěnd) *v.* mix together. (p. 118)

blizzard (blǐz′ ərd) *n.* a very heavy snowstorm with lots of wind. (p. 82)

block (blǒk) *n.* a section of a street between two cross streets. **GSL** (p. 172)

blood (blŭd) *n.* the red liquid in the human body that carries oxygen and keeps humans alive. **GSL** (p. 204)

bloom (blo͞om) *v.* open; blossom. (p. 136)

board (bôrd) *n.* the large panel in the front of a classroom that is used to write on. **GSL** (p. 44)

boat (bōt) *n.* a vehicle used to travel on water. **GSL** (p. 118)

body (bǒd′ ē) **1.** *n.* a mass that is separate from other masses. (p. 114) **2.** *n.* the human form. (p. 132) **3.** *n.* the part of an essay after the introduction and before the conclusion. (p. 220) **GSL**

bold (bōld) *adj.* set in darker type. **GSL** (p. 166)

bone (bōn) *n.* one of the hard materials that make up our skeleton. **GSL** (p. 130)

book (bo͝ok) *n.* a set of pages with writing on them that are held together between two covers. **GSL** (p. 44)

border (bôr′ dər) **1.** *v.* being next to something. (p. 164) **2.** *n.* the line separating countries, states, or other geographic areas. (p. 236) **GSL**

bored (bôrd) *adj.* feeling uninterested. (p. 94)

born (bôrn) *v.* brought into life by birth. (p. 98)

borrow (bǒr′ ō) *v.* use for a time before returning. **GSL** (p. 168)

both (bōth) *adj.* one and the other. **Dolch, GSL** (p. 86)

bothering (bo*th*′ ər ǐng) *v.* disturbing or annoying. (p. 96)

bottle (bǒt′ l) *n.* a glass or plastic container used to hold liquid. **GSL** (p. 182)

bottom (bǒt′ əm) *adj.* in the lowest position. **GSL** (p. 148)

bow (bō) *n.* a stringed device used to shoot an arrow. (p. 186)

box (bǒks) *n.* a square, cardboard container. **GSL** (p. 182)

boxed (bǒkst) *v.* contained inside a square. **GSL** (p. 200)

boy (boi) *n.* a male child. **GSL** (p. 38)

brain (brān) *n.* the organ inside the skull that controls thought and movement. **GSL** (p. 208)

branch (brănch) *n.* One of 3 parts of government. The 3 branches of government are the executive, legislative, and judicial branches. **GSL** (p. 210)

bread (brĕd) *n.* a basic type of food made from flour that is shaped into dough. The dough is baked in an oven, where it rises. **GSL** (p. 68)

break (brāk) *v.* fracture or crack. **GSL** (p. 60)

break down dissolve into simpler parts. (p. 206)

breakfast (brĕk′ fəst) *n.* the first meal of the day eaten in the morning. **GSL** (p. 70)

breathe (brē*th*) *v.* to inhale and exhale air. **GSL** (p. 204)

bring (brĭng) *v.* take with you. **Dolch, GSL** (p. 44)

broken (brō′ kən) *adj.* fractured or cracked. (p. 60)

brother (brŭ*th*′ ər) *n.* a male sibling. **GSL** (p. 86)

browse (brouz) *v.* research a topic by looking at various Internet sites. (p. 170)

brush (brŭsh) *v.* clean your teeth using a toothbrush and toothpaste. **GSL** (p. 134)

buckle down an idiom that means concentrate and work hard. (p. 196)

buffalo (bŭf′ ə lō′) *n.* a large mammal with a thick coat of hair, also known as a bison (p. 186)

building (bĭl′ dĭng) *n.* a structure built for people to inhabit. (p. 136)

built (bĭlt) *v.* made; constructed (present tense is *build*). (p. 136)

bus (bŭs) *n.* a long vehicle used to carry many people at once. **GSL** (p. 62)

bus stop the place where a bus picks people up or drops them off. (p. 62)

bushes (bŏŏsh′ əz) *n.* low shrubs with many branches (singular is *bush*). **GSL** (p. 194)

business (bĭz′ nĭs) *n.* the buying and selling of things. **GSL** (p. 234)

busy (bĭz′ ē) *adj.* having a lot to do. **GSL** (p. 88)

busy as bees an idiom that means everyone is working hard. (p. 196)

but (bŭt) *conj.* although; however. **Dolch, GSL** (p. 94)

butter (bŭt′ ər) *n.* a soft, yellow substance made from milk fat that is used for cooking or to spread on bread. **GSL** (p. 68)

button (bŭt′ n) *n.* an item on a computer screen that, when selected, allows you to view the information it indicates. **GSL** (p. 170)

buy (bī) *v.* to get something using money; purchase. **Dolch, GSL** (p. 54)

by (bī) *prep.* with the use or help of. **Dolch, GSL** (p. 62)

by hand drawn by a person. (p. 248)

C

cabinet (kăb′ ə nĭt) *n.* a team of people chosen by the president to work for him or her. (p. 212)

cactus (kăk′ təs) *n.* a plant with sharp needles that grows in the desert. (p. 162)

cafeteria (kăf′ ĭ tîr′ ē ə) *n.* the room in a school where lunch is served and eaten. (p. 46)

cake (kāk) *n.* a sweet, baked food made from flour, sugar, eggs, and other ingredients. It's often covered in frosting. **GSL** (p. 118)

calcium (kăl′ sē əm) *n.* a nutrient in food that helps keep teeth, bones, and hair healthy. (p. 130)

calculator (kăl′ kyə lā′ tər) *n.* a small electronic device used to do math. **GSL** (p. 198)

calendar (kăl′ ən dər) *n.* a table showing the months, weeks, and days in one year. (p. 98)

call (kôl) *v.* contact someone using a telephone. **Dolch** (p. 60)

call number the number a library uses to identify and find a book. (p. 168)

came (kām) *v.* past tense of *come*. See *come*. **Dolch** (p. 50)

can (kăn) **1.** *v.* is able. (p. 84) **2.** *n.* a round, metal container. (p. 182) **Dolch, GSL**

Canada (kăn′ ə də) *n.* a country in North America located north of the United States. (p. 164)

candy (kăn′ dē) *n.* sweet treats made from sugar. (p. 138)

can't (kănt) *v.* is not able (contraction of *cannot*). (p. 84)

canyon (kăn′ yən) *n.* a deep, narrow valley with steep cliff walls. (p. 112)

capacity (kə păs′ ĭ tē) *n.* how much something can hold. (p. 176)

capillaries (kăp′ ə lĕr′ ēz) *n.* tiny blood vessels. (p. 204)

capital (kăp′ ĭ tl) *n.* where the main government of a country or state is located. **GSL** (p. 136)

capitalize (kăp′ ĭ tl īz′) *v.* make a letter uppercase. (p. 216)

Capitol (kăp′ ĭ tl) *n.* the building where the United States Congress meets. (p. 136)

car (kär) *n.* a vehicle used to get from one place to another; automobile. **GSL** (p. 62)

card (kärd) *n.* a small, rectangular piece of cardboard. **GSL** (p. 226)

care (kâr) *v.* feel that something matters or is important. **GSL** (p. 96)

careful (kâr′ fəl) *adj.* with care or caution. (p. 106)

carry (kăr′ ē) *v.* hold something while moving it. **Dolch, GSL** (p. 252)

cart (kärt) *n.* a small-wheeled vehicle that is pushed by hand to hold groceries while shopping. **GSL** (p. 68)

cashier (kă shîr′) *n.* the person at a store whom you pay when you buy something. (p. 54)

cat (kăt) *n.* an animal with a long tail and whiskers that is a popular pet; feline. **GSL** (p. 118)

catalog (kăt′ l ôg′) *n.* an alphabetical listing of books in a library. (p. 168)

catch (kăch) *v.* capture, especially after chasing. **GSL** (p. 142)

caterpillar (kăt′ ər pĭl′ ər) *n.* a small, furry insect that eventually becomes a butterfly. (p. 172)

cattle (kăt′ l) *n.* cows. **GSL** (p. 178)

cause (kôz) *v.* make happen. **GSL** (p. 134)

caution (kô′ shən) *n.* close attention to avoid danger. **GSL** (p. 170)

celebrate (sĕl′ ə brāt′) *v.* observe a special event or holiday. (p. 190)

celebration (sĕl′ ə brā′ shən) *n.* a ceremony held to recognize a special event. (p. 138)

cell (sĕl) *n.* the smallest part of a living thing that is able to function by itself. (p. 232)

cell wall the hard, outer layer of a plant cell. (p. 232)

Celsius (sĕl′ sē əs) *adj.* about a scale for measuring temperature at which freezing is 0° and boiling is 100°. (p. 224)

center (sĕn′ tər) *n.* the middle. **GSL** (p. 248)

centimeter (cm) (sĕn′ tə mē′ tər) *n.* the unit of length that is one hundredth of a meter. (p. 172)

ceremony (sĕr′ ə mō′ nē) *n.* an act that's done for a special reason and is done the same way every time. **GSL** (p. 186)

certain (sûr′ tn) *adj.* particular. **GSL** (p. 226)

chain (chān) *n.* a connected series of mountains. **GSL** (p. 164)

chair (châr) *n.* a piece of furniture made for one person to sit on. **GSL** (p. 44)

chalk (chôk) *n.* a white stick used to write on a blackboard. **GSL** (p. 44)

chance (chăns) *n.* an opportunity. **GSL** (p. 188)

change (chānj) **1.** *n.* the money you get back after buying something. (p. 54) **2.** *v.* make different. (p. 202) **GSL**

character (kăr′ ək tər) *n.* a fictional person in a story. **GSL** (p. 244)

chart (chärt) *n.* a table containing information. (p. 50)

chased (chāsd) *v.* ran after, usually to catch. (p. 142)

check (chĕk) *v.* look at something again to make sure it's correct. **GSL** (p. 102)

check out take out of the library with the library's permission. (p. 168)

cheese (chēz) *n.* a solid food made from milk. **GSL** (p. 68)

chemical (kĕm′ ĭ kəl) *n.* any kind of matter. (p. 180)

chew (chōo) *v.* bite and grind something with your teeth, usually to make it easier to swallow. (p. 206)

chicken (chĭk′ ən) *n.* a bird that can't fly and is usually found on a farm. Eggs you eat come from chickens. **GSL** (p. 178)

chief (chēf) *n.* the leader of a tribe. **GSL** (p. 186)

Chief Justice *n.* the head of the Supreme Court justices. (p. 214)

childhood (chīld′ hŏod′) *n.* the part of your life when you are a child. **GSL** (p. 230)

children (chĭl′ drən) *n.* young people; kids (singular is *child*). **GSL** (p. 230)

chills (chĭlz) *n.* the shaking that comes from having a fever. (p. 58)

choice (chois) *n.* an option between 2 or more things. **GSL** (p. 224)

choose (chōoz) *v.* select; pick. **GSL** (p. 238)

circle (sûr′ kəl) *n.* a round, geometric shape. **GSL** (p. 248)

circle graph a chart in which a circle is divided into sections to represent data. It's also called a pie chart. (p. 126)

circled (sûr′ kəld) *adj.* having a circle drawn around it. (p. 200)

citizen (sĭt′ ĭ zən) *n.* a person who was born in a country or whose legal home is in that country. **GSL** (p. 238)

city (sĭt′ ē) *n.* a large busy area where many people live and work. **GSL** (p. 42)

clapping (clăp′ pĭng) *v.* striking the hands together to make a sound. (p. 122)

class (klăs) *n.* a gathering of students who meet to learn about a subject from a teacher. **GSL** (p. 38)

classify (klăs′ ə fī′) *v.* put into a group according to a characteristic. **GSL** (p. 218)

classroom (klăs′ rōom′) *n.* a room at school where class is taught. (p. 46)

clay (klā) *n.* a kind of mud that people use to make things, such as pottery. **GSL** (p. 186)

clean (klēn) *adj.* free of pollution. **Dolch, GSL** (p. 180)

clear (klîr) *adj.* not cloudy. **GSL** (p. 80)

clearly (klîr′ lē) *adv.* done in a way that's easy to understand. (p. 192)

click (klĭk) *v.* push the button on a mouse to make something happen on the computer screen. (p. 104)

climate (klī′ mĭt) *n.* the weather that's usual in a certain area. (p. 162)

clock (klŏk) *n.* a device that's used to tell the time of day. **GSL** (p. 100)

close (klōs) *v.* exit. **GSL** (p. 104)

close to just about; almost. (p. 78)

closed (klōsd) *adj.* has no break or opening; solid. (p. 250)

closely (klōs′ lē) *adv.* nearly; almost. (p. 198)

closing sentence the last sentence; conclusion. (p. 220)

cloud (cloud) *n.* a mass of water suspended in the atmosphere. **GSL** (p. 154)

cloudy (clou′ dē) *adj.* full of clouds. (p. 80)

clue (clōo) *n.* a helpful hint. (p. 102)

cluster (klŭs′ tər) *n.* a group of consonants. (p. 118)

coal (kōl) *n.* a fossil fuel found underground that looks like black rocks. **GSL** (p. 254)

coin (koin) *n.* round metal money. **GSL** (p. 54)

cold (kōld) **1.** *n.* a common illness in which you get a sore throat, cough, stuffy nose, and fever. (p. 56) **2.** *adj.* very cool. (p. 80) **Dolch, GSL**

coldest (kōl′ dəst) *adj.* the most cold. (p. 224)

collect (kŏl′ ĕkt′) *v.* look for and save many kinds of something. **GSL** (p. 66)

collection (kə lĕk′ shən) **1.** *n.* the last stage of the water cycle in which water gathers on the ground in pools, such as puddles and lakes. (p. 154) **2.** *n.* all the books and other texts in a library. (p. 168) **GSL**

colony (kŏl′ ə nē) *n.* a small village or community. **GSL** (p. 188)

color (kŭl′ ər) *n.* red, yellow, blue, and any mixture of these. **GSL** (p. 140)

Colorado River *n.* a large river in the western part of the United States that rises from the Rocky Mountains. (p. 164)

column (kŏl′ əm) *n.* a vertical list on a chart. (p. 200)

combine (kəm bīn′) *v.* put together to make one. **GSL** (p. 74)

come (kŭm) *v.* go toward the speaker or a place. **Dolch, GSL** (p. 46)

comet (kŏm′ ĭt) *n.* an object made of gases with a tail that moves through outer space. (p. 158)

comma (,) (kŏm′ ə) *n.* a punctuation mark used to show a pause in a sentence or to separate items in a series. (p. 216)

command (kə mănd′) **1.** *v.* give orders to; lead. (p. 212) **2.** *n.* a direction that tells you to do something. (p. 218) **GSL**

commander (kə măn′ dər) *n.* a leader. (p. 212)

commercial (kə mûr′ shəl) *n.* an advertisement on television. **GSL** (p. 234)

commit (kə mĭt′) *v.* do something. (p. 214)

common (kŏm′ ən) **1.** *adj.* shared by. (p. 148) **2.** *adj.* usual; ordinary. (p. 196) **GSL**

common factor a number that is a factor of two or more numbers. (p. 200)

common multiple a number into which two or more numbers can be divided with a remainder of zero. (p. 200)

communicate (kə myoŏ′ nĭ kāt′) *v.* pass on information. (p. 218)

commutative (kə myoō′ tə tiv) *adj.* refers to the order of numbers. (p. 202)

commute (kə myoōt′) *v.* go back and forth. (p. 202)

company (kŭm′ pə nē) *n.* a business. **GSL** (p. 234)

compare (kəm pâr′) *v.* look at what two or more things have in common. **GSL** (p. 52)

comparison (kəm păr′ ĭ sən) *n.* the showing of what two or more things have in common. **GSL** (p. 150)

compass (kŭm′ pəs) *n.* a mathematical tool to draw a circle. (p. 248)

compass rose a symbol that shows direction on a map. (p. 236)

compatible (kəm păt′ ə bəl) *adj.* goes together easily. (p. 198)

complete (kəm plēt′) *adj.* entire. **GSL** (p. 148)

complete sentence a sentence with a subject and a predicate. (p. 144)

completely (kəm plēt′ lē) *adv.* entirely. **GSL** (p. 194)

complex (kəm plĕks′) *adj.* having many parts; complicated. (p. 232)

composite (kəm pŏz′ ĭt) *adj.* having 2 or more factors. (p. 200)

compound sentence two sentences made into one using a conjunction to connect them. (p. 144)

compute (kəm pyoōt′) *v.* figure out an amount or number. (p. 198)

condensation (kŏn′ dən sā′ shən) *n.* the process by which a gas changes to a liquid. (p. 154)

confused (kən fyōōzd′) *adj.* being unable to understand. **GSL** (p. 94)

confusing (kən fyōō′ zĭng) *adj.* hard to understand. **GSL** (p. 222)

Congress (kŏng′ grĭs) *n.* the legislative branch of the U.S. government. (p. 210)

conjunction (kən jŭngk′ shən) *n.* a part of speech used to connect words or phrases. (p. 142)

connect (kə nĕkt′) *v.* link together. **GSL** (p. 240)

connected (kə nĕk′ təd) *v.* linked together. (p. 156)

consist (kən sĭst′) *v.* is made of. (p. 144)

consonant (kŏn′ sə nənt) *n.* any letter other than A, E, I, O, or U. (p. 118)

constant (kŏn′ stənt) *adj.* doesn't change. (p. 226)

Constitution (kŏn′ stĭ tōō′ shən) *n.* the document that sets the system of laws and principles of the U.S. government. (p. 214)

consumer (kən sōō′ mər) *n.* an animal that eats plants or other animals as part of a food chain. (p. 228)

contain (kən tān′) *v.* hold inside. **GSL** (p. 176)

container (kən tā′ nər) *n.* something in which material is held. (p. 182)

contest (kŏn′ tĕst′) *n.* a competition. (p. 52)

continent (kŏn′ tə nənt) *n.* one of seven large land masses that cover the earth. (p. 236)

continue (kən tĭn′ yōō) *v.* go on. **GSL** (p. 230)

continuous (kən tĭn′ yōō əs) *adj.* not ending. (p. 122)

control (kən trōl′) **1.** *n.* power over someone or something. (p. 188) **2.** *v.* make something work. (p. 208) **GSL**

convenient (kən vēn′ yənt) *adj.* made easy for one's purpose. **GSL** (p. 120)

convert (kən vûrt′) *v.* change from one type of thing to another. (p. 152)

cooking (kŏŏk′ ĭng) *v.* preparing food. (p. 116)

cool (kōōl) *adj.* slightly cold. **GSL** (p. 80)

copy (kŏp′ ē) *n.* a duplicate of something. **GSL** (p. 242)

core (kôr) *n.* the center. (p. 256)

corn (kôrn) *n.* a plant covered in yellow kernels that are eaten. **GSL** (p. 190)

corner (kôr′ nər) **1.** *n.* the point where two streets meet. (p. 64) **2.** *n.* the point where two lines meet. (p. 246) **GSL**

correct (kə rĕkt′) **1.** *adj.* right or true. (p. 78) **2.** *v.* make right. (p. 242) **GSL**

costs (kôsts) *v.* is worth. **GSL** (p. 54)

costume (kŏs′ tōōm′) *n.* an outfit worn on a particular occasion. (p. 138)

cotton (kŏt′ n) *n.* a plant with blossoms of soft, white balls from which clothing is made. **GSL** (p. 188)

coughing (kôf′ ĭng) *v.* pushing air from the lungs loudly and suddenly. **GSL** (p. 56)

could (kŏŏd) *v.* past tense of *can.* See *can.* **Dolch, GSL** (p. 64)

counselor (koun′ slər) *n.* someone that helps you talk about your problems. (p. 96)

count (kount) *v.* add up; figure out how many there are. **GSL** (p. 50)

counted (koun′ təd) *v.* past tense of *count.* See *count.* **GSL** (p. 78)

countries (kŭn′ trēz) *n.* plural of *country.* See *country.* **GSL** (p. 236)

country (kŭn′ trē) *n.* a nation. **GSL** (p. 42)

couple (kŭp′ əl) *n.* 2 of something. (p. 124)

court (kôrt) *n.* the place where a judge listens to legal cases and makes decisions based on the law. **GSL** (p. 214)

cousin (kŭz′ ĭn) *n.* the child of your aunt or uncle. **GSL** (p. 86)

cover (kŭv′ ər) **1.** *v.* be all over the top of something. (p. 112) **2.** *v.* put something over an object so you can't see it. (p. 134) **GSL**

criminal (krĭm′ ə nəl) *n.* someone who has been convicted of breaking a law. **GSL** (p. 214)

crops (krŏps) *n.* plants grown to eat or use. **GSL** (p. 190)

cross (krôs) *v.* pass through or over; intersect. **GSL** (p. 246)

crossing guard someone whose job is to help you cross the street safely. (p. 66)

crust (krŭst) *n.* the topmost layer. (p. 256)

culture (kŭl′ chər) *n.* the customs and practices of a particular group of people. (p. 116)

cup (kŭp) **1.** *n.* a container you drink from. (p. 70) **2.** *n.* a unit of volume that equals 8 ounces. (p. 176) **GSL**

current (kûr′ ənt) *n.* a steady, smooth movement. **GSL** (p. 208)

cursor (kûr′ sər) *n.* a blinking line on your computer screen that shows where a letter will appear when it's typed. (p. 104)

curved (kûrvd) *adj.* bent in a smooth, rounded way so that it's not straight. **GSL** (p. 246)

custom (kŭs′ təm) *n.* a practice of a particular culture. **GSL** (p. 116)

customary (kŭs′ tə mĕr′ ē) *adj.* usual. (p. 176)

customer (kŭs′ tə mər) *n.* a person buying something or receiving the services of a business. **GSL** (p. 234)

cut (kŭt) *v.* slice open. **Dolch, GSL** (p. 56)

cut down chop down trees; destroy. (p. 156)

cycle (sī′ kəl) *n.* a regularly repeated sequence of events. (p. 154)

cytoplasm (sī′ tə plăz′ əm) *n.* the jellylike fluid that fills a cell. (p. 232)

D

daily (dā′ lē) *adv.* happening every day. **GSL** (p. 132)

dairy (dâr′ ē) *adj.* made of milk. (p. 178)

dam (dăm) *n.* a barrier across a waterway that controls the flow of water. (p. 254)

dance (dăns) *n.* a type of movement usually done to music. **GSL** (p. 116)

dangerous (dān′ jər əs) *adj.* likely to cause harm; not safe. **GSL** (p. 106)

dark (därk) *adj.* having little or no light. **GSL** (p. 82)

data (dăt′ ə) *n.* collected information. (p. 126)

date (dāt) *n.* the day of the month. **GSL** (p. 98)

day (dā) *n.* a 24-hour period of time. **GSL** (p. 98)

death (dĕth) *n.* the end of life. **GSL** (p. 230)

debate (dĭ bāt′) *v.* argue the 2 sides of an issue. (p. 210)

decide (dĭ sīd′) *v.* to choose. **GSL** (p. 126)

decimal (dĕs′ ə məl) *n.* a part of a whole number. (p. 150)

decimal places the places for numbers after a decimal point, such as tenths and hundredths. (p. 150)

decimal point (.) the dot that separates the whole number from the decimal number. (p. 150)

declarative (dĭ klâr′ ə tĭv) *adj.* telling what happens. (p. 218)

declared (dĭ klârd′) *v.* said. **GSL** (p. 218)

decomposer (dē′ kəm pō′ zər) *n.* an animal that eats dead material. (p. 228)

decrease (dĭ krēs′) *v.* make less or smaller. **GSL** (p. 204)

deep (dēp) *adj.* extending far downward. **GSL** (p. 112)

deeper (dēp′ ər) *adj.* farther down. (p. 256)

deepest (dēp′ əst) *adj.* farthest down. (p. 256)

deer (dîr) *n.* large animals with hooves. The males have antlers, or large horns, growing from their heads. **GSL** (p. 194)

defense (dĭ fĕns′) *n.* the military. **GSL** (p. 212)

define (dĭ fīn′) *v.* give the meaning of. (p. 166)

definition (dĕf′ ə nĭsh′ ən) *n.* the meaning of something, such as a word. (p. 166)

degrees (dĭ grēz′) *n.* units of measurement that show location on a map. **GSL** (p. 236)

delete (dĭ lēt′) *v.* erase. (p. 122)

deliver (dĭ lĭv′ ər) *v.* bring to someone. **GSL** (p. 66)

demand (dĭ mănd′) *n.* people's need and desire for a product. **GSL** (p. 234)

demanded (dĭ măn′ dĭd) *v.* said that something must happen; ordered. (p. 218)

democracy (dĭ mŏk′ rə sē) *n.* a form of government in which citizens vote for their leader. (p. 238)

denominator (dĭ nŏm′ ə nā′ tər) *n.* the number on the bottom in a fraction. (p. 148)

department (dĭ pärt′ mənt) *n.* one part of an organization that does a particular job. **GSL** (p. 212)

depend on rely on. **GSL** (p. 156)

deposit (dĭ pŏz′ ĭt) *n.* extra money you receive for something that's given back to you after you recycle the item. (p. 182)

descended (dĭ sĕn′ dĭd) *v.* came from. **GSL** (p. 160)

describe (dĭ skrīb′) *v.* tell what something is like. **GSL** (p. 142)

desert (dĕz′ ərt) *n.* an area with a hot, dry climate. **GSL** (p. 112)

desk (dĕsk) *n.* a piece of furniture with a flat surface for writing and drawers for storing things. **GSL** (p. 44)

destroy (dĭ stroi′) *v.* ruin. **GSL** (p. 156)

detail (dĭ tāl′) *n.* particular information about something. **GSL** (p. 220)

determine (dĭ tûr′ mĭn) *v.* figure out. **GSL** (p. 152)

develop (dĭ vĕl′ əp) *v.* grow and change. **GSL** (p. 230)

dew (dōō) *n.* the condensation on grass and plants in the morning. (p. 154)

diagram (dī′ ə grăm′) *n.* a drawing used to explain something. (p. 222)

diameter (dī ăm′ ĭ tər) *n.* the width. (p. 248)

dictionary (dĭk′ shə nĕr′ ē) *n.* a reference book containing definitions and other information about words. **GSL** (p. 166)

did (dĭd) *v.* past tense of *do.* See *do.* **Dolch** (p. 60)

die (dī) *v.* stop living. **GSL** (p. 230)

diet (dī′ ĭt) *n.* the usual food and drink you eat. (p. 130)

difference (dĭf′ rəns) **1.** *n.* the number that's left after subtraction. (p. 74) **2.** *n.* a quality that is not alike. (p. 160) **GSL**

different (dĭf′ rənt) *adj.* not alike. **GSL** (p. 152)

difficult (dĭf′ ĭ kŭlt′) *adj.* hard; not easy. **GSL** (p. 102)

digest (dī jĕst′) *v.* the way your body breaks down food that's been eaten. (p. 206)

digit (dĭj′ ĭt) *n.* a number. (p. 50)

dime (dīm) *n.* a U.S. coin that is worth 10 cents. (p. 54)

dining room the room of a house where you eat. (p. 90)

dinner (dĭn′ ər) *n.* a meal eaten in the evening. **GSL** (p. 70)

direction (dĭ rĕk′ shən) *n.* the line along which something moves. **GSL** (p. 246)

directions (dĭ rĕk′ shənz) *n.* the steps for doing something; instructions. **GSL** (p. 108)

dirty (dûr′ tē) *adj.* not clean. (p. 180)

disagree (dĭs′ ə grē′) *v.* have a different opinion than someone else. **GSL** (p. 210)

discover (dĭ skŭv′ ər) *v.* find out for the first time. **GSL** (p. 222)

disk drive the slot in a computer where you put the disk. (p. 104)

diskette (dĭ skĕt′) *n.* the thing on which you store information from a computer. (p. 104)

display (dĭ splā′) *v.* show. (p. 126)

distance (dĭs′ təns) *n.* length. **GSL** (p. 172)

distribute (dĭ strĭb′ yoōt) *v.* divide things into parts and spread them out. (p. 202)

distributive (dĭ strĭb′ yə tĭv) *adj.* refers to a way to make math easier by using multiplication. (p. 202)

district (dĭs′ trĭkt) *n.* a region or area of land. **GSL** (p. 136)

District of Columbia (D.C.) *n.* a federal district in the eastern United States between Virginia and Maryland. Washington, D.C., is the capital of the United States. (p. 136)

diversity (dĭ vûr′ sĭ tē) *n.* a variety. (p. 160)

divide (÷) (dĭ vīd′) *v.* separate a number into equal parts. **GSL** (p. 76)

divided by split by. (p. 76)

divided into split into. (p. 166)

divisible (dĭ vĭz′ ə bəl) *adj.* able to be divided. (p. 200)

DNA *n.* a chemical in the cell that controls the action of cells and carries genetic information. (p. 232)

do (doō) *v.* perform. **Dolch, GSL** (p. 88)

doctor (dŏk′ tər) *n.* a person whose job it is to heal sick people. **GSL** (p. 58)

document (dŏk′ yə mənt) *n.* the entire text on a computer screen. (p. 104)

does (dŭz) *v.* third-person form of *do.* See *do.* **Dolch** (p. 60)

dog (dôg) *n.* an animal that barks and is a popular pet; canine. **GSL** (p. 126)

doing (doō′ ĭng) *v.* performing. **GSL** (p. 122)

dollar ($) (dŏl′ ər) *n.* paper money in the United States. **GSL** (p. 54)

done (dŭn) *v.* finished. **Dolch** (p. 48)

don't (dōnt) *contr.* contraction of *do not.* **Dolch** (p. 94)

dot (dŏt) *n.* a very small spot. (p. 150)

double (dŭb′ əl) *v.* make twice as much. **GSL** (p. 122)

down (doun) *adv.* in a lower direction. **Dolch, GSL** (p. 78)

downtown (doun′ toun′) *n.* the business center of a city or town. (p. 64)

dozen (dŭz′ ən) *n.* a set of twelve. **GSL** (p. 76)

draft (drăft) *n.* one of any attempts at writing a paper. (p. 242)

draw (drô) *v.* make a picture using a pencil; illustrate. **Dolch, GSL** (p. 248)

drawn (drôn) *v.* past participle of *draw.* See *draw.* (p. 164)

dress (drĕs) **1.** *n.* a one-piece type of clothing worn by women. (p. 72) **2.** *v.* wear clothing. (p. 116) **GSL**

dresses (drĕs əs) *n.* the plural form of *dress.* See *dress.* **GSL** (p. 194)

drill (drĭl) *n.* a routine. (p. 106)

drink (drĭngk) *v.* swallow liquid. **Dolch, GSL** (p. 70)

drive (drīv) *v.* operate a vehicle. **GSL** (p. 62)

drop (drŏp) *v.* let go of something so that it falls to the ground. **GSL** (p. 108)

dry (drī) *adj.* having little or no moisture. **GSL** (p. 162)

due date the date you need to return a book to the library. (p. 168)

dull (dŭl) *adj.* not interesting; boring. **GSL** (p. 144)

during (dŏor′ ĭng) *prep.* throughout the time of. **GSL** (p. 240)

duty (doō′ tē) *n.* a responsibility. **GSL** (p. 238)

E

each (ēch) *adj.* every one of a group considered individually. **GSL** (p. 50)

early (ûr′ lē) *adv.* happening at the beginning. **GSL** (p. 48)

earn (ûrn) *v.* get from working. **GSL** (p. 234)

easier (ēz′ ē ər) *adj.* simpler. (p. 202)

easily (ē′ zə lē) *adv.* without difficulty. (p. 198)

Eastern (ē′ stərn) *adj.* located in the east. **GSL** (p. 236)

easy (ē′ zē) *adj.* not hard; simple. **GSL** (p. 102)

eat (ēt) *v.* put something in your mouth and swallow. **Dolch, GSL** (p. 52)

edge (ĕj) *n.* a straight side. **GSL** (p. 248)

edit (ĕd′ ĭt) *v.* make corrections to writing in order to make it better. (p. 242)

education (ĕj′ ə kā′ shən) *n.* the process of learning. **GSL** (p. 212)

egg (ĕg) *n.* the oval-shaped thing that chickens produce that is often used for cooking and eating. **GSL** (p. 76)

either (ē′ thər) *pron.* one or the other. **GSL** (p. 224)

elder (ĕl′ dər) *n.* an older person. **GSL** (p. 116)

elect (ĭ lĕkt′) *v.* choose a person by voting. **GSL** (p. 212)

electricity (ĭ lĕk trĭs′ ĭ tē) *n.* an electric current used for power. (p. 254)

element (ĕl′ ə mənt) *n.* a particular part or characteristic. (p. 220)

elephant (ĕl′ ə fənt) *n.* a very large gray animal with a long trunk and 2 large teeth called tusks. **GSL** (p. 174)

else (ĕls) *adj.* other; different. **GSL** (p. 134)

embarrassed (ĕm băr′ əst) *adj.* self-conscious. (p. 94)

emergency (ĭ mûr′ jən sē) *n.* a situation that was not expected and needs attention immediately. (p. 60)

emotion (ĭ mō′ shən) *n.* a feeling. (p. 216)

employ (ĕm ploi′) *v.* give a job to. **GSL** (p. 234)

employee (ĕm ploi′ ē) *n.* someone hired to work. **GSL** (p. 234)

empty (ĕmp′ tē) *v.* remove the contents of. (p. 176)

encounter (ĕn koun′ tər) *v.* come in contact with. (p. 196)

encyclopedia (ĕn sī′ klə pē′ dē ə) *n.* one of a set of resource books with information about many things. (p. 168)

end (ĕnd) **1.** *v.* is over. (p. 84) **2.** *n.* the finish or conclusion of something. (p. 216) **GSL**

endangered (ĕn dān′ jərd) *adj.* so few in number that there may soon be no more. (p. 156)

ending (ĕn′ dĭng) **1.** *v.* finishing. (p. 122) **2.** *adj.* final. (p. 192) **3.** *n.* the conclusion of the story. (p. 244)

endpoint (ĕnd′ point′) *n.* a final place. (p. 246)

energy (ĕn′ ər jē) *n.* the ability to work or perform a physical activity; power. (p. 228)

England (ĭng′ glənd) *n.* a country in Europe that is on the island of Great Britain. (p. 190)

English (ĭng′ glĭsh) *n.* the native language of the United States and the United Kingdom; the study of this language. **GSL** (p. 48)

enjoy (ĕn joi′) *v.* like. **GSL** (p. 88)

enough (ĭ nŭf′) *adj.* sufficient to satisfy a need or desire. **GSL** (p. 198)

enter (ĕn′ tər) **1.** *v.* go into. (p. 134) **2.** *v.* type on a keyboard. (p. 168) **GSL**

entry (ĕn′ trē) *n.* a word and its definition, as it appears in a dictionary. (p. 166)

environment (ĕn vī′ rən mənt) *n.* all the living things in an area and all the things that surround them. (p. 156)

equal (ē′ kwəl) **1.** *v.* become the same as. (p. 74) **2.** *adj.* is the same as. (p. 76) **GSL**

equal rights the same laws and freedoms for everyone. (p. 138)

equally (ē′ kwəl lē) *adv.* the same as. (p. 76)

equation (ĭ kwā′ zhən) *n.* a math problem. (p. 226)

equator (ĭ kwā′ tər) *n.* the imaginary line that divides the earth. (p. 236)

equivalent (ĭ kwĭv′ ə lənt) *adj.* the same as; equal. (p. 152)

equivalent fractions fractions that are of equal value. (p. 148)

eraser (ĭ rā′ sər) *n.* the object used to erase. (p. 44)

erupt (ĭ rŭpt′) *v.* force out with sudden violence. (p. 256)

escape (ĭ skāp′) *v.* get away. **GSL** (p. 188)

essential (ĭ sĕn′ shəl) *adj.* necessary. (p. 220)

estimate (ĕs′ tə mĭt) **1.** *n.* a guess. (p. 78) **2.** *v.* to make an approximate guess. (p. 198)

ethnic (ĕth′ nĭk) *adj.* relating to a certain race or heritage. (p. 116)

European (yŏor′ ə pē′ ən) *adj.* of or related to Europe. (p. 188)

evaporation (ĭ văp′ ə rā shən) *n.* the act of changing from a liquid to a gas. (p. 154)

even (ē′ vən) *adj.* refers to any number with 2 as a factor. **GSL** (p. 200)

evening (ēv′ nĭng) *n.* the time of day between afternoon and night. **GSL** (p. 40)

evenly (ē′ vən lē) *adv.* without anything remaining. (p. 200)

event (ĭ vĕnt′) *n.* something that happens. **GSL** (p. 244)

ever (ĕv′ ər) *adv.* at any time. **GSL** (p. 224)

every (ĕv′ rē) *adj.* each one. **Dolch, GSL** (p. 50)

everyday (ĕv′ rē dā′) *adj.* common. **GSL** (p. 122)

everything (ĕv′ rē thĭng′) *pron.* all things. **GSL** (p. 134)

everywhere (ĕv′ rē wâr′) *adv.* in all places. **GSL** (p. 134)

exact (ĭg zăkt′) *adj.* without any error. **GSL** (p. 198)

example (ĭg zăm′ pəl) *n.* a problem or exercise used to show an idea. **GSL** (p. 166)

excited (ĭk sī′ tĭd) *adj.* happy and full of energy about something. **GSL** (p. 94)

excitement (ĭk sīt′ mənt) *n.* a feeling that is full of energy. (p. 142)

exclamation (ĕk′ sklə mā′ shən) *n.* an excited interjection. (p. 218)

exclamation point (!) the punctuation mark used at the end of an exclamation. (p. 216)

exclamatory (ĭk sklăm′ ə tôr′ ē) *adj.* relating to an exclamation. (p. 218)

executive (ĭg zĕk′ yə tĭv) *adj.* relating to the branch of government that carries out the laws. (p. 212)

exercise (ĕk′ sər sīz′) *n.* physical activity done to stay healthy. **GSL** (p. 132)

exhaust (ĭg zôst′) *n.* the fumes or gases released. (p. 180)

exit (ĕg′ zĭt) *n.* the door you use to leave a room or building. (p. 106)

expect (ĭk spĕkt′) *v.* think something is going to happen. **GSL** (p. 240)

experiment (ĭk spĕr′ ə mənt) *n.* a test to see if something is true. **GSL** (p. 108)

explain (ĭk splān′) *v.* tell about something. **GSL** (p. 240)

express (ĭk sprĕs′) *v.* make your thoughts and feelings known. **GSL** (p. 96)

expression (ĭk sprĕsh′ ən) **1.** *n.* a saying that means something particular; an idiom. (p. 196) **2.** *n.* one or more symbols that represent a number or the relationship between numbers. (p. 226) **GSL**

extend (ĭk stĕnd′) *v.* reach. **GSL** (p. 250)

extinct (ĭk stĭngkt′) *adj.* no longer exists. (p. 156)

extra (ĕk′ strə) *adj.* left over. **GSL** (p. 76)

extreme (ĭk strēm′) *adj.* far beyond what is normal or usual; severe. **GSL** (p. 162)

F

fabric (făb′ rĭk) *n.* the material used to make clothes. (p. 178)

factor (făk′ tər) **1.** *n.* a whole number that is multiplied. (p. 76) **2.** *n.* a whole number that can be divided into another. (p. 200)

factories (făk′ tə rēz) *n.* buildings where things are made in a large amount (singular is *factory*). **GSL** (p. 162)

factory worker someone who works in a factory. (p. 66)

Fahrenheit (făr′ ən hīt′) *adj.* relating to a temperature scale in which freezing is 32° and boiling is 212°. (p. 224)

fair (fâr) *adj.* according to rules and ethics; just. **GSL** (p. 214)

falcon (făl′ kən) *n.* a fast bird that hunts other birds and animals. (p. 126)

fall (fôl) **1.** *n.* the season between summer and winter; autumn. (p. 84) **2.** *v.* drop down from a higher place. (p. 154) **GSL**

false (fôls) *adj.* not true. **GSL** (p. 78)

familiar (fə mĭl′ yər) *adj.* easily recognized. **GSL** (p. 250)

family (făm′ lē) *n.* people you are related to. **GSL** (p. 86)

family room the room in the house where people spend time together, which usually has a couch and a television. (p. 90)

fan (făn) *n.* a person who goes to watch a sports event. **GSL** (p. 50)

far (fär) *adj.* not close; distant. **Dolch, GSL** (p. 62)

farmed (färmd) *v.* grew and harvested crops. (p. 190)

farmer (fär′ mər) *n.* a person whose job is to grow and harvest crops. (p. 178)

farming (fär′ mĭng) *n.* the practice of growing and harvesting crops. (p. 178)

farmland (färm′ lănd′) *n.* land where crops are grown and harvested. (p. 162)

fast (făst) *adj.* quick. **Dolch, GSL** (p. 100)

fastest (făs′ tĭst) *adj.* the most fast. (p. 150)

father (fä′ thər) *n.* the male parent. **GSL** (p. 86)

favorite (fā′ vrĭt) *adj.* most liked. **GSL** (p. 84)

feast (fēst) *n.* a large meal to celebrate something. **GSL** (p. 190)

feather (fĕth′ ər) *n.* the light, flat growth that covers a bird. **GSL** (p. 186)

feature (fē′ chər) *n.* a detail of something. (p. 162)

feed (fēd) *v.* give food to. **GSL** (p. 178)

feed on get nutrients from. (p. 228)

feel (fēl) *v.* have a sensation. **GSL** (p. 56)

feelings (fē′ lĭngz) *n.* emotions. (p. 94)

feet (fēt) **1.** *n.* units of length equal to 12 inches. (p. 172) **2.** *n.* the part of your body that you walk on. (singular is *foot*). (p. 194)

fell (fĕl) *v.* accidentally dropped oneself down. (present tense is *fall*. See *fall*). (p. 60)

female (fē′ māl′) *n.* a woman or girl. **GSL** (p. 230)

fever (fē′ vər) *n.* a high body temperature that means a person is sick. **GSL** (p. 56)

few (fyōō) *adv.* not many; several. **GSL** (p. 68)

fewer (fyōō′ ər) *adj.* less than. **GSL** (p. 52)

fiction (fĭk′ shən) *n.* a story that is not real. (p. 244)

field (fēld) *n.* a large, grassy area. **GSL** (p. 46)

fifteen (fĭf tēn′) *adj.* the number 15. (p. 152)

fifth (5th) (fĭfth) *adj.* corresponding in order to the number 5. (p. 52)

fifty (fĭf′ tē) *adj.* the number 50. (p. 152)

fight (fīt) *n.* an argument. **GSL** (p. 96)

file (fīl) *n.* a collection of data for a computer. (p. 104)

fill (fĭl) *v.* make full. **GSL** (p. 176)

final (fī′ nəl) *adj.* last. (p. 118)

finally (fī′ nəl lē) *adv.* at last. (p. 108)

find (fīnd) *v.* locate. **Dolch, GSL** (p. 46)

find out learn. (p. 108)

fine (fīn) *adj.* okay. **GSL** (p. 40)

fingernail (fĭng′ gər nāl′) *n.* the thin plate on the top of your fingertip. (p. 134)

finish line the line that must be crossed to finish a race. (p. 150)

fire (fīr) *n.* flames. **GSL** (p. 106)

fire extinguisher a container holding a liquid used to put out fires. (p. 106)

fireworks (fīr′ wûrks) *n.* explosives used in celebration that are shot into the air and explode into a pretty display of sparks. (p. 138)

first (1st) (fûrst) **1.** *adj.* corresponding in order to the number 1. (p. 52) **2.** *adj.* before anything else. (p. 108) **Dolch, GSL**

fish (fĭsh) *n.* an animal with fins that lives and breathes in water. **GSL** (p. 74)

fishing (fĭsh′ ĭng) *v.* trying to catch a fish with a pole, string, and a hook. (p. 114)

fit (fĭt) *adj.* healthy and in good physical shape. **GSL** (p. 132)

fitness (fĭt′ nĭs) *n.* good health and physical shape. (p. 132)

fixing (fĭk′ sĭng) *v.* repairing something that is broken. **GSL** (p. 88)

flag (flăg) *n.* a piece of cloth with colors and patterns that is the symbol of a group or country. **GSL** (p. 160)

flat (flăt) *adj.* having a level surface without slopes or hills. **GSL** (p. 112)

flexible (flek′ sə bəl) *adj.* able to bend easily. (p. 132)

flight (flīt) *n.* the trip an airplane takes to carry people somewhere. (p. 120)

flip (flĭp) *v.* turn over in the air. (p. 144)

float (flōt) *v.* held up by water. **GSL** (p. 256)

floating (flō′ tĭng) *v.* being held up by water. (p. 114)

floor (flôr) *n.* the surface you walk on inside a building. **GSL** (p. 90)

flow (flō) *v.* move smoothly and steadily like liquid. **GSL** (p. 204)

flower (flou′ ər) *n.* a blossom of a plant. **GSL** (p. 138)

flu (floo) *n.* an illness in which you get a high fever, chills, and muscle aches. (p. 58)

fluid ounce a unit of volume. (p. 176)

fly (flī) *v.* operate an airplane. **Dolch, GSL** (p. 66)

flying (flī ĭng) *v.* moving through the air. (p. 122)

follow (fŏl′ ō) **1.** *v.* do something according to instructions. (p. 108) **2.** *v.* come after. (p. 152) **GSL**

followed by having something come after. (p. 146)

food (food) *n.* what living things eat to stay alive. **GSL** (p. 116)

food chain a system in nature where living things stay alive by eating other living things. (p. 228)

foot (') (foot) *n.* a unit of length equal to 12 inches (plural is *feet*). **GSL** (p. 172)

football (foot′ bôl′) *n.* a sport in which 2 teams try to carry a ball to their end of a field without being stopped by the other team. (p. 124)

for (fôr) *prep.* used to indicate a purpose. **Dolch, GSL** (p. 60)

for example as a manner of demonstration. (p. 162)

force (fôrs) *n.* applied pressure. **GSL** (p. 252)

forced (fôrsd) *v.* made happen against one's will. (p. 188)

forecast (fôr′ kăst′) *n.* a weather prediction. (p. 80)

forefather (fôr′ fä′ thər) *n.* an ancestor. (p. 140)

forest (fôr′ ĭst) *n.* a large area covered with trees and plants. **GSL** (p. 162)

forever (fôr ĕv′ ər) *adv.* for a time without end; always. (p. 246)

forget (fər gĕt′) *v.* can't remember. **GSL** (p. 240)

fork (fôrk) *n.* a utensil with 2 or more prongs that is used for eating. **GSL** (p. 70)

form (fôrm) **1.** *v.* make or produce. (p. 154, 194) **2.** *n.* a type or kind. (p. 254) **GSL**

formal (fôr′ məl) *adj.* polite and serious. **GSL** (p. 196)

formed by made by. (p. 146)

forward (fôr′ wərd) *adj.* going towards the front. **GSL** (p. 202)

fossil fuel petroleum, coal, and natural gas. (p. 254)

fought (fôt) *v.* battled with physical force (present tense is *fight*). (p. 138)

fouls (foulz) *v.* makes dirty. (p. 180)

found (found) *v.* located (present tense is *find*). **Dolch** (p. 64)

founded (foun′ dəd) *v.* established or set up. (p. 140)

fourth (4th) (fôrth) *adj.* representing 4 in a series. (p. 52)

foxes (fŏk′ səs) *n.* small, doglike animals with bushy tails (singular is *fox*). (p. 194)

fraction (frăk′ shən) *n.* a way to show part of a whole, such as $\frac{1}{4}$. (p. 148)

free (frē) **1.** *adj.* spare or extra. (p. 88) **2.** *adj.* not controlled; being at liberty. (p. 188) **GSL**

freedom (frē′ dəm) *n.* the state of being free; liberty. **GSL** (p. 238)

freezing (frē′ zĭng) *adj.* very cold. **GSL** (p. 80)

fresh (frĕsh) *adj.* recently grown and harvested. **GSL** (p. 130)

fresh water (frĕsh′ wô′ tər) water that is not salty. (p. 114)

friend (frĕnd) *n.* someone with whom you like to spend time. **GSL** (p. 38)

friendly (frĕnd′ lē) *adj.* nice and polite. **GSL** (p. 92)

from (frŭm) *prep.* used to show where something started. **Dolch, GSL** (p. 42)

front (frŭnt) *n.* the area located before or ahead of something. **GSL** (p. 90)

front-end digit the first number in a figure or sum. (p. 198)

frowning (frou′nĭng) *v.* turning down the corners of your mouth to show unhappiness. (p. 92)

fruit (froot) *n.* the sweet part of a seed-bearing plant that is eaten. **GSL** (p. 68)

full (fool) *adj.* having no room left. **Dolch, GSL** (p. 48)

fun (fŭn) *adj.* enjoyable to do. **GSL** (p. 88)

function (fŭngk′ shən) *n.* what something does; its purpose. (p. 232)

funny (fŭn′ ē) *adj.* causing laughter; amusing. **Dolch, GSL** (p. 92)

fur (fûr) *n.* the short hair that covers the body of an animal. **GSL** (p. 188)

G

gallon (găl′ ən) *n.* a unit of volume that is equal to 4 quarts. **GSL** (p. 176)

gap (găp) *n.* a space between two things. **GSL** (p. 128)

garage (gə räzh′) *n.* a structure where cars are kept. **GSL** (p. 90)

garbage (gär′ bĭj) *n.* things that are thrown away; waste. (p. 180)

garbage can the container into which garbage is put. (p. 182)

garden (gär′ dn) *n.* an area where plants and flowers are grown by people. **GSL** (p. 84)

gardener (gärd′ nər) *n.* a person who grows plants and flowers. (p. 66)

gas (găs) *n.* a state of matter that is not a solid or a liquid. **GSL** (p. 108)

gases (găs′ əs) *n.* the plural form of *gas*. See *gas*. **GSL** (p. 158)

gas station a place to fill your car with gasoline. (p. 64)

gather (gă*th*′ ər) *v.* collect. **GSL** (p. 126, 186)

gave (gāv) *v.* made a present of (present tense is *give*). **Dolch** (p. 74)

gear (gîr) *n.* a wheel with teeth along the edge that mesh with teeth from other wheels to make a machine work. (p. 252)

geese (gēs) *n.* large water birds that look like swans but have shorter necks (singular is *goose*). (p. 78)

generation (jĕn′ ĕ rā shən) *n.* a group of people born and living about the same time. (p. 116)

generous (jĕn′ ər əs) *adj.* very giving and willing to share. **GSL** (p. 92)

geography (jē ŏg′ rə fē) *n.* the study of Earth's surface. (p. 164)

germs (jûrms) *n.* tiny bacteria that make you sick. (p. 134)

get (gĕt) *v.* receive. **Dolch, GSL** (p. 44)

gets rid of disposes of. (p. 206)

girl (gûrl) *n.* a young female. **GSL** (p. 38)

give (gĭv) *v.* place in the hands of; pass. **Dolch, GSL** (p. 44)

give me a hand an idiom that means "help me." (p. 196)

give out make known. (p. 170)

give up stop trying. (p. 222)

given (gĭv′ ən) *v.* past participle of *give*. See *give*. (p. 166)

gives off sends forth; emits. (p. 158)

glad (glăd) *adj.* pleased. **GSL** (p. 118)

glass (glăs) **1.** *n.* a cup for drinking made out of glass. (p. 70) **2.** *n.* a breakable material that's used to make many things, from bottles to windows. (p. 182) **GSL**

glasses (glăs′əs) *n.* a pair of lenses in a frame that you wear on your face to see better. **GSL** (p. 194)

globe (glōb) *n.* a map of the earth shaped like a ball. (p. 236)

glossary (glô′ sə rē) *n.* a list of words and their definitions found in the back of a book. (p. 120)

glove (glŭv) *n.* a fitted covering for your hand. (p. 106)

go (gō) *v.* move or proceed. **Dolch, GSL** (p. 44)

go between go in the middle of. (p. 146)

goes (gōz) *v.* proceeds. **Dolch** (p. 62)

goes after is put after. (p. 120)

goes before is put before. (p. 120)

goes between is put between. (p. 120)

goes on continues. (p. 246)

goggles (gŏg′ əlz) *n.* a pair of tight-fitting eyeglasses worn to protect your eyes. (p. 106)

going (gō′ ĭng) **1.** *v.* will happen in the future. (p. 80) **2.** *v.* taking a trip. (p. 84) **Dolch**

gold (gōld) *n.* a yellow element that is considered valuable. **GSL** (p. 188)

good (gŏŏd) *adj.* positive or happy. **Dolch, GSL** (p. 40)

goodbye (gŏŏd bī′) *interj.* what you say when you are leaving someone. (p. 40)

goods (gŏŏdz) *n.* products to be bought or sold. (p. 234)

got (gŏt) *v.* received (past tense of *get*). **Dolch** (p. 58)

govern (gŭv′ ərn) *v.* rule or lead. **GSL** (p. 238)

grade (grād) *n.* a mark of how well you did in a class or on a test. (p. 152)

graduate (grăj′ ŏŏ āt′) *v.* receive a diploma or degree for finishing school. (p. 98)

grain (grān) *n.* the seed from grasses, such as wheat or rice. **GSL** (p. 178)

gram (g) (grăm) *n.* a metric unit of weight that is equal to one thousandth of a kilogram. (p. 174)

grammar (grăm′ ər) *n.* a system of rules for language. **GSL** (p. 242)

Grand Canyon *n.* a large canyon located in the western United States. (p. 164)

grandchildren (grănd′ chĭl′ drən) *n.* the children of your child (singular is *grandchild*). (p. 116)

grandparent (grănd′ pâr′ ənt) *n.* a parent of one of your parents. (p. 86)

grass (grăs) *n.* the thin green leaves covering the ground that make a lawn. **GSL** (p. 112)

great (grāt) *adj.* very good. **GSL** (p. 40)

greater (grāt′ ər) *adj.* larger in value. (p. 78)

greatest (grāt′ əst) *adj.* largest. (p. 52)

greedy (grē′ dē) *adj.* taking more than you need or deserve. **GSL** (p. 244)

grew (grōō) *v.* planted and harvested (present tense is *grow*). (p. 190)

grid (grĭd) *n.* a chart made of horizontal and vertical lines crossing each other. (p. 152)

grocery (grō′ sə rē) *adj.* about the type of store that sells food and other household needs. (p. 68)

ground (ground) *n.* the solid surface of the earth that we walk on. **GSL** (p. 154)

grow (grō) *v.* become bigger. **Dolch, GSL** (p. 66)

grow up become an adult. (p. 230)

guarantee (găr′ ən tē′) *v.* promise. (p. 238)

guess (gĕs) *v.* answer without having enough information. **GSL** (p. 102)

guide (gīd) *v.* direct. **GSL** (p. 122)

guide word a word at the top of the page in a dictionary or glossary that tells you the first and last words on that page. (p. 166)

guilty (gĭl′ tē) *adj.* responsible for having done something wrong. **GSL** (p. 214)

Gulf of Mexico *n.* a part of the Atlantic Ocean that is between eastern Mexico and the southeastern United States. (p. 164)

gym (jĭm) **1.** *n.* a room in school used for athletic activities. (p. 46) **2.** *adj.* the type of class in school also known as physical education.(p. 48)

gymnast (jĭm′ năst′) *n.* a person who is trained and skilled at gymnastics. (p. 144)

habit (hăb′ ĭt) *n.* something you do so often that you do it without even thinking. **GSL** (p. 130)

had (hăd) *v.* was in possession of (present tense is *have*). **Dolch** (p. 74)

half gallon a unit of volume equal to 2 quarts. (p. 176)

hall (hôl) *n.* a long, narrow walkway; corridor. **GSL** (p. 46)

Halloween (hăl′ ə wēn′) a holiday on October 31st when you dress up in costumes. (p. 138)

halves (hăvz) *n.* plural of *half*. (p. 236)

hammer (hăm′ ər) *n.* a tool used for driving nails into a surface. **GSL** (p. 208)

hand (hănd) *n.* the part of your body attached to your wrist that has 5 fingers. **GSL** (p. 106)

hand in give to your teacher. (p. 146)

hand out give out to a class. (p. 146)

handsome (hăn′ səm) *adj.* attractive, for a man. (p. 86)

handwriting (hănd′ rī′ tĭng) *n.* writing done by hand. **GSL** (p. 242)

hang (hăng) *v.* fasten or suspend from above. **GSL** (p. 140)

happened (hăp′ ənd) *v.* occurred. (past tense of *happen*). **GSL** (p. 60)

happy (hăp′ ē) *adj.* in a good mood; glad. **GSL** (p. 94)

hard (härd) *adj.* stiff and solid. **GSL** (p. 112)

harm (härm) *v.* do damage; hurt. **GSL** (p. 180)

harmful (härm′ fəl) *adj.* causing damage or injury. (p. 134)

harvest (här′ vĭst) *v.* gather a crop. **GSL** (p. 178)

has (hăz) *v.* third-person form of *have*. **Dolch** (p. 56)

hate (hāt) *v.* strongly dislike. **GSL** (p. 72)

have (hăv) *v.* experience. **Dolch, GSL** (p. 40)

hay (hā) *n.* a dried grass fed to cows and horses. **GSL** (p. 178)

he (hē) *pron.* refers to a male. **Dolch, GSL** (p. 40)

headache (hĕd′ āk′) *n.* a feeling of pain in your head. **GSL** (p. 56)

heading (hĕd′ ĭng) *n.* a title that tells you the subject of a paper. (p. 220)

health (hĕlth) *n.* your physical and mental condition. **GSL** (p. 58)

healthy (hĕl′ thē) *adj.* in good physical and mental condition. (p. 130)

hear (hîr) *v.* listen to. **GSL** (p. 118)

heard (hûrd) *v.* past tense form of *hear*. See *hear*. (p. 82)

hearing (hîr′ ĭng) *n.* the ability to hear. **GSL** (p. 208)

heart (härt) *n.* the organ that pumps blood to all areas of your body. **GSL** (p. 204)

heartbeat (härt′ bēt′) *n.* the pulse of your heart pumping blood. (p. 204)

heavier (hĕv′ ē ər) *adj.* more heavy. (p. 174)

heavy (hĕv′ ē) *adj.* weighing a lot. **GSL** (p. 86, 174)

height (hīt) *n.* how tall someone or something is. **GSL** (p. 128)

hello (hĕ lō′) *interj.* what you say to greet someone. **GSL** (p. 40)

helmet (hĕl′ mĭt) *n.* a hard hat you wear on your head to protect it. (p. 132)

help (hĕlp) *v.* give assistance. **Dolch, GSL** (p. 60)

hemisphere (hĕm′ ĭ sfîr′) *n.* one half of the earth. (p. 236)

her (hûr) **1.** *adj.* possessive form of *she*. (p. 40) **2.** *pron.* the objective form of *she*. (p. 46) **Dolch**

herd (hûrd) *n.* a group of cattle or other livestock. (p. 178)

here (hîr) *adv.* at or in this place. **Dolch, GSL** (p. 44)

herself (hûr sĕlf′) *pron.* refers to her own self. (p. 96)

hexagon (hĕk′ sə gŏn′) *n.* a polygon with 6 sides. (p. 250)

hide (hīd) *n.* the removed skin and hair of an animal. **GSL** (p. 186)

higher (hī′ ər) *adj.* larger in number. (p. 150)

highest (hī′ əst) *adj.* largest in number. (p. 128)

hill (hĭl) *n.* a large mound of earth that is smaller than a mountain. **GSL** (p. 112)

him (hĭm) *pron.* objective form of *he*. **Dolch** (p. 46)

himself (hĭm sĕlf′) *pron.* refers to his own self. (p. 96)

his (hĭz) *pron.* possessive form of *he*. **Dolch** (p. 40)

historic (hĭ stôr′ ĭk) *adj.* having importance in history. (p. 136)

history (hĭs′ tə rē) *n.* the study of past events. **GSL** (p. 48)

hit the books an idiom that means *study*. (p. 196)

hobby (hŏb′ ē) *n.* an activity you do for fun. (p. 88)

hockey (hŏk′ ē) *n.* a team sport played on ice. (p. 124)

hold (hōld) *v.* contain. **Dolch, GSL** (p. 76, 176)

hold on refuse to release or let go. (p. 160)

holiday (hŏl′ ĭ dā′) *n.* a day of the year on which you celebrate an event or person. **GSL** (p. 138)

honor (ŏn′ ər) *v.* treat or remember with respect. **GSL** (p. 136)

horizontal (hôr' ĭ zŏn' tl) *adj.* going across, not up and down. **GSL** (p. 246)

hospital (hŏs' pĭ tl) *n.* the place where sick or injured people are taken to get well. **GSL** (p. 60)

hot (hŏt) *adj.* very warm; having a high temperature. **Dolch, GSL** (p. 80)

hottest (hŏt' əst) *adj.* having the highest temperature. (p. 224)

hour (our) *n.* an amount of time equal to 60 minutes. **GSL** (p. 100)

house (hous) **1.** *n.* a building that people live in. (p. 42) **2.** *n.* the 2 parts of the legislative branch of the U.S. government. (p. 210) **GSL**

House of Representatives *n.* one of the houses of Congress. (p. 210)

how (hou) *adv.* in what state or condition. **Dolch, GSL** (p. 40)

huge (hyo͞oj) *adj.* very large. (p. 166)

hugged (hŭgd) *v.* put your arms around someone and squeezed; embraced (present tense is *hug*). (p. 244)

human (hyo͞o' mən) *n.* a person. **GSL** (p. 156)

human being a person. (p. 230)

humid (hyo͞o' mĭd) *adj.* wet, damp, or moist. (p. 162)

hundred (hŭn' drĭd) *adj.* the number 100. (p. 152)

hundreds (hŭn' drĭdz) *adj.* represents the third place from the right in a place value. (p. 50)

hundredth (hŭn' drĭdth) *n.* a number that represents 1 of 100 parts. (p. 150)

hunted (hŭntd) *v.* chased for food or sport. **GSL** (p. 186)

hunter (hŭn' tər) *n.* someone or something who kills an animal for food or sport. (p. 228)

hurricane (hûr' ĭ kān') *n.* a storm with winds faster than 74 mph. (p. 82)

hurry (hûr' ē) *v.* go quickly. **GSL** (p. 48)

hurt (hûrt) *v.* got an injury. **Dolch, GSL** (p. 56)

hygiene (hī' jēn') *n.* the practice of keeping yourself clean and healthy. (p. 134)

I (ī) *pron.* refers to oneself. **Dolch, GSL** (p. 38)

idea (ī dē' ə) *n.* a thought. **GSL** (p. 220)

ideal (ī dēl') *n.* a goal. **GSL** (p. 160)

identify (ī dĕn' tə fī') *v.* recognize. (p. 144)

idiom (ĭd' ē əm) *n.* a phrase or expression having a special meaning. (p. 196)

if (ĭf) *conj.* in the event that. **Dolch, GSL** (p. 80)

ignore (ĭg nôr') *v.* to not pay attention. (p. 222)

ill (ĭl) *adj.* sick. **GSL** (p. 56)

illegal (ĭ lē' gəl) *adj.* against the law; not legal. (p. 214)

illustrate (ĭl' ə strāt') *v.* draw something in order to explain. (p. 126)

imaginary (ĭ măj' ə nĕr' ē) *adj.* fake or made-up; not real. **GSL** (p. 244)

immigrant (ĭm' ĭ grənt) *n.* someone who has moved to one country from another country. (p. 160)

imperative (ĭm pĕr' ə tĭv) *adj.* about the type of sentence that tells you what to do. (p. 218)

important (ĭm pôr' tnt) *adj.* having great value or significance. **GSL** (p. 220)

improve (ĭm pro͞ov') *v.* make better. **GSL** (p. 238)

in (ĭn) *prep.* during. **Dolch** (p. 98)

in case in the event of. (p. 106)

in general usually. (p. 122)

in order in the correct arrangement. (p. 150)

in shape physically fit. (p. 132)

in the same boat an idiom that means *in the same situation.* (p. 196)

in your head an idiom that means to figure something out by thinking about it. (p. 202)

inch (") (ĭnch) *n.* a unit of length equal to $\frac{1}{12}$ of a foot. **GSL** (p. 172)

include (ĭn klōōd′) *v.* take in as a part. **GSL** (p. 144)

incomplete (ĭn′ kəm plēt′) *adj.* unfinished; not complete. (p. 144)

incorrect (ĭn′ kə rĕkt′) *adj.* wrong; not correct. (p. 78)

incorrectly (ĭn′ kə rĕkt′ lē) *adv.* not done correctly. (p. 242)

increase (ĭn krēs′) *v.* become more. **GSL** (p. 204)

indent (ĭn dĕnt′) *v.* set the first line of a paragraph farther in from the margin. (p. 242)

independence (ĭn′ dĭ pĕn′ dəns) *n.* freedom. (p. 140)

Independence Day *n.* a holiday on July 4th to celebrate the United States' independence as a nation. (p. 138)

Indian (ĭn′ dē ən) *n.* a name often used for a Native American. (p. 186)

industry (ĭn′ də strē) *n.* business. **GSL** (p. 234)

infant (ĭn′ fənt) *n.* a baby. (p. 174)

inform (ĭn fôrm′) *v.* tell or let know. **GSL** (p. 216)

informal (ĭn fôr′ məl) *adj.* not formal; friendly. (p. 196)

information (ĭn′ fər mā′ shən) *n.* a collection of facts or data. (p. 124)

ingredient (ĭn grē′ dē ənt) *n.* what goes into a prepared food. (p. 130)

initial (ĭ nĭsh′ əl) *n.* the first letter of a word that is used by itself to represent that word. (p. 224)

injury (ĭn′ jə rē) *n.* a place on your body that you've hurt. (p. 60)

inner (ĭn′ ər) *adj.* on the inside of. (p. 256)

innocent (ĭn′ ə sənt) *adj.* didn't do anything wrong. (p. 214)

insect (ĭn′ sĕkt′) *n.* a bug. **GSL** (p. 156)

inside (ĭn sīd′) *n.* a house or building. **GSL** (p. 80)

instead of rather than. **GSL** (p. 194)

integer (ĭn′ tĭ jər) *n.* a positive or negative whole number, or zero. (p. 224)

interact (ĭn′ tər ăkt′) *v.* act with each other. (p. 156)

interest (ĭn′ trĭst) *n.* a state of curiosity about something. **GSL** (p. 220)

interesting (ĭn′ trĭ stĭng) *adj.* being of interest. (p. 144)

interjection (ĭn′ tər jĕk′ shən) *n.* a part of speech that expresses emotion and is able to stand alone. (p. 142)

Internet (ĭn′ tər nĕt′) *n.* a system of networks that connects computers all over the world. (p. 170)

interpret (ĭn tûr′ prĭt) *v.* find the meaning of. (p. 196)

interrogative (ĭn′ tə rŏg′ ə tĭv) *adj.* about the type of sentence that asks a question. (p. 218)

intersect (ĭn′ tər sĕkt′) *v.* cross. (p. 246)

intersecting (ĭn′ tər sĕk′ tĭng) *v.* crossing. (p. 246)

intersection (ĭn′ tər sĕk′ shən) *n.* the place where two lines cross. (p. 246)

intestine (ĭn tĕs′ tĭn) *n.* the organ in your body that helps you digest food and absorb its nutrients. (p. 206)

into (ĭn′ tōō) *prep.* inside of. **Dolch, GSL** (p. 76)

introduce (ĭn′ trə dōōs′) *v.* provide with a beginning. **GSL** (p. 220)

invite (ĭn vīt′) *v.* ask someone to come. **GSL** (p. 190)

irregular (ĭ rĕg′ yĕ lər) *adj.* about a verb with a root spelling that changes when the form of the verb changes. (p. 194)

is (ĭz) *v.* third-person singular form of *be*. See *be*. **Dolch** (p. 38)

is equal to (=) is the same as. (p. 226)

island (ī′ lənd) *n.* an area of land surrounded by water on all sides. **GSL** (p. 112)

it (ĭt) *pron.* used to refer to something already mentioned. **Dolch, GSL** (p. 40)

item (ī′ təm) *n.* a thing. (p. 198)

its (ĭts) *adj.* of or belonging to the thing just mentioned. **Dolch** (p. 102)

itself (ĭt sĕlf′) *pron.* the one the same as it. (p. 200)

J

jail (jāl) *n.* the place where criminals are put when they break the law. (p. 214)

jar (jär) *n.* a glass container with a lid. (p. 182)

jeans (jēnz) *n.* denim pants. (p. 72)

jelly (jĕl′ ē) *n.* a shapeless, sticky, semi-solid mass. (p. 232)

job (jŏb) *n.* what someone does to make money. (p. 66)

jog (jŏg) *v.* run at a slow, steady pace. (p. 132)

join (join) *v.* bring together. **GSL** (p. 142)

joke (jōk) *n.* something said to make people laugh. **GSL** (p. 92)

judge (jŭj) *n.* a person who hears and decides cases brought before a court of law. **GSL** (p. 214)

judicial (jōō dĭsh′ əl) *adj.* having to do with a court of law. (p. 214)

juice (jōōs) *n.* the liquid squeezed from fruit that is served as a drink. **GSL** (p. 68)

jumping (jŭm′ pĭng) *v.* springing off the ground using your legs and feet. **GSL** (p. 88)

jury (jŏor′ ē) *n.* the group of people who listen to a criminal trial and decide the verdict. (p. 214)

just (jŭst) *adv.* only. **Dolch, GSL** (p. 78)

justice (jŭs′ tĭs) **1.** *adj.* being fair. (p. 214) **2.** *n.* a judge. (p. 214) **GSL**

K

keep (kēp) *v.* make sure that something is continued. **Dolch, GSL** (p. 66)

key word a general word about what you're researching that you type into a search engine. (p. 170)

keyboard (kē′ bôrd′) *n.* the part of the computer with keys on which you type. (p. 104)

kill (kĭl) *v.* to cause the death of. **GSL** (p. 134)

kilogram (kg) (kĭl′ ə grăm′) *n.* a unit of weight equal to 1,000 grams. (p. 174)

kilometer (km) (kĭ lŏm′ ĭ tər) *n.* a unit of length equal to 1,000 meters. (p. 172)

kind (kīnd) **1.** *adj.* nice. (p. 92) **2.** *n.* a particular type. (p. 218) **Dolch, GSL**

kitchen (kĭch′ ən) *n.* the room in a house used for cooking. **GSL** (p. 90)

knife (nīf) *n.* something with a sharp edge used to cut food. **GSL** (p. 70)

know (nō) *v.* be aware of. **Dolch, GSL** (p. 42)

knowledge (nŏl′ ĭj) *n.* the state of knowing. **GSL** (p. 240)

known (nōn) *v.* recognized (present tense is *know*). **GSL** (p. 222)

L

label (lā′ bəl) **1.** *n.* an item used to identify something. (p. 124) **2.** *v.* mark something so that it can be identified. (p. 164)

labor (lā′ bər) *n.* the work employees do. (p. 234)

ladder (lăd′ ər) *n.* a structure with 2 sides connected by a series of bars that's used to climb, in order to reach a higher place. **GSL** (p. 232)

lake (lāk) *n.* a large body of water smaller than an ocean. **GSL** (p. 114)

lamp (lămp) *n.* a device that makes light. **GSL** (p. 90)

land (lănd) **1.** *v.* come down from the air and rest on a surface. (p. 144) **2.** *n.* the ground. (p. 180) **GSL**

landfill (lănd′ fĭl′) *n.* the place where everyone's garbage is put. (p. 182)

landform (lănd′ fôrm′) *n.* one of the features that makes up Earth's surface, such as a mountain or a canyon. (p. 164)

language (lăng′ gwĭj) *n.* communication through words. **GSL** (p. 196)

large (lärj) *adj.* big. **GSL** (p. 72)

last (lăst) *adj.* at the end of; final. **GSL** (p. 98)

last name the word or words by which a person is known that's passed down by family. (p. 120)

late (lāt) *adj.* arriving after you are supposed to. **GSL** (p. 48)

Latino (lə tē′ nō) *n.* a person with Latin American roots. (p. 160)

latitude (lăt′ ĭ tood′) *n.* a geographic distance measured north and south. (p. 236)

laughing (lăf ĭng) *v.* making happy sounds. **Dolch, GSL** (p. 92)

lava (lä′ və) *n.* the red hot liquid that comes out of volcanoes. (p. 256)

law (lô) *n.* a rule made by the government. **GSL** (p. 210)

lawyer (lô′ yər) *n.* someone who defends or prosecutes a person in a court of law. **GSL** (p. 214)

layer (lā′ ər) *n.* a single thickness of something. (p. 256)

lead (lēd) *v.* be in charge of; govern. **GSL** (p. 212)

learn (lûrn) *v.* gain knowledge. **GSL** (p. 108)

learned (lûrnd) *v.* past tense form of *learn*. See *learn*. **GSL** (p. 244)

least (lēst) *adj.* smallest. **GSL** (p. 52)

least common multiple the smallest number into which 2 or more numbers can be divided. (p. 200)

leather (lĕth′ ər) *n.* the dried skin of a cow used to make things, such as clothing. **GSL** (p. 178)

leave (lēv) *v.* have as a remainder. **GSL** (p. 74)

leaves (lēvz) *n.* the things that cover the branches of trees (singular is *leaf*). (p. 84)

left (lĕft) **1.** *adj.* located in the direction opposite right. (p. 64) **2.** *v.* remaining. (p. 74) **GSL**

left over remaining. (p. 76)

legend (lĕj′ ənd) *n.* a key that tells you what the marks on a map mean. (p. 164)

legislative (lĕj′ ĭ slā′ tĭv) *adj.* relating to the making of laws. (p. 210)

length (ləngkth) *n.* how long something is. **GSL** (p. 172)

less (lĕs) *adj.* smaller in number. **GSL** (p. 78)

lesson (lĕs′ ən) *n.* something important to be learned. **GSL** (p. 244)

let (lĕt) *v.* allow. **Dolch, GSL** (p. 60)

let out allow something to come out. (p. 256)

letter (lĕt′ ər) **1.** *n.* a message written and sent to someone. (p. 96) **2.** *n.* a symbol that represents a sound in a language. Letters are put together to make words. (p. 118) **GSL**

lever (lĕv′ ər) *n.* a handle to help you lift an object. (p. 252)

librarian (lī brâr′ ē ən) *n.* a person who works in a library. **GSL** (p. 168)

library (lī′ brĕr′ ē) *n.* a building where books are kept for people to borrow. **GSL** (p. 46)

library card a card given to you by the library that allows you to borrow books. (p. 168)

Library of Congress *n.* a huge government library. (p. 136)

lies (līz) *v.* rests on. **GSL** (p. 250)

life (līf) *n.* the period of time between birth and death. **GSL** (p. 240)

lift (lĭft) *v.* pick up. **GSL** (p. 252)

light (līt) **1.** *n.* brightness. (p. 82) **2.** *adj.* doesn't weigh much. (p. 174) **Dolch, GSL**

lighter (lī′ tər) *adj.* weighs less. (p. 174)

lightning (līt′ nĭng) *n.* the bright flash of light you see during a storm. (p. 82)

like (līk) **1.** *v.* prefer. (p. 72) **2.** *prep.* similar to. (p. 118) **Dolch, GSL**

limited (lĭm′ ĭ tĭd) *adj.* existing in an amount that has an end. **GSL** (p. 254)

Lincoln Memorial *n.* the building in Washington, D. C. built to honor Abraham Lincoln. (p. 136)

line (līn) *n.* a path of points. **GSL** (p. 246)

line plot a way to show a set of data. (p. 128)

line segment a line with a beginning and end. (p. 250)

line up *v.* make even columns. (p. 150)

link (lĭngk) **1.** *v.* connect. (p. 144) **2.** *n.* an Internet address that you can click on to take you to that site. (p. 170)

liquid (lĭk′ wĭd) **1.** *n.* a state of matter that is neither a solid nor a gas. (p. 176) **2.** *adj.* neither solid nor gas. (p. 256) **GSL**

list (lĭst) *n.* a group of written items. **GSL** (p. 68)

listed (lĭs′ tĭd) *v.* shown in a list. (p. 166)

listening (lĭs′ ə nĭng) *v.* hearing. **GSL** (p. 88)

liter (L) (lē′ tər) *n.* a metric unit of volume. (p. 176)

litter (lĭt′ ər) *v.* throw garbage on the ground. (p. 180)

little (lĭt′ l) *adj.* small. **Dolch** (p. 74)

little hand the hand on a clock that tells you the hour. (p. 100)

live (lĭv) *v.* have your home at; reside. **Dolch, GSL** (p. 42)

livestock (līv′ stŏk′) *n.* farm animals raised to make money, such as cows and horses. (p. 178)

living (lĭv′ ĭng) *adj.* alive. (p. 156)

living room a common room in a house used to relax or to entertain guests. (p. 90)

load (lōd) *n.* something you are carrying. **GSL** (p. 252)

loan (lōn) *v.* let someone borrow. **GSL** (p. 168)

located (lō′ kā′ tĭd) *v.* found in a particular place. (p. 136)

locker (lŏk′ ər) *n.* a small metal compartment at school that can be locked. (p. 46)

logging (lô′ gĭng) *n.* the practice of cutting down trees for wood. (p. 156)

lonely (lōn′ lē) *adj.* sad that you are alone. **GSL** (p. 94)

long (lông) *adj.* having a lot of length. **Dolch, GSL** (p. 86, 172)

long vowel a vowel with a long sound, such as the *a* in *cake*. (p. 118)

longer (lôn′gər) *adj.* having more length. **GSL** (p. 172)

longitude (lŏn′ jĭ tōōd′) *n.* a geographic distance measured east and west. (p. 236)

look (lŏŏk) **1.** *v.* appear. (p. 92) **2.** *v.* use the eyes to see. (p. 144) **Dolch, GSL**

look back check. (p. 222)

look for search for. (p. 102)

look up find information in a book. (p. 166)

loudly (loud′ lē) *adv.* in a way that makes a lot of noise. **GSL** (p. 192)

lower (lō′ ər) **1.** *adj.* less than. (p. 150) **2.** *v.* let down. (p. 252) **GSL**

lowercase (lō′ ər kās) *adj.* not capitalized. (p. 216)

lowest (lō′ əst) *adj.* least. (p. 128)

loyal (loi′ əl) *adj.* devoted. **GSL** (p. 238)

lumber (lŭm′ bər) *n.* wood. (p. 156)

lunch (lŭnch) *n.* the meal eaten in the afternoon. **GSL** (p. 70)

lunches (lŭn′ chəs) *n.* the plural form of *lunch*. See *lunch*. **GSL** (p. 194)

lungs (lŭngz) *n.* the organs used for breathing. **GSL** (p. 204)

Ⓜ

machine (mə shēn′) *n.* any device that makes work easier. **GSL** (p. 252)

made (mād) *v.* past tense form of *make*. See *make*. **Dolch** (p. 70)

magazine (măg′ ə zēn′) *n.* a collection of articles and pictures. (p. 168)

mail (māl) *n.* things received through the post office. **GSL** (p. 66)

mail carrier the person who delivers mail. (p. 66)

main (mān) *adj.* most important. **GSL** (p. 244)

main idea the most important idea. (p. 220)

major (mā′ jər) *adj.* large or important. (p. 162)

majority (mə jôr′ ĭ tē) *n.* more than half. (p. 124)

make (māk) *v.* prepare. **Dolch, GSL** (p. 70)

make sense is easy to understand. (p. 102)

make up resolve a fight. (p. 96)

male (māl) *n.* a man or boy. **GSL** (p. 230)

mall (môl) *n.* a large complex of stores. (p. 64)

manage (măn′ ĭj) *v.* direct or control as an authority. **GSL** (p. 212)

mantle (măn′ tl) *n.* the layer of Earth beneath its crust. (p. 256)

manufacture (măn′ yə făk′ chər) *v.* produce a product. (p. 234)

many (měn′ē) *adj.* large in quantity. **Dolch, GSL** (p. 68)

map (măp) *n.* a diagram of an area. **GSL** (p. 236)

mark (märk) *n.* a written symbol. **GSL** (p. 216)

market (mär′ kĭt) *n.* the place where goods are bought and sold. **GSL** (p. 234)

Martin Luther King, Jr., Day *n.* a holiday that honors the leader in the Civil Rights Movement. (p. 138)

mascot (măs′ kŏt′) *n.* a character representing a team. (p. 126)

mass (măs) *n.* the total amount of matter in something. **GSL** (p. 174)

material (mə tîr′ ē əl) *n.* a substance from which something can be made. **GSL** (p. 182)

math (măth) *n.* the study of numbers. (p. 48)

matter (măt′ ər) *n.* a problem. **GSL** (p. 56)

may (mā) *v.* be allowed to. **Dolch, GSL** (p. 46)

Mayflower (mā′ flou′ ər) *n.* the ship that carried the first Pilgrims to America. (p. 190)

me (mē) *pron.* referring to oneself. **Dolch** (p. 46)

meal (mēl) *n.* the food served and eaten at one time. **GSL** (p. 70)

mean (mēn) **1.** *adj.* not nice. (p. 92) **2.** *adj.* average. (p. 128) **3.** *v.* defined as. (p. 196) **GSL**

meaning (mē′ nĭng) *n.* a definition. (p. 166)

measure (mĕzh′ ər) **1.** *v.* find out how long something is. (p. 172) **2.** *n.* the length. (p. 248) **GSL**

measuring cup a cup with marks on it used for measuring. (p. 176)

meat (mēt) *n.* the flesh of an animal. **GSL** (p. 178)

meat-eater *n.* an animal that eats flesh; carnivore. (p. 228)

median (mē′ dē ən) *n.* the middle number. (p. 128)

medicine (měd′ ĭ sĭn) *n.* drugs given to sick people to make them feel better. **GSL** (p. 58)

meet (mēt) *v.* be introduced to someone. **GSL** (p. 38)

melt (mĕlt) *v.* change from a solid to a liquid. **GSL** (p. 256)

member (měm′ bər) *n.* someone who is part of a group. **GSL** (p. 186)

membrane (mĕm′ brān′) *n.* a thin covering of a cell. (p. 232)

memorial (mə môr′ ē əl) *n.* something done to remember a person or event. (p. 136)

memories (mĕm′ ə rēz) *n.* things you remember (singular is *memory*). (p. 116)

memorize (mĕm′ ə rīz′) *v.* make yourself remember something. (p. 194)

memory (mĕm′ ə rē) *n.* something that's remembered. **GSL** (p. 136)

mental math math you do in your head. (p. 198)

mentally (mĕn′ tl lē) *adv.* done in one's head. (p. 198)

mess around an idiom that means act in a playful, non-serious way. (p. 196)

message (mĕs′ ĭj) *n.* a note. **GSL** (p. 96)

messy (mĕs′ ē) *adj.* dirty or disorderly. (p. 90)

met (mĕt) *v.* past tense form of *meet*. See *meet*. (p. 190)

metal (mĕt′ l) *n.* a hard substance found in the earth. **GSL** (p. 256)

meter (m) (mē′ tər) *n.* a unit of length that is equal to 100 centimeters. (p. 172)

method (mĕth′ əd) *n.* a way to do something. (p. 222)

metric (mĕt′ rĭk) *adj.* belonging to a 10-based system of measurement. (p. 176)

metric ton a unit of weight equal to 1,000 kilograms. (p. 174)

Mexico (mĕk′ sĭ kō′) *n.* a country in North America that is south of the United States. (p. 164)

microscope (mī′ krə skōp′) *n.* an instrument used to see things that are too small to see with only your eyes. (p. 232)

middle (mĭd′ l) *adj.* center. **GSL** (p. 128)

midnight (mĭd′ nīt′) *n.* 12:00 a.m. (p. 100)

Midwest (mĭd wĕst′) *n.* a region of the north-central United States. (p. 162)

might (mīt) *v.* could possibly happen. **GSL** (p. 222)

migrated (mī′ grāt ĭd) *v.* came from one part of the country to another. (p. 190)

mild (mīld) *adj.* not hot or cold. **GSL** (p. 162)

mile (mīl) *n.* a unit of length equal to 5,280 feet. **GSL** (p. 172)

military (mĭl′ ĭ tĕr′ ē) *n.* armed forces. (p. 212)

milk (mĭlk) *n.* the white liquid we drink that usually comes from cows. **GSL** (p. 68)

milliliter (ml) (mĭl′ ə lē′ tər) *n.* a unit of length equal to one thousandth of a liter. (p. 176)

millimeter (mm) (mĭl′ ə mē′ tər) *n.* a unit of length equal to one thousandth of a meter. (p. 172)

mind (mīnd) *n.* the focus of your thoughts and ideas. **GSL** (p. 94)

minus (−) (mī′ nəs) *v.* take away. (p. 74)

minute (mĭn′ ĭt) *n.* a unit of time equal to 60 seconds. **GSL** (p. 100)

missing addend in algebra, the unknown quantity that needs to be solved. (p. 226)

Mississippi River *n.* a huge river in the United States. (p. 164)

misspell (mĭs spĕl′) *v.* spell incorrectly. (p. 122)

mistake (mĭ stāk′) *n.* an error. **GSL** (p. 242)

mix (mĭks) *v.* blend together. **GSL** (p. 108)

mixture (mĭks′ chər) *n.* the result of mixing things together. **GSL** (p. 160)

moccasin (mŏk′ ə sĭn) *n.* a soft shoe worn by Native Americans. (p. 186)

mode (mōd) *n.* the number occurring most often in a series. (p. 128)

molecule (mŏl′ ĭ kyool′) *n.* a tiny particle that makes up matter. (p. 232)

moment (mō′ mənt) *n.* a very short length of time. **GSL** (p. 122)

monitor (mŏn′ ĭ tər) *n.* a computer device that displays information on a screen. (p. 104)

month (mŭnth) *n.* a unit of time equal to about 30 days. **GSL** (p. 98)

mood (mōod) *n.* the way you feel. (p. 94)

moon (mōon) *n.* a body in space that revolves around Earth. **GSL** (p. 158)

more (môr) *adj.* larger in quantity. **GSL** (p. 52)

morning (môr′ nĭng) *n.* the early part of the day. **GSL** (p. 40)

most (mōst) *adj.* largest in quantity. **GSL** (p. 52)

mother (mŭth′ ər) *n.* the woman who gave birth to you. **GSL** (p. 86)

motherhood (mŭth′ ər hŏod′) *n.* the state of being a mother. **GSL** (p. 230)

motion (mō′ shən) *n.* the act of moving. **GSL** (p. 252)

motor (mō′ tər) *n.* an engine. **GSL** (p. 252)

mountain (moun′ tən) *n.* a natural mound in the earth much larger than a hill. **GSL** (p. 112)

mouse (mous) *n.* a device attached to a computer that allows you to move the pointer on the screen. **GSL** (p. 104)

mouth (mouth) *n.* the opening on the face that's used to eat and speak. **GSL** (p. 206)

move (mōov) *v.* carry from one place or position to another. **GSL** (p. 252)

moves over in math, goes to another number's place. (p. 152)

movie theater a place where people pay to see a movie on a large screen. (p. 64)

much (mŭch) **1.** *n.* an amount. (p. 54) **2.** *adj.* the size of an amount. (p. 68) **Dolch, GSL**

multicellular (mŭl′ tē sĕl′ yə lər) *adj.* having many cells. (p. 232)

multiple (mŭl′ tə pəl) **1.** *n.* a number that can be divided by another number with no remainder. (p. 200) **2.** *adj.* many. (p. 232)

multiplication (mŭl′ tə plĭ kā′ shən) *n.* a kind of math in which a number is added to itself a certain number of times. **GSL** (p. 202)

multiply (mŭl′ tə plī′) *v.* add a number to itself a certain number of times. **GSL** (p. 76)

muscle (mŭs′ əl) *n.* the tissue around the bones that gives the body strength and the ability to move. (p. 132)

museum (myōo zē′ əm) *n.* a place where art or other objects are kept for people to see. (p. 64)

mushroom (mŭsh′ rōom′) *n.* a fungus that consists of a stem and a cap. (p. 228)

music (myōo′ zĭk) *n.* arranged sound into a steady, unified rhythm. **GSL** (p. 116)

must (mŭst) *v.* need to. **Dolch, GSL** (p. 60)

my (mī) *pron.* belonging to me. **Dolch** (p. 38)

myself (mī sĕlf′) *pron.* that one identical to me. **Dolch** (p. 56)

myth (mĭth) *n.* something people often think is true, but is not. (p. 244)

N

name (nām) **1.** *n.* what a person is called. (p. 38) **2.** *v.* describe. (p. 142) **GSL**

named after given a name because it was the name of someone important. (p. 136)

napkin (năp′ kĭn) *n.* a piece of paper or cloth that you use to wipe your mouth while eating. (p. 70)

nation (nā′ shən) *n.* a country. **GSL** (p. 160)

national (năsh′ ə nəl) *adj.* relating to a nation. (p. 140)

national park land declared public property by the government. (p. 164)

native (nā′ tĭv) *adj.* originally from an area. **GSL** (p. 160)

Native Americans *n.* the people who lived in North America first; Indians. (p. 190)

natural (năch′ ər əl) *adj.* grown in nature; not artificial. (p. 130)

natural gas a fossil fuel. (p. 254)

nature (nā′chər) *n.* the environment. **GSL** (p. 186)

near (nēr) *adj.* close. **GSL** (p. 62)

nearest hundred when rounding, it's the closest number that is a multiple of one hundred. (p. 78)

nearest ten when rounding, it's the closest number that is a multiple of ten. (p. 78)

necessary (něs′ ĭ sĕr′ ē) *adj.* something that is needed. **GSL** (p. 210)

need (nēd) *v.* have to. **GSL** (p. 46)

needed (nē′dĕd) *v.* required. (p. 222)

negative (něg′ ə tĭv) *adj.* less than zero. (p. 224)

negative sign (−) the symbol used to indicate a number is negative. (p. 224)

neither (nē′ *th*ər) *adj.* not one or the other. **GSL** (p. 224)

nerve (nûrv) *n.* the tissue in your body that helps you to feel. (p. 208)

nervous (nûr′ vəs) *adj.* worried because you are thinking about something. (p. 94)

neuron (no͝or′ ŏn′) *n.* a nerve cell. (p. 208)

never (něv′ ər) *adv.* not ever. **Dolch, GSL** (p. 70)

new (no͞o) *adj.* never used until now. **Dolch, GSL** (p. 72)

newspaper (no͞oz′ pā′ pər) *n.* a daily publication of news. **GSL** (p. 168)

next (někst) *adj.* after this. **GSL** (p. 108)

next to beside. (p. 64)

nice (nīs) *adj.* good. **GSL** (p. 40)

nickel (nĭk′ əl) *n.* a coin worth 5 cents. (p. 54)

no (nō) *adv.* used to express refusal. **Dolch, GSL** (p. 40)

nonrenewable (nŏn′ rĭ no͞o′ ə bəl) *adj.* no more can be made once it's all used. (p. 254)

noon (no͞on) *n.* 12:00 p.m. **GSL** (p. 100)

nor (nôr) *conj.* not either. **GSL** (p. 224)

North Pole *n.* the northern end of Earth's axis of rotation. (p. 236)

Northeast (nôrth ēst′) *n.* a region of the northeast United States, including the New England states, New York, and sometimes Pennsylvania and New Jersey. (p. 162)

Northern (nôr′ thərn) *adj.* located in the north. **GSL** (p. 236)

Northwest (nôrth wĕst′) *n.* a region of the northwest United States, including Washington, Oregon, and Idaho. (p. 162)

not (nŏt) *adv.* in no way. **Dolch, GSL** (p. 40)

notebook (nōt′ bo͝ok′) *n.* a book of blank pages for writing. **GSL** (p. 44)

notes (nōts) *n.* things you write down to help you remember information. **GSL** (p. 240)

nothing (nŭth′ ĭng) *pron.* not anything. **GSL** (p. 88)

noun (noun) *n.* in grammar, it is a person, place, or thing. **GSL** (p. 142)

now (nou) *adv.* at this moment. **Dolch, GSL** (p. 48)

nucleus (no͞o′ klē əs) *n.* the center of a cell that works as the cell's brain. (p. 232)

number (nŭm′ bər) *n.* a digit, such as 1, 2, or 3. **GSL** (p. 50)

number line a way to order data. (p. 78)

numerator (no͞o′ mə rā′ tər) *n.* in a fraction, the number above the bar. (p. 148)

nurse (nûrs) *n.* a person you go to when you are sick. **GSL** (p. 56)

nutrient (no͞o′ trē ənt) *n.* a vitamin you get from food. (p. 206)

nutritious (no͞o trĭsh′ əs) *adj.* healthy. (p. 130)

O

o'clock (ə klŏk′) *adv.* of or according to the clock. (p. 100)

obey (ō bā′) *v.* behave obediently. **GSL** (p. 238)

object (ŏb′ jĕkt′) *n.* a thing. **GSL** (p. 158)

observe (əb zûrv′) *v.* watch and see. **GSL** (p. 108)

observed (əb zûrvd′) *v.* celebrated or recognized a holiday. (p. 138)

obtuse angle an angle larger than 90° and less than 180°. (p. 248)

occur (ə kûr′) *v.* happen. (p. 128)

occurring (ə kûr′ĭng) *v.* happening. (p. 122)

ocean (ō′ shən) *n.* a huge body of salt water that covers more than 70% of Earth's surface. **GSL** (p. 114)

octagon (ŏk′ tə gŏn′) *n.* a polygon with 8 sides. (p. 250)

odd (ŏd) *adj.* any number not divisible by 2. (p. 200)

of (ŭv) *prep.* containing. **Dolch, GSL** (p. 68)

off (ôf) *adv.* no longer functioning. **Dolch, GSL** (p. 104)

offer (ô′ fər) *v.* give. **GSL** (p. 170)

office (ô′ fĭs) *n.* the room in the school where the secretary and principal are found. **GSL** (p. 46)

often (ôf′ ən) *adv.* many times; frequently. **GSL** (p. 70)

oil (oil) *n.* a nonrenewable form of energy. **GSL** (p. 254)

old (ōld) *adj.* no longer new. **Dolch, GSL** (p. 72)

on (ŏn) *adv.* in operation. **Dolch** (p. 104)

once (wŭns) *adv.* one time. **Dolch, GSL** (p. 48)

once in a while occasionally. (p. 146)

one eighth ($\frac{1}{8}$) one of 8 parts of one whole. (p. 148)

one fourth ($\frac{1}{4}$) one of 4 parts of one whole; quarter. (p. 148)

one half ($\frac{1}{2}$) one of 2 parts of one whole. (p. 148)

one tenth ($\frac{1}{10}$) one of 10 parts of one whole. (p. 148)

one third ($\frac{1}{3}$) one of 3 parts of one whole. (p. 148)

ones (wŭnz) *adj.* represents the first place from the right in a place value. (p. 50)

only (ōn′ lē) *adv.* just that and no more. **Dolch, GSL** (p. 76)

open (ō′ pən) *v.* make available for use. **Dolch, GSL** (p. 104)

opening (ō′ pə nĭng) *n.* a hole or break in a figure. (p. 250)

operation (ŏp′ə rā′shən) *n.* a process in math, such as addition or subtraction. **GSL** (p. 226)

opinion (ə pĭn′ yən) *n.* what you think about something. **GSL** (p. 218)

opposite (ŏp′ə zĭt) *n.* altogether different in nature. For example, *up* is the opposite of *down*. **GSL** (p. 166)

or (ôr) *conj.* used to show a choice. **Dolch, GSL** (p. 48)

orbit (ôr′ bĭt) *n.* the path of a body around another body in space. (p. 158)

order (ôr′ dər) *n.* a particular arrangement. **GSL** (p. 52)

ordered (ôr′ dərd) *v.* arranged. **GSL** (p. 120)

ordinal (ôr′ dn əl) *adj.* relating to the order of a number. (p. 52)

organ (ôr′ gən) *n.* a part of your body that performs a special function. **GSL** (p. 204)

organelle (ôr′ gə nĕl′) *n.* a part of a cell with a special job. (p. 232)

organism (ôr′ gə nĭz′ əm) *n.* a living thing. (p. 228)

organize (ôr′ gə nīz′) *v.* put in order. **GSL** (p. 242)

origin (ôr′ ə jĭn) *n.* the place where something comes from. **GSL** (p. 160)

original (ə rĭj′ ə nəl) *adj.* first. (p. 160)

other (ŭ*th*′ ər) **1.** *adj.* different (p. 200) **2.** *n.* someone that's not you. (p. 238) **GSL**

ounce (ouns) *n.* a small unit of measurement. **GSL** (p. 174)

our (our) *adj.* yours and mine. **Dolch** (p. 68)

ourselves (our sĕlvz′) *pron.* yourself and myself. (p. 96)

outdoor (out′ dôr) *adj.* outside. (p. 224)

outer (ou′ tər) *adj.* on the outside of. (p. 256)

outlier (out′ lī′ ər) *n.* the largest number in a set. (p. 128)

outline (out′ līn′) *n.* a list of ideas you make before you write a paper. **GSL** (p. 242)

outside (out′ sīd) *n.* the exterior, not in a house or building. **GSL** (p. 80)

over (ō′ vər) **1.** *adj.* finished. (p. 48) **2.** *prep.* covering various parts of. (p. 102) **Dolch, GSL**

own (ōn) **1.** *n.* something belonging to you. (p. 102) **2.** *v.* have or possess. (p. 226) **Dolch, GSL**

oxygen (ŏk′ sĭ jən) *n.* the air you breathe. (p. 204)

P

pad (păd) *n.* something you wear on a knee or elbow to protect it. **GSL** (p. 132)

pain (pān) *n.* the state of hurting. **GSL** (p. 56)

paint (pānt) *v.* make pictures with paint and a brush. **GSL** (p. 66)

pair (pâr) *n.* two of something. **GSL** (p. 118, 200)

pals (pălz) *n.* friends. (p. 76)

pants (pănts) *n.* clothing you wear on your legs. (p. 72)

paper (pā′ pər) **1.** *n.* a sheet for writing on. (p. 44) **2.** *adj.* comes from a material made mainly from wood. (p. 182) **GSL**

parade (pə rād′) *n.* many people marching in the street to celebrate something. (p. 138)

paragraph (păr′ ə grăf′) *n.* a short block of writing that expresses one idea. (p. 220)

parallel (păr′ ə lĕl′) *adj.* side by side. (p. 246)

parallelogram (păr′ ə lĕl′ ə grăm′) *n.* a polygon with 2 pairs of equal sides. (p. 250)

paramedic (păr′ ə mĕd′ ĭk) *n.* a person who arrives in an ambulance to help during an emergency. (p. 60)

parent (pâr′ ənt) *n.* your mother or your father. **GSL** (p. 86)

parenting (pâr′ ən tĭng) *n.* the act of raising children. (p. 230)

park (pärk) *n.* an outdoor area with grass and trees that's set aside for people to use. **GSL** (p. 64)

part (pärt) *n.* a piece or portion. **GSL** (p. 76, 148)

part of speech the classification of a word, such as a noun or verb. (p. 142)

participate (pär tĭs′ ə pāt′) *v.* join in. (p. 238)

particular (pər tĭk′ yə lər) *adj.* a certain way. **GSL** (p. 120)

partner (pärt′ nər) *n.* someone who you're paired with for something. **GSL** (p. 38)

party (pär′ tē) **1.** *n.* a gathering of people to celebrate. (p. 98) **2.** *n.* an organized political group. (p. 212) **GSL**

pass (păs) **1.** *v.* put into effect. (p. 210) **2.** *v.* go through. (p. 248) **GSL**

passed down taught to younger generations. (p. 116)

past tense the form of a verb that shows the action already happened. (p. 166)

path (păth) *n.* a route or way made for a particular purpose. **GSL** (p. 158)

patient (pā′ shənt) *n.* the person a doctor is treating. **GSL** (p. 58)

patriotic (pā′ trē ŏt′ ĭk) *adj.* devoted to your country. **GSL** (p. 140)

pattern (păt′ ərn) *n.* something that is copied and repeated over and over. **GSL** (p. 192)

pay (pā) *v.* give money for something. **GSL** (p. 54)

pen (pĕn) *n.* an instrument for writing that uses ink. **GSL** (p. 44)

penalty (pĕn′ əl tē) *n.* what you have to pay because you did something wrong. (p. 214)

pencil (pĕn′ səl) *n.* an instrument used for writing that has an eraser on top. **GSL** (p. 44)

penny (pĕn′ ē) *n.* a coin worth one cent. **GSL** (p. 54)

pentagon (pĕn′ tə gŏn′) *n.* a polygon with 5 sides. (p. 250)

per (pûr) *prep.* for each. **GSL** (p. 152)

percent (pər sĕnt′) *n.* a portion out of 100; per hundred. (p. 152)

percent symbol (%) the symbol used to indicate percent. (p. 152)

perfect (pûr′ fĭkt) *adj.* without any mistakes; flawless. **GSL** (p. 248)

period (.) (pĭr′ ē əd) *n.* the punctuation mark used at the end of a sentence. (p. 216)

permission (pər mĭsh′ ən) *n.* written or verbal consent. **GSL** (p. 170)

perpendicular (pûr′ pən dĭk′ yə lər) *adj.* intersecting. (p. 246)

phone number the number you have to dial on a phone to talk to someone. (p. 42)

phrasal verb a verb that is put with another word to have a special meaning. (p. 146)

phrase (frāz) *n.* a group of words that can't stand on its own as a sentence. (p. 144)

physical (fĭz′ ĭ kəl) **1.** *adj.* relating to the body. (p. 132) **2.** *adj.* solid; referring to something you can see. (p. 164)

pick (pĭk) *v.* choose. **Dolch, GSL** (p. 126)

pick up take in your hand. (p. 146)

pictograph (pĭk′ tə grăf′) *n.* a way to show data that uses pictures. (p. 126)

picture (pĭk′ chər) *n.* a drawing or other kind of image. **GSL** (p. 126, 222)

pie (pī) *n.* a dessert usually made of fruit. (p. 52)

piece (pēs) *n.* a part. **GSL** (p. 148)

piece of cake an idiom that means something is easy. (p. 196)

Pilgrims (pĭl′ grəmz) *n.* one of the first groups of people from Europe who made their home in America. (p. 190)

pilot (pī′ lət) *n.* a person who flies an airplane. (p. 66)

pint (pīnt) *n.* a unit of volume that equals 16 ounces. **GSL** (p. 176)

pipe down an idiom telling someone to be quiet. (p. 196)

pizza (pēt′ se) *n.* a baked food consisting of crust, sauce, and cheese. (p. 148)

place (plās) **1.** *n.* a spot within a number that has a certain value. (p. 50) **2.** *v.* put. (p. 120) **3.** *n.* location. (p. 246) **GSL**

plain (plān) *n.* a flat area of land. **GSL** (p. 112)

plan (plăn) *n.* a strategy for doing something. **GSL** (p. 102)

plane (plān) *n.* a surface that goes on forever in all directions. (p. 250)

plane figure a shape that lies flat. (p. 250)

planet (plăn′ ĭt) *n.* a body in space that revolves around a star. (p. 158)

plant (plănt) **1.** *n.* a living thing that takes in carbon dioxide and releases oxygen. (p. 66, 228) **2.** *v.* put seeds in the ground so that they will grow into plants. (p. 190) **GSL**

plant life a living thing that takes in carbon dioxide and releases oxygen. (p. 156)

plant-eater *n.* an animal that eats plants; herbivore. (p. 228)

plastic (plăs′ tĭk) *n.* a material used to make many things because it is cheap and does not break easily. (p. 182)

plate (plāt) **1.** *n.* a round dish to put food in. (p. 70) **2.** *n.* a section of the earth's crust that slowly shifts over millions of years. (p. 256) **GSL**

play (plā) *v.* participate in a sport. **Dolch, GSL** (p. 84)

player (plā′ ər) *n.* a person in a game or sport. (p. 50)

please (plēz) *adv.* a polite thing to say when you ask something. **Dolch, GSL** (p. 42)

pledge (plĕj) *n.* a promise. (p. 140)

Pledge of Allegiance *n.* a promise you make to the U.S. flag that means you'll be loyal to the United States. (p. 140)

plot (plŏt) *n.* the series of events in a story. (p. 244)

plural (ploŏr′ əl) *adj.* more than one. **GSL** (p. 194)

plural form in grammar the words that show more than one. (p. 166)

plus (+) (plŭs) *conj.* in addition to. (p. 74)

P.M. *abbr.* used for times in the afternoon and evening. (p. 100)

point (point) *n.* an exact location in space. **GSL** (p. 246)

police (pə lēs′) *n.* the people who maintain law and order. **GSL** (p. 60)

police officer an officer of the law. (p. 66)

policy (pŏl′ ĭ sē) *n.* a plan for how to do things. (p. 212)

political (pə lĭt′ ĭ kəl) *adj.* relating to politics. **GSL** (p. 210)

politician (pŏl′ ĭ tĭsh′ ən) *n.* a person who makes laws and runs the government. **GSL** (p. 210)

poll (pōl) *n.* a survey. (p. 124)

pollute (pə loōt′) *v.* make dirty. (p. 180)

pollution (pə loō′ shən) *n.* all the harmful things people do to the air, water, and land to make them dirty. (p. 180)

polygon (pŏl′ ē gŏn′) *n.* a shape with 3 or more sides. (p. 250)

pond (pŏnd) *n.* a body of water smaller than a lake. (p. 114)

poor (poŏr) *adj.* not having much money. **GSL** (p. 188)

popular (pŏp′ yə lər) *adj.* liked by many people. **GSL** (p. 124)

pork (pôrk) *n.* the meat from pigs. (p. 178)

portion (pôr′ shən) *n.* a part. (p. 152)

position (pə zĭsh′ ən) *n.* place. **GSL** (p. 120)

positive (pŏz′ ĭ tĭv) *adj.* greater than zero. (p. 224)

post office the place that receives and delivers mail. (p. 64)

pound (pound) *n.* a unit of weight equal to 16 ounces. **GSL** (p. 174)

pour (pôr) *v.* let spill from a container. **GSL** (p. 108)

power (pou′ ər) *n.* energy. **GSL** (p. 254)

practice (prăk′ tĭs) *v.* do something many times so that you'll become good at it. **GSL** (p. 132)

practicing (prăk′ tĭ sĭng) *v.* doing something many times in order to become good at it. (p. 88)

precede (prĭ sēd′) *v.* come before. (p. 142)

precipitation (prĭ sĭp′ ĭ tā′ shən) *n.* rain, snow, sleet, or hail. (p. 154)

predator (prĕd′ ə tər) *n.* an animal that hunts other animals for food. (p. 228)

predicate (prĕd′ ĭ kĭt) *n.* in a sentence, it's the verb and the object of the verb. (p. 144)

prefer (prĭ fûr′) *v.* like more than something else. **GSL** (p. 124)

pregnant (prĕg′ nənt) *adj.* going to have a baby. (p. 230)

prejudice (prĕj′ ə dĭs) *n.* the unfair treatment of people because of the group they belong to. **GSL** (p. 160)

prepare (prĭ pâr′) *v.* get ready for. **GSL** (p. 240)

preposition (prĕp′ ə zĭsh′ ən) *n.* a part of speech that shows the relation of things. (p. 142)

present 1. (prĕz′ ənt) *adj.* happening now; current. (p. 122) **2.** (prĭ zĕnt′) *v.* show. (p. 242) **GSL**

present continuous verbs ending in *ing*. (p. 122)

present simple verbs used for habitual actions. (p. 122)

presentation (prĕz′ ən tā′ shən) *n.* a project or paper you present in front of your class. (p. 242)

preserve (prĭ zûrv′) *v.* keep whole and safe. **GSL** (p. 156)

president (prĕz′ ĭ dənt) *n.* the leader of the United States. **GSL** (p. 212)

press (prĕs) *n.* all types of journalism. **GSL** (p. 238)

pressure (prĕsh′ ər) *n.* a push or force. **GSL** (p. 256)

pretty (prĭt′ ē) *adj.* attractive. **Dolch, GSL** (p. 72)

prevent (prĭ vĕnt′) *v.* keep from happening. **GSL** (p. 134)

preview (prē′ vyōō′) *v.* look at text quickly to get an idea of what it's about before you read it. (p. 240)

prewrite (prē rīt′) *v.* the first stage of writing in which you make outlines and write down ideas. (p. 242)

prey (prā) *n.* an animal that is being hunted by another animal. (p. 228)

price (prīs) *n.* how much something costs. **GSL** (p. 54)

prime (prīm) *adj.* having only 2 factors. (p. 200)

prime meridian *n.* the line that divides Earth and gives the longitude west and east. (p. 236)

print (prĭnt) *v.* send the text or images on your computer screen to a printer to make it appear on paper. **GSL** (p. 104)

printer (prĭn′ tər) *n.* a machine that allows you to print what's on your computer screen. (p. 104)

private (prī′ vĭt) *adj.* secret. **GSL** (p. 170)

prize (prīz) *n.* something you win. **GSL** (p. 52)

problem (prŏb′ ləm) *n.* a math question that needs to be solved. **GSL** (p. 102, 222)

process (prŏs′ ĕs′) *n.* the way something is done. (p. 240)

produce (prə dōōs′) *v.* make. **GSL** (p. 228)

producer (prə dōō′ sər) *n.* a living thing that makes its own food. (p. 228)

product (prŏd′ əkt) *n.* the result of a multiplication problem. **GSL** (p. 76)

prohibited (prō hĭb′ ĭ tĭd) *v.* not allowed. (p. 106)

pronoun (prō′ noun′) *n.* a part of speech that takes the place of a noun. (p. 142)

pronounce (prə nouns′) *v.* saying a word. **GSL** (p. 192)

pronunciation (prə nŭn′ sē ā′ shən) *n.* the way you say words. **GSL** (p. 192)

properly (prŏp′ ər lē) *adv.* correctly. **GSL** (p. 232)

property (prŏp′ ər tē) *n.* a math rule that is always true. **GSL** (p. 202)

protect (prə tĕkt′) *v.* keep safe. **GSL** (p. 106)

proud (proud) *adj.* filled with or showing esteem. **GSL** (p. 140)

provide (prə vīd′) *v.* give. **GSL** (p. 222)

puddle (pŭd′ l) *n.* a small pool of water on the ground. (p. 154)

pull (pŏŏl) *v.* apply force to something so that it comes toward you. **Dolch** (p. 60)

pulley (pŏŏl′ ē) *n.* a simple machine that is a wheel over which a rope is pulled to help lift something. (p. 252)

pulse (pŭls) *n.* each beat of your heart as it pumps blood. (p. 204)

pump (pŭmp) *n.* a machine that moves liquid by squeezing it out a portion at a time. **GSL** (p. 204)

pumpkin (pŭmp′ kĭn) *n.* a large, round, orange gourd often used to make pie or carved to look like a face in celebration of Halloween. (p. 190)

punctuation (pŭngk′ chōo ā′ shən) *n.* the marks used to end or show a pause in a sentence. (p. 216)

purpose (pûr′ pəs) *n.* the reason for doing something. **GSL** (p. 240)

push (pŏosh) *v.* apply force to something so that it moves away from you. **GSL** (p. 252)

put (pŏot) *v.* place. **Dolch, GSL** (p. 44)

put away put something back where it belongs. (p. 146)

put down place something on a surface. (p. 146)

put together combine. (p. 192)

quadrilateral (kwŏd′ rə lăt′ ər əl) *n.* a polygon that has 4 sides. (p. 250)

quantity (kwŏn′ tĭ tē) *n.* an amount. **GSL** (p. 226)

quart (kwôrt) *n.* a unit of volume that equals 32 ounces. **GSL** (p. 176)

quarter (kwôr′ tər) *n.* a coin worth 25 cents. **GSL** (p. 54)

quarter after 15 minutes past the hour. (p. 100)

quarter to 15 minutes before the hour. (p. 100)

question (kwĕs′ chən) *n.* something asked. **GSL** (p. 218)

question mark (?) the punctuation at the end of a sentence that asks a question. (p. 216)

quickly (kwĭk′ lē) *adv.* done with speed. **GSL** (p. 192)

quiet (kwī′ ĭt) *adj.* doesn't make much noise; silent. **GSL** (p. 92)

quite (kwīt) *adv.* completely. (p. 198)

quotation marks (" ") the marks you put at the beginning and end of a quote. (p. 216)

quotient (kwō′ shənt) *n.* the number of times one number can be divided into another. (p. 76)

race (rās) **1.** *n.* an event in which people run to see who can finish first. (p. 150) **2.** *n.* a group of people classified by the color of their skin. (p. 160) **GSL**

radio (rā′ dē ō) *n.* a device with no picture that you can listen to for music or news. **GSL** (p. 82)

radius (rā′ dē əs) *n.* a segment from the circle's center. (p. 248)

rain forest (rān′ fôr′ ĭst) *n.* a jungle. (p. 156)

raindrop (rān′ drŏp′) *n.* the individual beads of water that make up rain. (p. 154)

rainfall (rān′ fôl′) *n.* the total amount of rain that falls. (p. 162)

rainy (rā′ nē) *adj.* having a lot of rainfall. **GSL** (p. 80)

raise (rās) **1.** *v.* take care of children until they're adults. (p. 230) **2.** *v.* lift. (p. 252) **GSL**

raking (rā′ kĭng) *v.* gathering leaves on the ground into a pile. **GSL** (p. 122)

ran (răn) *v.* past tense form of *run*. See *run*. **Dolch** (p. 82)

range (rānj) *n.* the entire value within a set of data. (p. 128)

rapidly (răp′ ĭd lē) *adv.* done in a fast way. **GSL** (p. 142)

rarely (râr′ lē) *adv.* almost never happening. **GSL** (p. 70)

rate (rāt) *n.* the pace at which something is moving or working. **GSL** (p. 204)

ratio (rā′ shē ō′) *n.* the relationship between two quantities expressed as the quotient of one divided by the other. (p. 152)

ray (rā) *n.* a part of a line. **GSL** (p. 246)

react (rē ăkt′) *v.* respond to something. (p. 208)

reaction (rē ăk′shən) *n.* a response. (p. 208)

read (rēd) *v.* look at words in order to understand what they mean. **Dolch, GSL** (p. 42)

reader (rē′ dər) *n.* the audience for something written. (p. 220)

real (rēl) *adj.* something that is actual. **GSL** (p. 244)

really (rē′ lē) **1.** *adv.* very. (p. 174) **2.** *adv.* actually. (p. 222)

reason (rē′ zən) *n.* why you do something. **GSL** (p. 240)

reasonable (rē′ zə nə bəl) *adj.* logical or sensible. (p. 222)

receive (rĭ sēv′) *v.* get from someone. **GSL** (p. 144)

recognize (rĕk′ əg nīz′) *v.* become familiar with. **GSL** (p. 146)

record (rĭ kôrd′) **1.** *v.* write down. (p. 126) **2.** (rĕk′ ərd) *adj.* best ever done. (p. 150) **GSL**

rectangle (rĕk′ tăng′ gəl) *n.* a polygon with 4 sides and 4 right angles. (p. 250)

recycle (rē sī′ kəl) *v.* use again. (p. 182)

recycling bin the place where garbage that can be recycled is put. (p. 182)

reduce (rĭ dōos′) *v.* make smaller. **GSL** (p. 148)

reference (rĕf′ rəns) *adj.* referring to something you use for information. **GSL** (p. 168)

reflect (rĭ flĕkt′) *v.* think about something you've read. **GSL** (p. 240)

reflex (rē′ flĕks′) *n.* an automatic response. (p. 208)

region (rē′ jən) *n.* a geographic area or part of the country. (p. 162)

register (rĕj′ ĭ stər) *v.* go through a process that will allow you to do something. (p. 238)

regroup (rē grōop′) *v.* arrange in a new set. (p. 202)

regular (rəg′ yə lər) *adj.* following a standard set of rules; normal. **GSL** (p. 194)

reject (rĭ jĕkt′) *v.* refuse to accept. (p. 210)

related (rĭ lā′ tĭd) *v.* connected. **GSL** (p. 144, 226)

relative (rĕl′ ə tĭv) *n.* someone you are related to, like an aunt or cousin. **GSL** (p. 116)

relax (rĭ lăks′) *v.* be at ease. (p. 88)

released (rĭ lēsd) *v.* let out. (p. 180)

religion (rĭ lĭj′ ən) *n.* the practice of having faith in a god. **GSL** (p. 188)

rely on depend upon. (p. 170)

remainder (R) (rĭ mān′ dər) *n.* a number that's left over after dividing. (p. 76)

remember (rĭ mĕm′ bər) *v.* think about information or an event from the past; recall. **GSL** (p. 240)

remind (rĭ mīnd′) *v.* make someone remember something. **GSL** (p. 140)

remove (rĭ mōov′) *v.* to move from a position or place. (p. 134)

renewable (rĭ nōo′ ə bəl) *adj.* referring to something that can't run out. (p. 254)

reorder (rē ôr′ dər) *v.* put in a different order. (p. 202)

repeat (rĭ pēt′) *v.* do again. **GSL** (p. 154)

replace (rĭ plās′) *v.* put in the place of something else. **GSL** (p. 142)

report (rĭ pôrt′) **1.** *v.* tell. (p. 216) **2.** *n.* a paper written about a topic. (p. 242) **GSL**

represent (rĕp′ rĭ zĕnt′) **1.** *v.* symbolize. (p. 140) **2.** *v.* speak on the behalf of someone. (p. 214) **GSL**

representative (rĕp′ rĭ zĕn′ tə tĭv) *n.* a politician who represents a specific state or region. **GSL** (p. 210)

reproduce (rē′ prə dōos′) *v.* make or produce offspring. **GSL** (p. 230)

require (rĭ kwīr′) *v.* must have; need. (p. 216)

reread (rē rēd′) *v.* read again. (p. 240)

resource (rē′ sôrs′) *n.* something in a place that people use to help them live. (p. 186)

respect (rĭ spĕkt′) *v.* treat with honor. **GSL** (p. 238)

responsibilities (rĭ spŏn′ sə bĭl′ ĭ tēz) *n.* duties (singular is *responsibility*). (p. 238)

rest (rĕst) *v.* sleep or quiet relaxation. **GSL** (p. 58)

restaurant (rĕs′ tə ränt′) *n.* a place that serves food. **GSL** (p. 64)

result (rĭ zŭlt′) *n.* an outcome. **GSL** (p. 124)

return (rĭ tûrn′) *v.* give back. **GSL** (p. 168)

reuse (rē yōōz′) *v.* use again. (p. 182)

review (rĭ vyōō′) *v.* study or look at. **GSL** (p. 240)

revise (rĭ vīz′) *v.* make corrections. (p. 242)

revolve (rĭ vŏlv′) *v.* go around something in a circle. (p. 158)

rewrite (rē rīt′) *v.* write again. (p. 152)

rhyme (rīm) *v.* the action of two words having the same end sound. (p. 118)

rice (rīs) *n.* the seed of a grass grown for food. **GSL** (p. 178)

rich (rĭch) *adj.* having lots of money. **GSL** (p. 188)

ride (rīd) *v.* to be a passenger in a vehicle. **Dolch, GSL** (p. 62)

right (rīt) **1.** *n.* the direction opposite left. (p. 64) **2.** *adj.* correct. (p. 102) **3.** *n.* a just or legal claim. (p. 238) **Dolch, GSL**

right angle an angle with a measurement of 90°. (p. 248)

right now at this moment. (p. 122)

ring (rĭng) *n.* a hollow circle around something. **GSL** (p. 158)

rise (rīz) *v.* float upward. **GSL** (p. 154)

river (rĭv′ ər) *n.* a large stream of water that empties into a lake or ocean. **GSL** (p. 114)

rock (rŏk) *n.* a hard, naturally formed mineral; stone. **GSL** (p. 112)

Rocky Mountains *n.* a large mountain range in the western United States. (p. 164)

role (rōl) *n.* the function or purpose. (p. 218)

rotate (rō′ tāt) *v.* turn in a circle. (p. 158)

rough (rŭf) *adj.* violent. **GSL** (p. 114)

round (round) *v.* estimate. **Dolch, GSL** (p. 78)

round down estimate to a lower number. (p. 78)

round up estimate to a higher number. (p. 78)

row (rō) *n.* a horizontal grouping. **GSL** (p. 200)

ruin (rōō′ ĭn) *v.* destroy. **GSL** (p. 180)

rule (rōōl) *n.* a direction for conduct that must be followed. **GSL** (p. 106)

ruler (rōō′ lər) *n.* a stick with marks on it used for measuring. (p. 172)

run (rŭn) *n.* to move at a pace much faster than walking. **Dolch, GSL** (p. 82)

run into connect and become part of. (p. 114)

run on use as a fuel. (p. 254)

run out use something until you don't have anymore. (p. 254)

runner (rŭn′ ər) *n.* a person who runs. (p. 150)

S

sad (săd) *adj.* not happy; upset. **GSL** (p. 94)

safe (sāf) *adj.* protected from harm. **GSL** (p. 106)

said (sĕd) *v.* past tense form of *say*. See *say*. **Dolch** (p. 82)

sale (sāl) *n.* a reduction in price for goods. **GSL** (p. 54)

salesperson (sālz′ pûr′ sən) *n.* a person who works in a store and sells things. (p. 234)

salt (sôlt) *n.* a white mineral that's crushed and used to flavor food **GSL** (p. 114)

salt water water with salt in it, such as the water in an ocean. (p. 114)

salute (sə lōōt′) *v.* the way people in the military greet one another. (p. 140)

same (sām) *adj.* exactly alike. **GSL** (p. 152)

sand (sănd) *n.* the yellow or white grains that cover a beach. **GSL** (p. 112)

satellite (săt′ l īt′) *n.* a way to send and receive information through space. (p. 158)

save (sāv) *v.* keep and store. **GSL** (p. 104)

saw (sô) *v.* past tense form of *see*. **Dolch, GSL** (p. 82)

say (sā) *v.* speak about. **Dolch, GSL** (p. 50)

scale (scāl) **1.** *n.* a way to organize and show data. (p. 124) **2.** *n.* an instrument used to weigh things. (p. 174) **GSL**

scan (scăn) *v.* look over something quickly; skim. (p. 166)

scavenger (skăv′ ən jər) *n.* an animal that looks for dead animals to eat. (p. 228)

schedule (skĕj′ ōol) *n.* a list of things to do and when to do them. (p. 48)

science (sī′ əns) *n.* a class in which you study the way the world works. **GSL** (p. 48)

score (skôr) *n.* the number of points each team has in a game. (p. 50)

screen (skrēn) *n.* the computer monitor. **GSL** (p. 104)

scroll (skrōl) *v.* move a page up or down on a computer. (p. 170)

sea (sē) *n.* the body of water that's part of an ocean. **GSL** (p. 114)

seal (sēl) *n.* a design or emblem that represents someone or something. (p. 140)

search (sûrch) *v.* look for. **GSL** (p. 168)

search engine a site on the Internet that helps you find websites with information you're trying to find. (p. 170)

season (sē′ zən) *n.* spring, summer, fall, or winter. **GSL** (p. 84)

second (2nd) (sĕk′ ənd) **1.** *adj.* in a series, located after the first and before the third. (p. 52) **2.** *n.* a short unit of time. Sixty seconds equal a minute. (p. 100) **GSL**

section (sĕk′ shən) *n.* a part of a whole. (p. 126)

see (sē) *v.* look at. **Dolch, GSL** (p. 64)

seed (sēd) *n.* the tiny thing from which a plant grows. **GSL** (p. 190)

seem (sēm) *v.* appear. **GSL** (p. 92)

segment (sĕg′ mənt) *n.* a piece of a line with two endpoints. (p. 246)

select (sĭ lĕkt′) *v.* choose. (p. 222)

selfish (sĕl′ fĭsh) *adj.* unwilling to share. **GSL** (p. 92)

Senate (sĕn′ ĭt) *n.* a part of the legislative branch of the government. (p. 210)

senator (sĕn′ ə tər) *n.* a person who serves in the Senate. (p. 210)

sensation (sĕn sā′ shən) *n.* a physical feeling. (p. 208)

sense (sĕns) *n.* one of the 5 ways to notice the world around you: see, hear, touch, smell, or taste. **GSL** (p. 208)

sentence (sĕn′ təns) *n.* a complete thought that has a subject and a predicate. **GSL** (p. 144)

separate (sĕp′ ə rāt′) *v.* take apart. **GSL** (p. 192)

separated (sĕp′ ə rāt′ əd) *v.* taken apart. (p. 146)

separately (sĕp′ rĭt lē) *adv.* not together. **GSL** (p. 202)

series (sîr′ ēz) *n.* a list of things. (p. 216)

serious (sîr′ ē əs) *adj.* without humor. (p. 92)

serve (sûrv) *v.* work for. **GSL** (p. 212)

service (sûr′ vĭs) *n.* work a customer pays for. **GSL** (p. 234)

serving (sûr′ vĭng) *n.* the amount of something you eat at one time. (p. 130)

set (sĕt) **1.** *n.* a group of related numbers. (p. 128) **2.** *n.* a group of similar things. (p. 248) **GSL**

setting (sĕt′ ĭng) *n.* where a story occurs. (p. 244)

settled (sĕt′ ld) *v.* make a home in a new place. **GSL** (p. 186)

settler (sĕt′ lər) *n.* one who settles in a new region. (p. 188)

several (sĕv′ rəl) *adj.* many. **GSL** (p. 124)

shaded (shād′ əd) *v.* darkened. **GSL** (p. 152)

shall (shăl) *v.* past tense form of *should.* See *should.* **Dolch, GSL** (p. 84)

shallow (shăl′ ō) *adj.* not deep. **GSL** (p. 114)

shape (shāp) *n.* a form. **GSL** (p. 250)

share (shâr) *v.* give some of what you have to someone else. **GSL** (p. 92)

shared (shârd) *v.* past tense form of *share.* See *share.* (p. 190)

she (shē) *pron.* referring to a female. **Dolch, GSL** (p. 40)

sheep (shēp) *n.* animals similar to goats, but covered in thick wool. **GSL** (p. 228)

shelter (shĕl′ tər) *n.* anything with a roof that will protect you from the weather. **GSL** (p. 82)

shelves (shĕlvz) *n.* the flat boards on which books are kept in rows (singular is *shelf*). **GSL** (p. 168)

shift (shĭft) *v.* move. (p. 152)

shine (shīn) *v.* look bright, like a light; twinkle. **GSL** (p. 158)

ship (shĭp) *n.* large boat. **GSL** (p. 188)

shirt (shûrt) *n.* a piece of clothing that you wear on the top half of your body. **GSL** (p. 72)

shoe (shoo) *n.* something you wear on your foot. **GSL** (p. 72)

shore (shôr) *n.* the place where the ocean meets land. **GSL** (p. 112)

short (shôrt) *adj.* having a small height. **GSL** (p. 128)

short vowel a vowel with a short sound, such as the *a* in *cat.* (p. 118)

shorter (shôr′ tər) *adj.* having less height. (p. 172)

shortest (shôr′ tĭst) *adj.* having the least height. (p. 128)

should (shood) *v.* used to express the requirement of an action. **GSL** (p. 58)

show (shō) *v.* illustrate or demonstrate. **GSL** (p. 50, 126)

shown (shōn) *v.* past tense form of *show.* See *show.* (p. 164)

shy (shī) *adj.* uncomfortable talking to people. (p. 92)

sibling (sĭb′ lĭng) *n.* a brother or sister. (p. 86)

sick (sĭk) *adj.* not feeling well; ill. **GSL** (p. 56)

side (sīd) *n.* a line that forms the boundary of a plane figure. **GSL** (p. 250)

sidewalk (sīd′ wôk′) *n.* a paved path beside a road for people to walk on. (p. 62)

sight (sīt) *n.* the ability to see. **GSL** (p. 208)

sign (sīn) **1.** *n.* a symbol used in math that tells you what operation to perform. (p. 74) **2.** *n.* in grammar, another word for *mark.* (p. 216) **GSL**

signed (sīnd) *adj.* indicates whether a number is positive or negative. (p. 224)

silent (sī′ lənt) *adj.* not making any noise; quiet. **GSL** (p. 118)

similar (sĭm′ ə lər) *adj.* somewhat alike. (p. 192)

similarities (sĭm′ ə lăr′ ĭ tēz) *n.* characteristics of 2 or more things that are somewhat alike. (p. 160)

simple (sĭm′ pəl) *adj.* basic; not complex. **GSL** (p. 232)

simple sentence a sentence with one idea. (p. 144)

simplest form the smallest possible form of a fraction. (p. 148)

simplify (sĭm′ plə fī′) *v.* make easier. (p. 222)

singing (sing′ ĭng) *v.* saying words in a musical tone. **Dolch** (p. 88)

single (sĭng′ gəl) *adj.* only one. **GSL** (p. 232)

singular (sĭng′ gyə lər) *adj.* being only one. (p. 194)

sink (sĭngk) *n.* a small tub with a faucet in the kitchen or bathroom used to wash things. **GSL** (p. 90)

sister (sĭs′ tər) *n.* a female sibling. **GSL** (p. 86)

sit down seat yourself in a chair. (p. 146)

sitting (sĭt′ tĭng) *v.* being in a seated position. **Dolch** (p. 86)

size (sīz) *n.* how big something is. **GSL** (p. 174)

skin (skĭn) *n.* the layer of flesh that covers the outside of your body. **GSL** (p. 134)

skip (skĭp) *v.* miss. (p. 130)

skip-count *v.* count by more than one number at a time. (p. 200)

skirt (skûrt) *n.* a piece of clothing worn by females that hangs down from the waist. **GSL** (p. 72)

sky (skī) *n.* the upper atmosphere. **GSL** (p. 154)

slang (slăng) *n.* informal speaking. (p. 196)

slave (slāv) *n.* someone who is forced to work for no money and is treated like property. **GSL** (p. 188)

sledding (slĕd′ ĭng) *v.* sliding down a snow-covered hill on a sled. (p. 84)

sleeping (slē′ pĭng) *v.* resting so that your eyes are closed and you aren't aware of anything around you. **Dolch** (p. 88)

slice (slīs) *v.* cut. (p. 148)

slow (slō) *adj.* moving at a low speed. **GSL** (p. 100)

slow down go slower. (p. 252)

slowest (slō′ ĭst) *adj.* the most slow. (p. 150)

slowly (slō′ lē) *adv.* done in a slow way. **GSL** (p. 192)

small (smôl) *adj.* little. **Dolch, GSL** (p. 72)

smell (smĕl) *n.* something you sense with your nose. **GSL** (p. 208)

smiling (smī′ lĭng) *v.* curving the sides of your mouth up to show you're happy. **GSL** (p. 92)

smog (smŏg) *n.* air pollution made of smoke and fog. (p. 180)

smoke (smōk) *n.* the clouds that rise into the air when something is burning. **GSL** (p. 180)

smooth (smōōth) *adj.* totally flat. **GSL** (p. 114)

snack (snăk) *n.* a small amount of food you eat between meals. (p. 130)

sneezing (snēz′ ĭng) *v.* blowing air out of your nose or mouth suddenly. (p. 56)

snowflake (snō′ flāk′) *n.* an individual piece of snow that falls from the sky. (p. 154)

snowing (snō′ ĭng) *v.* frozen precipitation falling from the sky. **GSL** (p. 82)

so (sō) *adv.* to a large degree. **Dolch, GSL** (p. 92)

soap (sōp) *n.* a bar or a liquid used to clean skin. **GSL** (p. 134)

soccer (sŏk′ ər) *n.* a team sport in which a ball is kicked across a field. (p. 124)

society (sə sī′ ĭ tē) *n.* all people and communities put together. **GSL** (p. 210)

sock (sŏk) *n.* a covering you put on your foot under your shoe. **GSL** (p. 72)

sofa (sō′ fə) *n.* a long, soft chair made for more than one person to sit on. (p. 90)

soft (sôft) *adj.* not hard. **GSL** (p. 112)

softly (sôft′ lē) *adv.* quietly. **GSL** (p. 192)

soil (soil) *n.* dirt. **GSL** (p. 112)

solar power energy that comes from the sun. (p. 254)

solar system all the planets that revolve around the sun. (p. 158)

soldier (sōl′ jər) *n.* somebody in the military who fights in wars. **GSL** (p. 138)

solid (sŏl′ ĭd) *adj.* hard all the way through. **GSL** (p. 256)

solution (sə lōō′ shən) *n.* an answer to a problem. **GSL** (p. 222)

solve (sŏlv) *v.* answer a math problem. **GSL** (p. 102)

some (sŭm) *adj.* part, but not all. **Dolch, GSL** (p. 68)

someday (sŭm′ dā′) *adv.* referring to one day in the future. (p. 254)

someone (sŭm′ wŭn) *pron.* a person. **GSL** (p. 88)

something (sŭm′ thĭng) *pron.* a thing. **GSL** (p. 88)

sometimes (sŭm′ tīmz′) *adv.* now and then; occasionally. **GSL** (p. 70)

soon (sōōn) *adv.* in the near future. **Dolch, GSL** (p. 58)

sore (sôr) *adj.* painful. **GSL** (p. 58)

sorry (sŏr′ ē) *adj.* feeling bad about something you did. **GSL** (p. 96)

sort (sôrt) *v.* put into groups. **GSL** (p. 120)

sound (sound) *n.* a specific noise. **GSL** (p. 118)

sound out read a word out loud to help you pronounce it correctly. (p. 192)

soup (sōōp) *n.* a liquid food that usually has pieces of meat or vegetables in it. **GSL** (p. 68)

source (sôrs) *n.* the place where something comes from. (p. 254)

South Pole *n.* the southern end of Earth's axis of rotation, in Antarctica. (p. 236)

Southeast (south ēst′) *n.* an area in the southeastern United States. (p. 162)

Southern (sŭth′ ərn) *adj.* located in the south. (p. 236)

Southwest (south wĕst′) *n.* an area in the southwestern United States. (p. 162)

space (spās) **1.** *n.* the place where stars and planets exist; the universe. (p. 158) **2.** *n.* a distance between two things. (p. 248) **GSL**

speak (spēk) *v.* talk. **GSL** (p. 118)

special (spĕsh′ əl) *adj.* different. **GSL** (p. 116)

species (spē′ shēz) *n.* a kind of living thing. (p. 156)

speech (spēch) **1.** *n.* a talk given in front of an audience about a specific topic. (p. 138) **2.** *n.* the act of expressing yourself with words. (p. 238) **GSL**

speed up go faster. (p. 252)

spell (spĕl) *v.* put letters together to form words. **GSL** (p. 122)

spelled (spĕld) *v.* how letters are put together to form a word. (p. 242)

spelling (spĕl′ ĭng) *adj.* having to do with the way letters are put together to form words. (p. 194)

spill (spĭl) *v.* drop liquid from a container. **GSL** (p. 106)

spin (spĭn) *v.* go around in circles while staying in one place. **GSL** (p. 158)

spinal cord part of the nervous system that is inside the backbone. (p. 208)

split (splĭt) *v.* divided. **GSL** (p. 220)

spoon (spōōn) *n.* a rounded utensil for eating soft foods or scooping liquids. **GSL** (p. 70)

sprained (sprānd) *adj.* pulled or torn. (p. 60)

spread (sprĕd) *v.* make something travel to many places. **GSL** (p. 134)

spread out stretch outward. (p. 202)

spring (sprĭng) *n.* the warmer season after winter when everything grows. **GSL** (p. 84)

sprint (sprĭnt) *v.* to run really fast for a short time. (p. 150)

square (skwâr) *n.* a polygon with 4 equal sides. **GSL** (p. 250)

stage (stāj) *n.* one phase or period during a process. **GSL** (p. 154)

stairs (stârz) *n.* steps. **GSL** (p. 46)

stamp (stămp) *n.* the small sticker put on mail before you send it. (p. 174)

stand for represent. (p. 126)

stand up go from a sitting position to a standing position. (p. 146)

standing (stăn′ dĭng) *v.* be on your feet. **GSL** (p. 86)

star (stär) **1.** *n.* a shape that has 5 points. (p. 140) **2.** *n.* an object in space that is smaller than a planet. (p. 158) **GSL**

start with have as a beginning. (p. 120)

starts (stärts) *v.* begins. **Dolch, GSL** (p. 84)

statement (stāt′ mənt) *n.* something said. (p. 218)

states (stāts) *v.* says. **GSL** (p. 220)

station (stā′ shən) *n.* the place where a train or subway stops to let people on and off. **GSL** (p. 62)

statue (stăch′ ōō) *n.* a figure made out of a material, such as metal or wood that's made to look like someone or something. (p. 136)

Statue of Liberty *n.* a statue on Ellis Island, in New York, that greets immigrants when they arrive in the United States. It symbolizes freedom. (p. 140)

stay (stā) *v.* remain. **GSL** (p. 194)

steep (stēp) *adj.* being very tall with a sharp, upward angle. **GSL** (p. 112)

step (stĕp) *n.* a stage in a process. **GSL** (p. 108)

stomach (stŭm′ ək) *n.* the place in your body where your food goes to be digested. **GSL** (p. 206)

stomachache (stŭm′ ək āk′) *n.* a pain in your stomach. (p. 56)

stop (stŏp) *v.* quit moving or going. **Dolch, GSL** (p. 62)

store (stôr) *n.* a place that sells something. **GSL** (p. 64)

stories (stôr′ ēz) *n.* the plural form of *story.* See *story.* **GSL** (p. 116)

storm (stôrm) *n.* heavy precipitation with strong winds. **GSL** (p. 82)

story (stôr′ ē) *n.* a telling of an event, whether true or fiction. **GSL** (p. 244)

straight (strāt) *adj.* having no bends or curves. **GSL** (p. 246)

straight angle an angle with a measure of 180°. (p. 248)

stream (strēm) *n.* a small river. **GSL** (p. 114)

street (strēt) *n.* a road. **GSL** (p. 62)

stretch (strĕch) *v.* bend your body in order to loosen your muscles. **GSL** (p. 132)

strict (strĭkt) *adj.* very forceful about discipline. **GSL** (p. 92)

stripes (strīps) *n.* repeated lines across something. **GSL** (p. 140)

strong (strông) *adj.* healthy. **GSL** (p. 130)

student (stōōd′ nt) *n.* a person who goes to school. **GSL** (p. 38)

study (stŭd′ ē) *v.* read about and learn a subject. **GSL** (p. 48)

style (stīl) *n.* a particular type; fashion. (p. 116)

subject (sŭb′ jĭkt) **1.** *n.* a class at school. (p. 48) **2.** *n.* in a sentence, it's what does the action. (p. 144) **3.** *n.* what something is about; topic. (p. 168) **GSL**

substitute (sŭb′ stĭ tōōt′) *v.* put in the place of something else. (p. 226)

subtract (səb trăkt′) *v.* take away. (p. 74)

subway (sŭb′ wā′) *n.* a train that goes underground and takes people all over a city. (p. 62)

such as for example. (p. 164)

sugar (shŏŏg′ ər) *n.* a white substance used to make foods and drinks sweet. **GSL** (p. 68)

sum (sŭm) *n.* a total. (p. 74)

summarize (sŭm′ ə rīz′) *v.* tell about what you read in just a few sentences. (p. 128)

summer (sŭm′ ər) *n.* the hot season following spring. **GSL** (p. 84)

sum up tell you everything about it. (p. 220)

sun (sŭn) *n.* the star that warms Earth and around which all planets in the solar system revolve. **GSL** (p. 158)

sunlight (sŭn′ līt′) *n.* the light from the sun that reaches Earth. (p. 228)

sunny (sŭn′ ē) *adj.* bright and cloudless. (p. 80)

sunrise (sŭn′ rīz′) *n.* the moment when the sun comes up and it becomes light outside. (p. 100)

sunset (sŭn′ sĕt′) *n.* the moment when the sun goes down and it becomes dark outside. (p. 100)

supply (sə plī′) *n.* an amount of something. **GSL** (p. 234)

support (sə pôrt′) *v.* give reasons and evidence for something. **GSL** (p. 220)

Supreme Court *n.* the highest federal court in the United States. (p. 214)

sure (shŏŏr) *adj.* positive. **GSL** (p. 226)

surf (sûrf) **1.** *v.* ride on a wave using a long board. (p. 114) **2.** *v.* visit sites on the Internet. (p. 170)

surface (sûr′ fəs) *n.* the outside of something. **GSL** (p. 236)

surround (sə round′) *v.* being on all sides. **GSL** (p. 112)

survey (sûr′ vā′) *n.* a poll in which many people are asked the same questions to find out their opinions about a topic. (p. 126)

survive (sər vīv′) *v.* stay alive. (p. 156)

sustain (sə stān′) *v.* keep in existence; maintain. (p. 158)

swallow (swŏl′ ō) *v.* allow something to travel down your throat. **GSL** (p. 206)

sweater (swĕt′ ər) *n.* a piece of warm clothing made of wool or cotton that is like a heavy shirt. (p. 72)

sweetheart (swēt′ härt′) *n.* a person you are dating. (p. 138)

sweets (swēts) *n.* desserts and candy. **GSL** (p. 130)

swimming (swĭm′ ĭng) *v.* the act of moving through water by kicking your legs and moving your arms. **GSL** (p. 114)

switch (swĭch) **1.** *n.* a button to turn something on or off. (p. 104) **2.** *v.* reverse. (p. 202)

syllable (sĭl′ ə bəl) *n.* one of the sounds that make up a word. (p. 192)

symbol (sĭm′ bəl) *n.* something that represents something else. (p. 140)

synonym (sĭn′ ə nĭm′) *n.* a word that has the same meaning as another word. (p. 166)

system (sĭs′ təm) *n.* a group of things that are related and work together to make up something larger. **GSL** (p. 156)

T

table (tā′ bəl) *n.* an organized way to present data. **GSL** (p. 126)

tablespoon (tā′ bəl spōōn′) *n.* a cooking measurement equal to 3 teaspoons or $\frac{1}{2}$ a fluid ounce. (p. 176)

take apart break down into pieces. (p. 192)

take out remove something from where it's kept. (p. 146)

talk (tôk) *v.* speak. **GSL** (p. 42)

tall (tôl) *adj.* having a lot of height. **GSL** (p. 128)

tallest (tôl′ ĭst) *adj.* having the most height. (p. 128)

tally marks (////) marks used on a chart to represent data. (p. 124)

tank (tăngk) *n.* a glass box filled with water in which fish are kept. (p. 74)

tape measure a long ribbon with marks on it used to measure things. (p. 172)

task (tăsk) *n.* a job. (p. 240)

taste (tāst) *v.* sense something with your mouth and tongue. **GSL** (p. 208)

taxes (tăk′ sĭz) *n.* money you must pay the government so they can pay for things society needs. **GSL** (p. 238)

taxi (tăk′ sē) *n.* a car you can hire to drive you somewhere. **GSL** (p. 62)

teacher (tē′ chər) *n.* a person who teaches students about a subject. (p. 38)

team (tēm) *n.* a group of people working together as one. (p. 132)

teaspoon (tē′ spoōn′) *n.* a cooking measurement equal to $\frac{1}{3}$ of a tablespoon. (p. 176)

teenager (tēn′ ā′ jər) *n.* a person between the ages of 13 and 19. (p. 230)

tell (tĕl) *v.* give information by saying it. **Dolch, GSL** (p. 42)

temperature (tĕm′ prə choŏr′) *n.* how hot or cold something is. **GSL** (p. 58, 224)

tennis (tĕn′ ĭs) *n.* a sport played by hitting a ball over a net using rackets. (p. 124)

tens (tĕnz) *adj.* represents the second place from the right in a place value. (p. 50)

tense (tĕns) *n.* the form of a verb that tells when it happened. (p. 122)

tenth (10th) (tĕnth) *n.* one of 10 parts of a whole. (p. 150)

term (tûrm) **1.** *n.* a period of time that a person is made to serve. (p. 212) **2.** *n.* one quantity in a math problem. (p. 226) **GSL**

text (tĕkst) *n.* printed words. (p. 240)

than (thăn) *conj.* used after a comparative adjective or adverb to introduce something of unequal comparison. **GSL** (p. 52)

thank (thăngk) *v.* used to show you appreciate something that someone did or said. **Dolch, GSL** (p. 42)

Thanksgiving Day *n.* a U.S. holiday in November, celebrating a feast between the Pilgrims and Native Americans in 1621. (p. 190)

that (thăt) *adj.* used to refer to something mentioned. **Dolch, GSL** (p. 54)

the (thē *before vowel*; thə *before consonant*) *art.* a term used before a particular noun. **Dolch, GSL** (p. 38)

their (thâr) *adj.* belonging to them. **Dolch** (p. 78)

them (thĕm) *pron.* used to refer to others as a group. **Dolch** (p. 46)

theme (thēm) *n.* the author's message in a story. (p. 244)

themselves (thĕm sĕlvz′) *pron.* those who are identical with them. (p. 96)

then (thĕn) *adv.* next. **Dolch, GSL** (p. 108)

there (thâr) *pron.* used to introduce a sentence. **Dolch, GSL** (p. 50)

thermometer (thər mŏm′ ĭ tər) *n.* an instrument to measure temperature. (p. 58)

these (thēz) *adj.* plural form of *this.* See *this.* **Dolch** (p. 54)

they (thā) *pron.* used to refer to ones previously mentioned. **Dolch** (p. 42)

thin (thĭn) *adj.* not weighing much; skinny. **GSL** (p. 86)

thing (thĭng) *n.* an item. **GSL** (p. 216)

think (thĭnk) **1.** *v.* believe. (p. 92) **2.** *v.* reflect on something. (p. 102) **Dolch, GSL**

third (3rd) (thûrd) *adj.* corresponding in order to the number 3. (p. 52)

thirty (thûr′ tē) *n.* a half past the hour. (p. 100)

this (thĭs) *adj.* used to refer to the person or thing present. **Dolch, GSL** (p. 54)

those (thōz) *adj.* plural form of *that.* See *that.* **Dolch, GSL** (p. 54)

thought (thôt) *n.* something you think. (p. 218)

thousands (thou′ zəndz) *adj.* represents the fourth place from the right in a place value. (p. 50)

throat (thrōt) *n.* the front part of the neck. **GSL** (p. 206)

throw away get rid of. (p. 182)

throw in the towel an idiom that means *quit*. (p. 196)

thunderstorm (thŭn′ dər stôrm′) *n.* a storm with heavy rain, thunder, and lightning. (p. 82)

tide (tīd) *n.* the changing level of a body of water. **GSL** (p. 114)

tidy (tī′ dē) *adj.* neat. **GSL** (p. 90)

tiger (tī′ gər) *n.* a large wild cat with stripes. (p. 126)

time (tīm) **1.** *n.* a way to express what part of the day or night you are in. (p. 100) **2.** *n.* how long it took to do something. (p. 150) **GSL**

time clock a special clock used to time runners. (p. 150)

times (×) (tīmz) *v.* multiply by. (p. 76)

tin (tĭn) *n.* a thin, cheap metal often used to make cans. **GSL** (p. 182)

tiny (tī′ nē) *adj.* very small. (p. 232)

tipi (tē′ pē) *n.* a cone-shaped hut in which some tribes of Native Americans used to live. (p. 186)

tired (tīrd) *adj.* in need of sleep. **GSL** (p. 130)

title (tīt′ l) **1.** *v.* to name a chart or graph. (p. 124) **2.** *n.* the name of a book or story. (p. 244) **3.** *n.* a word put before someone's name to show respect. (p. 216) **GSL**

to (tōō) *prep.* in the direction of. **Dolch, GSL** (p. 44)

tobacco (tə băk′ ō) *n.* a leaf that is dried and then smoked in a pipe or cigarette. **GSL** (p. 188)

today (tə dā′) *n.* this day. **Dolch, GSL** (p. 98)

toe (tō) *n.* one of the 10 digits attached to the end of your feet. **GSL** (p. 200)

together (tə gĕth′ ər) *adv.* in a single group. **Dolch, GSL** (p. 42)

told (tōld) *v.* past tense form of *tell*. See *tell*. (p. 218)

tomorrow (tə mŏr′ ō) *n.* the day after today. **GSL** (p. 98)

ton (tŭn) *n.* 2,000 pounds. **GSL** (p. 174)

too (tōō) **1.** *adv.* also. (p. 42) **2.** *adv.* more than enough; excessively. (p. 252) **Dolch, GSL**

toothbrush (tōōth′ brŭsh′) *n.* an instrument used to clean your teeth. (p. 134)

top (tŏp) *adj.* in the highest position. **GSL** (p. 148)

topic (tŏp′ ĭk) *n.* the main idea or subject. (p. 220)

topic sentence a sentence that introduces the topic. (p. 220)

tornado (tôr nā′ dō) *n.* a spinning column of wind moving at such a high speed that it's able to destroy things in its path. (p. 82)

toss (tôs) *v.* gently throw. (p. 180)

total (tōt′ l) *adj.* entire. **GSL** (p. 54)

touch (tŭch) **1.** *v.* come in contact with. (p. 134) **2.** *n.* the ability to feel something using your hand. (p. 208) **GSL**

touched (tŭcht) *v.* past tense form of *touch*. See *touch*. **GSL** (p. 244)

tour (tōōr) *v.* visit. **GSL** (p. 136)

tourist (tōōr′ ĭst) *n.* a person on vacation somewhere. (p. 136)

toward (tə wôrd′) *prep.* in the direction of. **GSL** (p. 120)

toxin (tŏk′ sĭn) *n.* a harmful substance that pollutes. (p. 180)

traded (trā′ dĭd) *v.* given something in exchange for something else. **GSL** (p. 188)

tradition (trə dĭsh′ ən) *n.* the passing down of something in a culture. (p. 116)

train (trān) *n.* a long vehicle with many cars that runs on a track. **GSL** (p. 62)

transform (trăns fôrm′) *v.* change from one form to another. (p. 206)

translate (trăns′ lāt) *v.* figure out what something means and change it into something else. **GSL** (p. 208)

transport (trăns pôrt′) *v.* move something from one place to another. (p. 252)

trash (trăsh) *n.* garbage. (p. 180)

trash collector a person who takes away garbage and gets rid of it. (p. 66)

travel (trăv′ əl) *v.* move; go from one place to another. **GSL** (p. 206)

treasury (trĕzh′ ə rē) *n.* the department of a government in charge of money. **GSL** (p. 212)

trial (trī′ əl) *n.* a process that happens in a court of law to decide if someone is guilty of a crime. **GSL** (p. 214)

triangle (trī′ ăng′ gəl) *n.* a polygon with 3 sides. (p. 250)

tribe (trīb) *n.* a group of families that share a common ancestry and culture. **GSL** (p. 186)

true (trōō) *adj.* correct. **GSL** (p. 78)

try (trī) *v.* attempt. **Dolch, GSL** (p. 102)

try on put clothes on to see if you like them. (p. 72)

tube (tōōb) *n.* a hollow stick. **GSL** (p. 204)

turkey (tûr′ kē) *n.* a large bird often used for food. (p. 190)

turned (tûrnd) changed. **GSL** (p. 244)

turn in give to your teacher. (p. 242)

turn off stop something from working; shut off. (p. 146)

turn on give power to something to make it work. (p. 146)

turns into becomes. (p. 154)

twice (twīs) *adv.* two times. (p. 248)

type (tīp) **1.** *v.* use a keyboard to enter text. (p. 104) **2.** *n.* a kind. (p. 218) **GSL**

ugly (ŭg′ lē) *adj.* not attractive. **GSL** (p. 72)

umbrella (ŭm brĕl′ ə) *n.* a device you hold over your head to keep you dry when it's raining. **GSL** (p. 80)

uncle (ŭng′ kəl) *n.* the brother of your mother or father. **GSL** (p. 86)

under (ŭn′ dər) *prep.* beneath. **Dolch, GSL** (p. 90)

understand (ŭn′ dər stănd) *v.* figure out. **GSL** (p. 102)

unemployed (ŭn′ ĕm ploid′) *adj.* without a job. (p. 234)

unhealthy (ŭn hĕl′ thē) *adj.* not good for you. (p. 130)

unicellular (yōō′ nĭ sĕl′ yə lər) *adj.* having one cell. (p. 232)

uniform (yōō′ nə fôrm′) *n.* a type of outfit you have to wear for a certain job. (p. 138)

unique (yōō nēk′) *adj.* special because it's different. (p. 146)

unit (yōō′ nĭt) *n.* a group that is part of a larger group. **GSL** (p. 176)

unity (yōō′ nĭ tē) *n.* the coming together as one. **GSL** (p. 160)

unknown quantity in algebra, the number you have to solve that's represented by a letter. (p. 226)

unlimited (ŭn lĭm′ ĭ tĭd) *adj.* without end. (p. 254)

until (ŭn tĭl′) *prep.* up to the time of. **GSL** (p. 98)

unusual (ŭn yōō′ zhōō əl) *adj.* out of the ordinary; strange. (p. 194)

up (ŭp) *adv.* in a higher place or direction. **GSL** (p. 80)

upon (ə pŏn′) *prep.* on. **Dolch, GSL** (p. 44)

uppercase (ŭp′ ər kās′) *adj.* capital. (p. 216)

upset (ŭp sĕt′) *adj.* unhappy. **GSL** (p. 94)

us (ŭs) *pron.* the objective form of *we*. **Dolch** (p. 46)

use (yo̅o̅z) *v.* apply something toward a purpose. **Dolch, GSL** (p. 44)

use up use something until there is none left. (p. 254)

used (yo̅o̅zd) *v.* past tense for *use.* See *use.* (p. 166)

useful (yo̅o̅s′ fəl) *adj.* having purpose; helpful. (p. 206)

useless (yo̅o̅s′ lĭs) *adj.* having no purpose; worthless. (p. 206)

usually (yo̅o̅′ zho̅o̅ əl lē) *adv.* happening most times. **GSL** (p. 70)

V

Valentine's Day *n.* a February 14th holiday celebrating love. (p. 138)

valuable (văl′ yo̅o̅ ə bəl) *adj.* worth a lot of money. **GSL** (p. 182)

value (văl′ yo̅o̅) *n.* an amount. **GSL** (p. 50, 128)

vapor (vā′ pər) *n.* a state of matter (p. 154)

variable (vâr′ ē ə bəl) *n.* something that changes. (p. 226)

varies (vâr′ ēz) *v.* changes a lot. (p. 226)

vegetable (věj′ tə bəl) *n.* an edible part of a plant. (p. 68)

vein (vān) *n.* one of the tubes that carries blood to the heart. (p. 204)

verb (vûrb) *n.* an action word. **GSL** (p. 142)

vertex (vûr′ těks′) *n.* the point of an angle. (p. 248)

vertical (vûr′ tĭ kəl) *adj.* in an up and down direction. (p. 246)

very (věr′ ē) *adv.* to a large degree. **Dolch, GSL** (p. 106)

vessel (věs′ əl) *n.* something used to carry something. **GSL** (p. 204)

Veterans Day *n.* a U.S. holiday in honor of military veterans. (p. 138)

vice president the person ranking below the president. (p. 212)

village (vĭl′ ĭj) *n.* a small community of homes. **GSL** (p. 186)

vinegar (vĭn′ ĭ gər) *n.* a sour-tasting acid. (p. 108)

visit (vĭz′ ĭt) *v.* go to see. **GSL** (p. 58)

vitamin (vī′ tə mĭn) *n.* a nutrient. (p. 130)

voice (vois) *n.* your ability to speak. **GSL** (p. 192)

volcano (vŏl kā′ nō) *n.* an opening in Earth's crust where lava will sometimes pour out. (p. 256)

vote (vōt) *n.* one person's choice made in a survey or election. **GSL** (p. 126)

voting (vō′ tĭng) *n.* the act of making your choice for a candidate in an election. **GSL** (p. 238)

vowel (vou′ əl) *n.* any of the letters A, E, I, O, or U. **GSL** (p. 118)

vulture (vŭl′ chər) *n.* a large scavenger bird. (p. 228)

W

wage (wāj) *n.* the money earned from a job. **GSL** (p. 234)

wait (wāt) *v.* remain somewhere because you expect something to happen. **GSL** (p. 62)

walk (wôk) *v.* move from one place to another on your feet. **Dolch, GSL** (p. 62)

wall (wôl) *n.* a surface that makes up one side of a room. **GSL** (p. 90)

want (wônt) *v.* desire. **Dolch, GSL** (p. 66)

war (wôr) *n.* the fighting between countries in which many people die. **GSL** (p. 138)

warm (wôrm) *adj.* somewhat hot. **Dolch, GSL** (p. 80)

warm up get ready. (p. 132)

warning (wôr′ nĭng) *n.* advice to look out for a certain danger. (p. 82)

was (wŭz) *v.* a past tense form of *is.* See *is.* **Dolch** (p. 98)

washing (wô′ shǐng) *v.* cleaning using soap and water. **Dolch, GSL** (p. 88)

Washington, D.C. *n.* the capitol of the United States. (p. 136)

Washington Monument *n.* a tall stone monument in Washington, D.C., built in honor of George Washington. (p. 136)

waste (wāst) *n.* the part of food that is left over after digestion. **GSL** (p. 206)

watch (wŏch) *n.* a type of clock you wear on your wrist. (p. 100)

watching (wŏch′ ĭng) *v.* looking at. **GSL** (p. 88)

water (wô′ tər) *n.* a clear liquid that covers much of Earth. (p. 154)

wave (wāv) *n.* a moving rise of water over the top of a large body of water. **GSL** (p. 114)

way (wā) *n.* method. **GSL** (p. 102)

we (wē) *pron.* you and me. **Dolch, GSL** (p. 42)

weak (wēk) *adj.* not strong. **GSL** (p. 58)

wear (wâr) *v.* put on your body. **GSL** (p. 72)

weather (wĕth′ ər) *n.* the conditions outside, such as temperature and precipitation. **GSL** (p. 80)

Web (wĕb) *n.* the Internet. (p. 170)

web address the address of a particular website. (p. 170)

web browser software you use to connect to the Internet. (p. 170)

website (wĕb′ sīt′) *n.* a particular place on the Internet. (p. 170)

week (wēk) *n.* a 7-day period. **GSL** (p. 98)

weigh (wā) *v.* determine how heavy something is. **GSL** (p. 174)

weight (wāt) **1.** *n.* a heavy object you lift for exercise. (p. 132) **2.** *n.* the measurement of how heavy something is. (p. 174) **GSL**

welcome (wĕl′ kəm) *v.* receive a person with kindness. **GSL** (p. 40)

well (wĕl) *adv.* good. **Dolch, GSL** (p. 56)

well-balanced *adj.* having a good or healthy combination. (p. 130)

well known known by many people; famous. (p. 170)

went (wĕnt) *v.* past tense form of *go.* See *go.* **Dolch** (p. 82)

were (wîr) *v.* a past tense form of *are.* See *are.* **Dolch** (p. 98)

Western (wĕs′ tərn) *adj.* located in the west. **GSL** (p. 236)

what (wŭt) *pron.* which particular one. **Dolch, GSL** (p. 38)

wheat (wēt) *n.* a type of grass, the grain of which is used to make bread. **GSL** (p. 178)

wheel (wēl) *n.* something round used to move things. **GSL** (p. 252)

when (wĕn) *pron.* at what point in time. **Dolch, GSL** (p. 48)

where (wâr) *pron.* in which location. **Dolch, GSL** (p. 42)

whether (wĕth′ ər) *conj.* if. **GSL** (p. 198)

which (wĭch) *pron.* what particular one or ones. **Dolch, GSL** (p. 52)

while (wīl) *conj.* during the time that. **GSL** (p. 240)

White House *n.* the house where the president of the United States lives and works. (p. 212)

who (hōō) *pron.* which person. **Dolch, GSL** (p. 38)

whole (hōl) *adj.* entire. **GSL** (p. 148)

whole number a number without a decimal or fraction. (p. 50)

why (wī) *adv.* for what reason. **Dolch, GSL** (p. 94)

wigwam (wĭg′ wŏm′) *n.* a type of hut that Native Americans lived in. (p. 186)

will (wĭl) *v.* used to show intention. **Dolch, GSL** (p. 80)

windmill (wĭnd′ mĭl′) *n.* a machine that runs on the energy made by a wheel of blades turned by the wind. (p. 254)

window (wĭn′ dō) *n.* a box on your computer screen. **GSL** (p. 104)

wind up finally result in. (p. 206)

windy (wĭn′ dē) *adj.* having a large amount of wind. **GSL** (p. 82)

winter (wĭn′ tər) *n.* the cold season following autumn. **GSL** (p. 84)

wish (wĭsh) **1.** *v.* desire or hope for. (p. 84) **2.** *n.* a hope or desire for something. (p. 244) **Dolch, GSL**

with (wĭth) *conj.* to. **Dolch, GSL** (p. 96)

without (wĭth out′) *conj.* not with. **GSL** (p. 210)

wolves (wŏolvz) *n.* wild animals that look like dogs. (p. 228)

wondered (wŭn′ dərd) *v.* was curious about. **GSL** (p. 218)

won't (wônt) *contr.* will not. (p. 80)

wool (wŏol) *n.* the fur of sheep. **GSL** (p. 178)

word problem a math problem explained in the form of a situation. (p. 222)

work (wûrk) *v.* do a job. **Dolch, GSL** (p. 66)

work out exercise. (p. 132)

worship (wûr′ shĭp) *v.* practice religion. **GSL** (p. 188)

would (wŏod) *v.* past tense of *will*. See *will*. **Dolch. GSL** (p. 84)

wrapper (răp′ ər) *n.* a piece of paper or plastic that covers an object or a piece of food. (p. 180)

wrist (rĭst) *n.* the joint that connects your hand to your arm. **GSL** (p. 204)

write (rīt) *v.* form words on paper. **Dolch, GSL** (p. 42)

writer (rī′ tər) *n.* a person whose job is to write. (p. 220)

writing (rī′ tĭng) *n.* text on paper. (p. 242)

written (rĭt′ n) *v.* expressed through writing. (p. 224)

wrong (rông) *adj.* incorrect. **GSL** (p. 94)

WWW *abbr.* abbreviation that stands for World Wide Web. (p. 170)

yard (yärd) **1.** *n.* the grassy area around a house. (p. 90) **2.** *n.* a unit of length equal to 3 feet. (p. 172) **GSL**

yardstick *n.* a stick that is one yard long and is used to measure things. (p. 172)

year (yēr) *n.* a period of 365 days. **GSL** (p. 98)

Yellowstone *n.* a national park located in the western United States. (p. 164)

yes (yĕs) *adv.* it is so. **Dolch, GSL** (p. 40)

yesterday (yĕs′ tər dā′) *n.* the day before today. **GSL** (p. 98)

you (yōo) *pron.* used to refer to the person you are talking to. **Dolch** (p. 38)

young (yŭng) *adj.* not old. **GSL** (p. 86)

your (yŏor) *pron.* possessive form of *you*. See *you*. (p. 38)

yours (yŏorz) *pron.* the one or ones belonging to you. **Dolch** (p. 72)

yourself (yŏor sĕlf′) *pron.* that one that is the same as you. (p. 56)

yourselves (yŏor sĕlvz′) *pron.* plural form of *yourself*. See *yourself*. (p. 96)

zero (zîr′ ō) *n.* none. **GSL** (p. 224)

A – C

Social Studies Words

D – F

Social Studies Words

G – I

Social Studies Words

J – L

Social Studies Words

M – O

Social Studies Words

Acknowledgments

ILLUSTRATION CREDITS

16, 21, 23, ©Sean O'Neill 41, 55, 57, 63, 77, 81, 87, 115, 139, 155, 163, 173, 177, 209 ©Kathryn Marlin

PHOTO CREDITS

4 *top* ©U.S. Mint Handout/ Reuters/Corbis *right* ©Courtesy of the US Mint *left* ©Courtesy of Sandia National Laboratories *bottom* ©Courtesy of the US Mint *bottom left* © Richard Hutchings/CORBIS 4-5 *center* ©Joseph Sohm; Visions of America/CORBIS 5 *top* ©Bill Aron/PhotoEdit Inc. *bottom* ©Royalty-Free/CORBIS 6 *top* ©Catherine Karnow/CORBIS *center* ©Flip Schulke/CORBIS *bottom* ©Pete Stone/CORBIS 7 *left* ©Tom Bean/CORBIS *right* ©Royalty-free/ CORBIS 8 *top* ©Yang Liu/ CORBIS *center* © Steve Vidler/SuperStock *bottom* ©Leland Bobbe/CORBIS *left* ©Tom Stewart/CORBIS 9 *left* ©Tom Stewart/CORBIS *right* ©Gary Hicks/Science Photo Library 10 -11 ©Getty Images 12 igloo ©Stuart Westmorland/CORBIS 12 jam, lamp, owl, pots, vase, x-ray, yarn ©Creatas 12 all other images ©Getty Images 18 olives ©Royalty-Free/Corbis 18 banana ©Getty Images 18 all other images ©Dynamic Graphics 20 ©Eileen Ryan Photography 22 ©Eileen Ryan Photography 34 *top* ©Lawrence Manning/CORBIS 34 *bottom* © SERGIO MORAES/Reuters/Corbis 35 *top* ©royalty-free/CORBIS 35 *center* ©royalty-free/CORBIS 35 *bottom* ©royalty-free/CORBIS 36 –37 ©Getty Images 42 *left* ©Michael Keller/ CORBIS *center* © Royalty-Free/CORBIS *right* © Getty Images 44 *center* ©Eileen Ryan Photography *bottom* ©Getty Images 48 *top left* ©Ariel Skelley/CORBIS *top center* ©Eileen Ryan Photography *top right* ©Eileen Ryan Photography *bottom left* ©Tom Stewart/CORBIS *bottom right* ©Charles Gupton/CORBIS 50 *center* ©Roger Ressmeyer/CORBIS *bottom* ©Getty Images *right* ©Joseph Sohm; Visions of America/CORBIS 52 *left* ©Getty Images *center* ©James L. Amos/CORBIS 54 *center* ©Courtesy of Sandia National Laboratories *center* ©Courtesy of the US Mint *left* ©U.S. Mint Handout/ Reuters/Corbis *bottom* ©Courtesy of the US Mint *right* ©Peter M. Fisher/CORBIS 56 *top right* ©Eileen Ryan Photography *bottom right* ©Eileen Ryan Photography *bottom center* ©Creatas *bottom left* ©Eileen Ryan Photography 58 *left* ©Creatas *bottom center* ©Creatas *right* ©Royalty-Free/CORBIS 60 *center* ©Tim Wright/ CORBIS *right* ©LWA-JDC/CORBIS 62 *top left* ©Bill Aron/PhotoEdit Inc. *top right* ©Michael Newman/PhotoEdit Inc. *center* ©Eileen Ryan Photography *bottom left* ©Creatas *bottom right* ©Art Stein/ZUMA/ CORBIS 64 *top* ©taxi *top right* ©The Image Bank *bottom left* ©Scott Roper/ CORBIS *bottom center* ©Jose Luis Perez/ CORBIS *bottom right* ©Royalty-Free/CORBIS 66 *top right* ©Bill Melton/ Index Stock Imagery *center* ©Richard Nowitz/ CORBIS *right* ©Paul A. Souders/ CORBIS *bottom left* ©Henry Diltz/ CORBIS *bottom right* ©Ariel Skelley/ CORBIS

68 bread, cheese, & milk ©Getty Images all other images ©Christian Burnham 70 *bottom left* ©Royalty-Free/Corbis *top right* ©Roy Morsch/ Corbis *center right* ©Lois Ellen Frank/ Corbis *bottom right* ©Royalty-Free/Corbis 74 background ©Getty Images 76 *left* ©Getty Images 78 *right* ©Chase Swift/CORBIS 80 *left* ©Creatas *right* ©Joe Gemignani/ CORBIS 82 *top right* ©Royalty-Free/CORBIS *bottom left* © NOAA Photo Library, NOAA Central Library;OAR/ERL/National Severe Storms Laboratory (NSSL) *bottom right* ©Royalty-Free/CORBIS 84 *top right* ©Ed Bock/ CORBIS *bottom left* ©Tom Stewart/ CORBIS *bottom right* ©Paul Barton/CORBIS 88 *top right* ©Royalty-Free/CORBIS *center* ©Gabe Palmer/CORBIS *bottom left* ©Paul Barton/CORBIS *bottom right* ©Cheque/ CORBIS 90 *bottom left* ©Royalty-free/ CORBIS *bottom* ©Royalty-free/ CORBIS *bottom right* ©Patrick Olear/PhotoEdit Inc. 92 *top right* ©Roy Morsch/CORBIS *center* ©Ronnie Kaufman/CORBIS *bottom left* ©Reuters/CORBIS *bottom right* ©Lawrence Manning/CORBIS 94 *top* ©Gary Houlder/ CORBIS *top right* ©Tom Stewart/ CORBIS *bottom left* ©Creatas *bottom* ©David Young-Wolf/Photoedit *bottom right* ©Creatas 96 *top right* ©Eileen Ryan Photography *bottom left* ©Jose Luis Pelaez, Inc. /CORBIS *bottom right* ©Getty Images 98 *left* ©Walter Hodges/CORBIS *center* ©Firefly Productions/CORBIS *right* ©Patrik Giardino/CORBIS 100 *top, bottom, & right* ©Getty Images 102 106 *top right* ©Royalty-Free/CORBIS *bottom left* ©Royalty-Free/CORBIS *bottom center* ©Creatas *bottom right* ©Getty Images 108 110 –111 ©Getty Images 112 *top right* © Brian A. Vikander/CORBIS *center* ©Royalty-Free/CORBIS *bottom left* © Photowood Inc./CORBIS *bottom right* © Danny Lehman/CORBIS 114 *left* © Ariel Skelley/CORBIS *right* © Buddy Mays/CORBIS *bottom* © Royalty-Free/CORBIS 116 *top right* ©Paul A. Souders/CORBIS *bottom right* ©Lindsay Hebberd/CORBIS *bottom left* ©Kerstin Geier; Gallo Images/CORBIS 118 *left* ©Royalty-Free/CORBIS *bottom right* ©Royalty-Free/CORBIS 120 *bottom* ©Getty Images 122 *bottom* ©The Image Bank *bottom right* ©Ted Horowitz/CORBIS 130 *bottom* ©Creatas 132 *bottom* ©Creatas *right* ©Catherine Wessel/CORBIS 134 *top right* ©Ariel Skelley/CORBIS *bottom left* ©Robert Stevens/CORBIS *bottom right* ©Lester V. Bergman/CORBIS 136 *bottom* ©Getty Images 138 *top right* ©Jose Luis Pelaez/CORBIS *center* ©Getty Images *bottom left* ©Flip Schulke/CORBIS *bottom right* ©Ramin Talaie/CORBIS 140 *top right* ©Getty Images *center* ©Bettman/Corbis *left* ©Creatas *bottom left* © Bohemian Nomad Picturemakers/CORBIS *bottom right* ©Royalty-Free/CORBIS 148 *center* © Royalty-Free/CORBIS 152 *bottom* © Getty Images 154 *top right* ©National Oceanic & Atmospheric Administration *bottom right* ©David Turnley/CORBIS *bottom left* ©Patrik Giardino/CORBIS